SELECTIVE MEMORY: A LIFE IN FILM

SUE MILLIKEN has been producing films in Australia since the 1970s.

She is a past president of the Screen Producers' Association of Australia and was made a Life Member in 1991. She is a former Chair of the Australian Film Commission and served on the Film and Literature Board of Review. She has been honoured with the Australian Film Institute's Raymond Longford Award for her contribution to the Australian film industry and was awarded the Australian Government's Centenary Medal in 2003.

Sue Milliken has produced such films as *The Odd Angry Shot* (1979), *The Fringe Dwellers* (1985), *Black Robe* (1991), *Sirens* (1994), *Dating the Enemy* (1995), *Paradise Road* (1997) and *Crocodile Dreaming* (2007).

Sue was made an Officer of the Order of Australia (AO) in the 2008 Queen's New Year's Honours List for her services to the film and television industry through a range of organisations, as an advocate for the development of the industry, for support and encouragement of Indigenous filmmakers, and as a producer.

SELECTIVE MEMORY
A LIFE IN FILM

SUE MILLIKEN

HYBRID
PUBLISHERS

Published by Hybrid Publishers

Melbourne Victoria Australia

© Sue Milliken 2013

www.hybridpublishers.com.au

First published 2013

National Library of Australia Cataloguing-in-Publication data:
Author: Milliken, Sue.
Title: Selective memory: a life in film / Sue Milliken.
ISBN: 9781921665875 (pbk.)
Notes: Includes index.
Subjects: Milliken, Sue.
Motion picture producers and directors – Australia – Biography.
Motion picture industry – Australia.
Motion pictures – Production and direction – Australia.

Dewey Number: 791.43023092

Cover design: Grant Gittus ©
Typeset in Adobe Caslon Pro 12/16
Printed in Australia by McPherson's Printing Group

CONTENTS

AUTHOR'S NOTE

These recollections comprise some of my memories of the very lively time which was the Australian film industry in the period 1970 to 2000. Over the years I kept an intermittent diary and as the dramas around me escalated, I found myself given to recording the day's events. They form part of the basis for this work.

As with the film *Rashomon* and Laurence Durrell's novels *The Alexandria Quartet*, other participants may have widely varying memories and opinions of the same events, which I readily acknowledge.

Any period of time is a mosaic, in which the pieces can be made to fit by the people who were there, in the shape that works for them.

This is how I saw it.

Sue Milliken
Queens Park, Sydney
April 2013

FOREWORD

I AM OFTEN SURPRISED at the number of people who ask me, in relation to films, "What's the difference between a director and a producer?" These are invariably sophisticates who have no difficulty in distinguishing a conductor from a composer or a publisher from an author.

Briefly, the difference is – a producer is the person who oversees the entire film. It is his/her responsibility to see that the film is shot on schedule and within the budget. He/she has to deal with numerous contracts and numerous people on the set – behind and in front of the camera – and with the financiers – who may be from half a dozen different countries or organisations and can be relied on to endlessly examine the daily reports, often convinced that their money is being wastefully spent.

The director is, or should be, the person who has artistic control of the film. He/she directs the actors' performances, decides which locations will best serve the story, works closely with the production designer on choices of sets and locations, and liaises with the cameraman on the angles chosen, the lighting of the scenes and the colours employed to establish mood.

These definitions, admittedly being written by a director and perhaps open to dispute, make it sound as if the producer is a dull functionary while the director is a sensitive artist. Frequently this may indeed be the case but a first-rate producer – and Sue Milliken certainly qualifies in this category – is something more. Organisational skill is unquestionably a prime requisite, yet is in curiously short supply. I've never ceased being astonished at the number of producers I have worked with – on expensive films – whose expertise in this field was so limited that they would appear to be more suited to sweeping the studio floor than supervising hundreds of people and being responsible for an investment of millions of dollars.

The key factor is unquestionably the relationship between the producer and the director. If the producer is not aware of the director's vision for the film, then the whole enterprise can easily crash in flames. Too many producers regard the director as more of an impediment to the production than a creative benefactor. Too often the director is urged to compromise on the number of camera angles, to reduce the number of "takes" of the actors, to eliminate some of the more expensive sets – in general, to make all sorts of concessions that will result in the film moving faster and therefore more likely to be finished on time and on budget. I am ignoring, for the purposes of this introduction, the fact that many directors do develop manic personalities during the course of filming, leading to excesses that result in disaster.

A well known if rather extreme example would be *Heaven's Gate* written and directed by Michael Cimino in 1980. Cimino could not be curbed and the film cost $44 million, the most expensive film ever made at that time. Its gross US revenue was $1.5 million. United Artists, the oldest studio in Hollywood, went out of business as a result.

Sue Milliken has produced three films that I have directed: *The Fringe Dwellers*, *Black Robe* and *Paradise Road*. I am proud of all three and am aware that their quality can be attributed largely to Sue's understanding of what it was I was trying to achieve with each film. She knew the scripts in enormous detail and was sensitive to my various requests – another day for this scene, a few more extras here, a reorganisation of some days of the schedule because I've thought of something that will improve a sequence – and so on. I don't want to give the impression that she was a slavish toady to my whims. *Certainly not the case.* But she listens carefully to every request, is quick to disagree (vehemently) if she thinks it unreasonable and quick to agree if she thinks the film will benefit, even though this will almost invariably involve her in the complications of altering schedules, shifting finance from one sequence to another and so on.

All three films we made together came in on time and on budget. All have been shown internationally.

Perhaps the period when directors most dread producers is during the editing. Generally, producers keep quiet during the actual filming of scenes because, I believe, they find this process confusing. It's all done in bits and pieces, angles change frequently, there are repetitions, curiously mute moments etc. etc. Quite a bit of technical knowledge is necessary here to fully understand the process, and few producers have acquired this knowledge. Many have spent so much time in committee rooms chasing after finance or so much time in expensive restaurants courting investors that the technicalities of making a film have been ignored.

However, once the film can be viewed on an editing machine, far too many producers are under the delusion they are masters of storytelling. H.G. Wells wrote, "There is no passion to equal the passion of a literary editor to alter the work of a writer". To paraphrase this, there is no passion to equal that of a producer to alter a director's work during the editing of the film. Over the years I've had all sorts of battles with producers who use their position of representing the financiers to "improve" the cut of the film. Invariably, the director is editing the film with an image of the entire film in his head. Every cut made has to be done so that it affects not just the scene of which it is a part, but the film as a whole. Far too many producers will insist on changes that will damage this flow. Worse, I've watched aghast as they go through rejected takes of the actors and insist that the line readings chosen be replaced by others. I've actually worked on films where fine performances have been destroyed by a producer's selection of less effective "takes".

The most creative producers I've worked with have been Richard Zanuck (*Driving Miss Daisy*), Dino DeLaurentiis (*Crimes of the Heart*) ... and Sue Milliken. None of them haunted the editing room interfering shot by shot, but sensibly watched each successive cut of the film in a theatre from beginning to end without a break. This is the way audiences watch a film and is the only logical way to make adjustments. All three of these producers would then deliver their verdict on the work. All three would invariably make sensible and helpful suggestions regarding the flow of the drama, the relationships of the characters, the details of the performances, the areas that were slow and repetitive, the areas that were too fast – and so on ... This fascinating book by Sue Milliken – one of the few written by a film producer – is a forthright and witty account of the career, so far, of an immensely capable and talented producer, whose skills are held in awe by everyone in the Australian film industry and whose name is known and respected by production companies world-wide. With a few exceptions – Darryl F. Zanuck, Alexander Korda, David O. Selznick and maybe one or two others – producers never become household names in the manner of so many actors and quite a few directors, but without them, few films would be made at all.

Bruce Beresford

PROLOGUE

14 May 1996

On Location, Cairns. Night Shooting.

THE PRODUCTION OFFICE IS BEDLAM. *The accounts department, production team and locations people are all working in a room smaller than a hotel bedroom. Everyone is constantly on the phone. Most of the time a man is repairing the photocopier in the only floor space in the corner. I spend most of the day working from my room. The house phone is by the bed and I have to plug my mobile phone in across the room at the dressing table. The lead for my mobile phone doesn't quite reach the table where my computer is set up. I spend a lot of time getting up from the computer to answer the house phone, or answering the door. Sometimes I'm on my mobile phone plugged in at the dressing table, the house phone rings and there is someone at the door simultaneously.*

I spend a couple of hours on set and leave about 8 p.m. On my way back to the hotel/production office I duck into the drive-in bottle shop to pick up a bottle of Dewars. The Cate Blanchett problem on top of the Jean Simmons problem is finally one too many and I'm hanging out for a Scotch. I have just parked the car when my assistant calls to say that the completion guarantor wants to speak to me and is waiting in his room at the Gray D'Albion Hotel in Cannes, where he is attending the Film Festival. I spend twenty minutes on the phone to Cannes from the car park of the grog shop, slumped in my rent-a-car, hoping no one from the film crew will see me.

Finally back in my room, I send faxes to Fox Searchlight and Village Roadshow. Dinner is a packet of cashews from the mini bar and two Scotch and sodas. Bed at 11.30 p.m.

I plan to get up at 2.30 a.m. to call my co-producer, Greg Coote in Los Angeles, but he beats me to it. I am in a deep sleep and actually dreaming when the phone rings at 1.30. Greg hasn't looked at the new itinerary and has been ringing all over Port Douglas trying to find me. He's pissed off. We discuss the casting of Margaret Drummond. When I get off the phone from Greg, I ring the casting agent in LA to tell him we won't be going with Joan Plowright, and that we are offering the role to Pauline Collins.

Go back to sleep. At 2.15 the phone rings. It's Greg again. The studio wants Joan Plowright. I call the casting agent back and tell him it's opened up again. He says he'll ring Joan and check if she will do the role for the money. It's now 3 a.m.

I drag my exhausted body out of bed, throw on some jeans and go down to the production office. No one there. The only time I've ever wanted the office on a night shoot and it's empty. They are all on set. I drive to the set to give the director, Bruce Beresford, the news – the studio is insisting on the actor he doesn't want.

In between takes, Bruce and I spend the next two hours on the phone to Greg. The tennis match goes back and forth. Bruce is adamant, Joan Plowright is too old for the character. The studio executives have heard of her, that's why they want her. The casting agent calls. Miss Plowright has just been offered something else; that would solve the problem. I tell Greg the decision is urgent because whoever the actor is, she has to get on a plane to Queensland in twenty-four hours.

Several calls later, I leave the set at 5 a.m. and get to bed around 6. At 8.30 Greg rings to say that the studio has approved Pauline Collins. I get dressed, go down to the production office and tell them, then get on the phone to Norman at Village Roadshow about the deal.

Another day – or is it the same one? – has begun on Paradise Road.

ONE

Not a Writer at the ABC

THE 1960S WERE A TIME of opportunity. With an expanding economy and full employment, Donald Horne's Lucky Country was a lazy, unimaginative, sun-filled place where most Australians lived a comfortable and complacent life on the gentle swell of post-war prosperity.

The cultural cringe was at its rampant peak. To impress, a thing had to be "imported" – and that meant imported from Europe, preferably Britain, or of course from our saviours in wartime, the USA.

In 1965 I was twenty-five. I had been working as a secretary for a couple of small-time property developers whose domain was the western suburbs of Sydney. My job was to mind their one-room office in the city while they subdivided paddocks in Fairfield, laid down the minimum of drains and concrete, and then sold them to the booming numbers of young people moving into the suburbs. My job was not only not very interesting – there was little to do. To pass the time, I began writing freelance feature articles and submitting them to the *Sydney Morning Herald* which, to my surprise, not only bought them, but published them.

I moaned to a friend about my job.

"Why don't you join the ABC as a scriptwriter?" he said. I looked at him as if he'd said, why don't you join the astronaut program.

"Well, you're a writer. The ABC employs writers."

A writer. Hardly. But then I thought, well, why not? Prior to that moment, I'd never thought that broadcasting could be a career for someone like me. But I made the phone call which changed my life.

—⟨∞⟩—

I had grown up in the country, first in the town of Wingham on the north coast of NSW where my mother's family had lived since the 1850s and where they owned and ran the Wingham Hotel. My father's family were farmers from near Forster. When I was fourteen and my brother Robert was seven, we moved fifty miles away to a dairy and beef cattle property in the hills behind Gloucester.

Showing off my seat on a horse, aged four.

After boarding school I did a secretarial course at Miss Hales' Secretarial College in Sydney. It was not academia, but an unforeseen upside was learning to touch type, which was to become a surprising advantage in the age of computers.

Once I was through with Miss Hales – we parted without regret on either side – and as soon as I could get the fare together, I sailed for London on the P&O liner *Strathnaver*, a one-class passenger ship full of young Australians off to see the world. The voyage was, in the manner of the time, a six-week-long party. The end-of-empire hijinks on board were interspersed with revelatory excursions to Colombo, Bombay, Aden and Cairo.

And so travel became my tertiary education. Once in London I discovered theatre, music, opera and ballet. Some of the greatest artists of the twentieth century were then performing in the London theatre. Tickets were easy to get for the cheap seats. I saw Menuhin, Ashkenazy, Pavarotti, Victoria de Los Angeles and the incomparable Nureyev, among many. In a time before the tourist hordes, it was possible to wander into the National Gallery, the Sistine Chapel, the Louvre, the Prado, and to view the great art of humanity at leisure. Tickets to Teatro La Fenice could be picked up in the afternoon before the performance.

It was not all culture, however. A night of partying in Rome ended with a swim in the Trevi Fountain; in Athens it meant watching the sunrise from the steps of the Parthenon. Just six young people, a bottle of retsina and a two-thousand-year-old building. Such possibilities are but a memory in today's over-crowded, security-ridden world.

A family tragedy changed everything. My mother was killed in an accident while driving up the steep cutting on our property. I flew back to Australia and spent a year at home with my father and younger brother, Robert, while we tried to re-stabilise our lives without the dynamic and loving presence of the person who had been the centre of our world.

Eventually I was able to go back to live in Sydney, which brought me in due course to the property developers and my telephone call to the ABC.

At the ABC head office in Elizabeth Street, the small grey employment woman peered at me across her in-tray. "Oh no, dear, we don't employ scriptwriters," she said. She didn't even glance at my clippings book which I was waving confidently at her. Oh well, no surprises there. I bent down to pick up my handbag to leave. Then the woman added, "But we do have a vacancy for a temporary typist grade one." She must have made the connection: if you were a writer, you could type.

I didn't hesitate. It had to be better than the property developers, one of whom had recently started chasing me round the desk.

"I'll take it," I said.

The ABC had established its place in Australian life as the voice which crossed the far distance: solid, reliable and friendly. The vestiges of Australian culture which had survived the post-war era pretty much lived in, or at least around, the ABC. Until the arrival of television in 1956, radio plays were what sustained people at home at night, if they were not listening to the competing quiz shows of Bob Dyer and Jack Davey, the most popular radio entertainers of the day. On weekdays at twelve, every housewife west, north and south of Parramatta downed tools for "episode one thousand and trillion of Gwen Meredith's (pause) Blue Hills".

However, the world of the ABC which I entered – like Dorothy in *The Wizard of Oz* – alert, interested and keen to do well – bore little resemblance to the august organisation's benign public image.

I spent my first year filling in typing jobs wherever I was sent. I read the internal jobs bulletin each fortnight to see if any scriptwriting opportunities would fall out of the sky. Curiously this did not happen, but I did get a good look at the workings of the organisation.

I learnt that the ABC was administered by a middle management which epitomised the irony of Donald Horne's title. A bunch of mostly male bureaucrats, permanent public servants, they were on a cushy job for life. Many had come from the PMG (Postmaster General's Department) or from failed careers in the Holy of Holies, the BBC.

To middle management, rules, regulations and paperwork were an end in themselves and took no account of the needs of programming. Like good bureaucrats everywhere, the top of their game was to say no. Programs were generated in spite of the system. "If all programs stopped tomorrow," someone said, "it would take three months for Broadcast House to notice." No one considered this an exaggeration.

However, the production people were another thing altogether. Young, lively, clever and bursting with the drive to make programs, they existed in a parallel universe. Middle management despised and feared them and devoted itself more or less full-time to keeping them under control. The broadcasters and program makers fought back with all the considerable cunning they could muster. It was war, and it was waged daily.

Among the departments I was sent to was O&M – Organisation and Methods – high up in Broadcast House. Here a lot of paper was moved around, very slowly. The highlight of the day was a game of carpet bowls in the corridor at lunchtime, to which all the men looked forward with enthusiasm. Even as a novice, I was surprised by the leisurely pace of this most Kafkaesque of departments.

After O&M I was sent for a couple of months to the architects' office, which was quite a lot more interesting. The ABC employed architects full-time, several of them. They and the sound engineers inhabited a little cottage inside the enclave of the Gore Hill television studios. I think they were responsible for the various concert halls where the state orchestras played, and probably for partitioning the ever-expanding offices required by O&M. As the ABC was then housed in twenty-six rented buildings across Sydney and God knows how many others across the country, I suppose someone had to deal with that.

At the time of my visit with them, the Sydney Opera House construction crisis was in full swing and our office was in it up to its neck. Even understanding the political imperatives of the time, it seems a daft idea to have demanded a multi-purpose auditorium to handle both opera and concerts in a so-called opera house. The main hall was required to provide perfect acoustics for a symphony orchestra *and* the mechanics required to stage grand opera – and seat 2,800 people at the same time. That was the brief given to Jørn Utzon. What were they thinking? Design disasters were being discovered on a daily basis. Utzon would soon resign.

The ABC was hell-bent on having a perfect concert hall for its orchestras, otherwise, it threatened, it would pull out of the Opera House altogether and remain in the Sydney Town Hall. ("Good riddance," someone should have said.) But I expect they had the government over a barrel. Terrified of the blowout of costs of construction of the Opera House, the loss of revenue from ABC concerts would have been the last straw.

One day, one of the sound engineers who worked with the architects, a small chap with curly hair who was an amateur organist, came bursting into the office. "Do you realise there is no plan for an organ in the Opera House?" he announced theatrically to the room at large.

Seventeen faces looked up at him. "Tut, tut," they said.

There was a perfectly good organ in the Sydney Town Hall. But the ABC had to have one in the Opera House, even though (or perhaps, because?) its existence made the auditorium incompatible with staging opera.

The organ duly replaced the elaborate stage machinery which, rumour had it, was towed out to sea and sunk. The biggest auditorium became the ABC's concert hall, the drama theatre became the opera theatre, with its tiny stage and cramped orchestra pit, and drama moved to the concourse level.

Now when I queue with fifty other women for the loo at interval at the opera, it reminds me that toilets had inadvertently been omitted from the drawings, and when I watch the chorus of *Aida* banging into each other on stage like a tin of gaudily clad sardines, I think about that sound engineer, and what was lost.

Just as I was beginning to become frustrated with my lack of progress at the ABC, a family friend arranged an introduction to the playwright Robert Wales, who had taken a job at ABC as Head of TV Promotions in order to feed his family while he was writing plays. Bob needed an assistant in the Promotions Department and asked me if I would be interested. It wasn't exactly scriptwriting, but it was a way out of the typing pool.

This was my introduction to the television studios at Gore Hill. The building, facing the Pacific Highway, was constructed in a huge square. It had a corridor around and between the two large studios, with offices off the corridor. The design meant that, in order to get anywhere, you did a lot of walking. It was good for the legs and very convivial, as people took an interest in the passing parade and often called you in for a chat and, more importantly, a gossip. By gossip, I mean as described by Diana Athill in her memoir *Stet*, about her life in British publishing: "… gossip in its highest and purest form: a passionate interest, lit by humour and above malice, in human behaviour." Well, mostly but not always, above malice … Gossip about people and goings-on was the lifeblood of the ABC, and a staple of everyone in the film industry. How else is one to find out anything?

The atmosphere at Gore Hill was effervescent, a world away from glum old administration. The excitement of seeing programs created, in any form, was a revelation. People were friendly, interested and helpful. And they were funny. They approached their work with zest and an eye to the frequent absurdities of the business. Oh wow, this is for me, I thought.

I had found my place.

Bob's sidekick in TV Promotions, a dry, chain-smoking former journalist called Mickey Davis, kindly let me write some of the on-air material, and she kept a close eye on me just in case I put the Mr Squiggle copy with the Contrabandits graphic.

Many years later, when I heard a voice-over on the ABC saying, "When Sergeant Plod discovers Constable Tripe kissing PC Body in the radio room, there is high drama on *The Bill*." I laughed and thought, things haven't changed much in forty years.

I spent quite a lot of time in the Film Library, picking up and returning graphics and trailers, and there I met and became friends with Louise Mutton, whose boyfriend, John Seale, was a tall camera assistant with an enquiring look. John was soon to become a camera operator, the best of the best, tanned and graceful in a pair of shorts and desert boots behind the geared head of the big Mitchell camera. Much later, he was to become the Academy Award-winning cinematographer of films like *The English Patient*, *Rain Man*, *Witness* and *Cold Mountain*.

Outside of work (and occasionally during – everyone at the ABC had a creative sideline as well as their paying job), Bob Wales was finishing off a play called *The Cell*, a mystery set in a convent, which played to critical approval at the Ensemble Theatre. On weekends he and his wife, Joan, sailed the harbour on their small yacht on which, to my delight, I was often invited. Summer Sundays usually involved sailing to Quarantine Bay where we anchored by a beach which hadn't changed since Arthur Phillip. A swim over the side would be followed by lunch and a glass of wine, and a beat back to Double Bay behind the nor'-easter in the late afternoon.

It was after one of these congenial outings that we came ashore to the news that the Prime Minister, Harold Holt, had gone missing off a beach in Victoria, which seems as hard to grasp now as it was then.

TV Promotions was fun, but then I discovered production. The studios were always busy with new shows and sometimes I was able to go on set and watch a program being recorded. Observing the collaborative buzz of a lot of people working together, totally focused to produce a performance, often sharing laughter, and then seeing the result live in front of me, was magic. Before long I wisely jettisoned the scriptwriting plan. Good scriptwriters are very, very rare, and it is better to be a good anything than a second-rate something. And better to pursue an opportunity than to beat your head against a door which is unlikely ever to open.

Whenever there was any kind of production position advertised in the ABC jobs bulletin I applied for it, but for a long time I failed even to get an interview. Patiently I plugged on, somehow knowing this would be for me. Persistence was rewarded when a position for a script assistant in the Education Department was advertised. This was the lowest rung on the production food chain, TV Education being a backwater whose brief was to provide schools programs and material for *University of the Air*. Obviously no one else applied, as I got it. I was as excited as if I'd been offered a job as a producer at MGM.

TV Education was run by Frank Watts, a mild-mannered, middle-aged former school teacher, and his deputy Kay Kinnane, a six-foot redhead. Kay, a pioneering executive at the ABC, was to become the first ever female Senior Officer. Fey, dry and a bit vague, she might have been the first to start changing the culture of management, and the staff liked and respected her. She was generally referred to as Big Amy, the remnant of some long-dead joke from Damon Runyon. Although the programming in Education was pretty mundane, the producers were not. They were clever and keen to make the best of what they were given.

Producers in the ABC were actually a combination producer and director. They generated their own programs, often wrote them, organised them, and then went behind the camera or cameras and directed the filming or TV recording. They were assisted in these activities by a script assistant, so-called, who actually was a production assistant. The scripto typed the script, made the facilities bookings, fought with the service departments for crew and equipment, kept a detailed description of the shots for the editor, and then sat in the studio and readied the cameras for the director's instructions to the vision switcher. Then they mopped up, filled out the paperwork and made sure the show ended up where it was supposed to.

University graduates went into the ABC as specialist trainees, treated like yearling thoroughbreds in a racing stable, moved assiduously from creative department to creative department, and tutored in the ways of broadcasting. All the specialist trainees at that time were male. The scriptos, on the other hand, were a subculture – clever girls who for whatever reason had bypassed university and taken junior jobs to get into production. They wound up knowing as much or sometimes a lot more about the craft than the trainees, and they held the various production departments together with their organising skills, quick wit and ability to work the system.

My first assignment in Education was to do a shot list for some filming around Sydney. The director was a burly Canadian, Alex Cann, the husband of talent agent June Cann. Alex and June had met on the set of *Eureka Stockade* in 1948 where Alex was the first assistant director and June the continuity girl. Alex had been an actor and stuntman in Hollywood before coming to Australia. He had subsequently fallen on the bottle and his family on hard times; Big Amy, a friend of June's, had given him this job to help out. I later appreciated her support for Alex when I came to know June as one of the nicest and most decent people who ever worked in the film industry.

The cameraman on our little shoot, Keith Gow, was what my mother would have referred to as an old commo – a veteran of the Waterside Workers' Film Unit – and the survivor of an accident in New Guinea when the propeller of a taxiing plane hit his camera while he was filming, driving the eyepiece into his face. The three of us must have made an odd group, two diverse but battle-scarred filmmakers and a novice who didn't know one end of a camera from the other. It was a leisurely shoot, and much time was spent over morning teas in coffee shops while Alex and Keith swapped stories of old movies and documentaries in exotic places. Blotting Paper just sat there, listening and fascinated.

I was assigned to producer Tom Haydon on a series of programs for *University of the Air* to be recorded in an outside broadcast (OB) van at the University of NSW. Tom was very tall and lanky, with big hands which stuck out of shirtsleeves too short for him. He had a mop of curly brown hair and a motormouth. Full of enthusiasm for everything he did, he never stopped talking and gesticulating, his hands waving about as fast as the dialogue. Or monologue. He became a brilliant documentary maker, in and outside the ABC, with credits including *The British Empire*, *The Talgai Skull* and *The Last Tasmanian*. He died of cancer in 1991, aged fifty-three.

I had been working in his office for a couple of days when he said casually, "Get on to Facilities and get me a Siemens reel-to-reel." At my uncertain look, he added, "Tape recorder." Two days later, after several calls to Facilities (having been told they didn't have one, that I couldn't have one if they did, that they wouldn't have one available for six months, that they never made them available to TV Education) I turned up in Tom's office with the tape recorder. He grinned at me. "Very good," he said. "I don't want the tape recorder. Facilities are bastards to deal with, and those machines are impossible to get hold of. I just set you the test. I thought, let's see if she can do it. If she can, she'll be okay."

Tom's and my *University of the Air* show consisted of three cameras in a lecture theatre at the University of NSW, and a professor talking and using a blackboard. Various shots of the professor and the blackboard were intercut with graphics illustrating whatever it was he was talking about. This was all pre-ordained and scripted, and typed by me. Even in my euphoric state at being "in production", it was pretty clear that this was the bottom of the barrel, but I didn't care. My job in the OB van which recorded this masterpiece was to sit next to Tom and grab his index finger when it jabbed towards the button switching to the wrong camera. I spent a lot of time sitting outside the van smoking with the tech crew while Tom took lengthy telephone calls from his solicitor. He was going through a divorce which had its own timing tensions as he was anxious to marry his very pregnant girlfriend before the immediately imminent birth of their baby. (These things were important, back then.) Both productions were completed on time and on schedule.

One day I was in the staff canteen at lunchtime when I was introduced to a new producer in TV Education, Wolfgang Storch. Wolf, an Austrian, had recently arrived in Australia from the US.

13

A Fulbright Scholar, he had an interesting past, having survived the Dresden bombing as a child, and as a student having escaped from East Berlin as the wall was going up. "You'd better go now," his mother had said. He had not seen her since. He had a nervous personality and was quietly derided by the other producers, who thought his Austrian nationality was a cover for being German (and by extension, a Nazi), and who made jokes about his anxieties. He was known to chew a handkerchief into holes when directing filming.

After my time with Tom and the professor, I was assigned to work for Wolf. He had lots of plans for programs but the department, not for the first or last time, had no production budget. So we sat around, working on ideas, me typing them up and sending them off to some filing cabinet somewhere. One day when, as usual, there didn't seem to be anything to do when we got to the office, and it was a perfect summer's day, the sensible thing seemed to be to go to the beach. Before long we were going to the beach most days, and coming in once a fortnight to pick up our pay and check the in-tray. There was never anything in it.

When the weather was unsuitable for the beach, I spent the days painting my new terrace house in Paddington. Terrace houses were very unfashionable, and Paddington was a run-down slum. This meant the houses were cheap, with the inner city advantage of being close to everything. When I visited my bank manager to arrange a loan to buy the house, he was totally against the idea. "Oh no," he said. "We don't lend money for terrace houses. Why don't you buy a nice unit, dear?" Demonstrating the persistence which had secured me the tape recorder, and with a bit of lateral thinking about the financing, I got him to do what I wanted, not what he wanted.

I don't remember actually making any programs with Wolf. After we had spent several months of pleasurable indolence on full pay – pleasurable but also frustrating, because we would rather have been making films – the ABC created a new documentary production unit headed by the broadcaster and left-wing rebel, Allan Ashbolt. Tom Haydon and another Education producer, John Worrall, were transferred to the new unit. Swiftly adapting to the opportunism necessary to survive, I managed to jump ship along with them, and we crossed the road to a new office on the Forbes Street corner of William Street, and the new department, Special Projects.

Ashbolt was the kind of person you would die to work with. He'd had a colourful career in the ABC. Described as a "radical activist", he was a courageous natural leader with a social conscience and profound political beliefs. He was tall and graceful, and he had an actor's voice which made him a distinctive broadcaster. In those days of permanent public servants where no one could be fired, ABC management was terrified of him. His obituary in *Inside the ABC* says: "He was twice removed from *Four Corners* and from time to time attempts were made to sideline him when questions were raised over content of programs under his control." The creation of the new unit was almost certainly another attempt to sideline him. For the moment, ABC management had pretty much cornered him, and his ability to create controversy was temporarily in check.

I got an early demonstration of Ashbolt's politics. I had written an article about a fight between the Kosciusko Park Trust and skiers which the *Sydney Morning Herald* had bought but not published. When the SMH journalists went out on strike, the paper, without consulting me, made my piece the op-ed lead story, with a big by-line. I was thrilled and I showed it to Ashbolt.

"Scab," was all he said.

There was another employee in the Special Projects Unit, a small, skinny, scruffy writer called Bob Ellis. Wherever Bob went he was accompanied by a brown Globite school case which contained tattered drafts of scripts and, I suspected, a stale sandwich and a decomposing apple core. One of his funnier pieces of writing described the ABC top brass as "claret-pickled pontiffs of the ninth floor", penned in an article for *The Bulletin* in which he was musing in a taxi on his way to Elizabeth Street, where he was to be carpeted for some misdemeanour. It was pretty obvious that Bob had also been parked in Special Projects because no one knew what else to do with him.

Also in the new team was a raffish Italian, Giancarlo Manara. The story went that the general manager of the ABC, Sir Charles Moses, on a visit to Italy, had been introduced to Giancarlo at a party and had said to him over the vino, "If you're ever in Australia, come and see me." Two years later, Giancarlo presented himself in Moses' office. At the time he spoke no English and he was very deaf, the result of an accident with a horse. The ABC didn't know what to do with him, but Moses, in the benign spirit of the time, gave him a job anyway. For a while Giancarlo ran the Italian-language newspaper, *La Fiamma*, while doing what Wolf and I did – picking up his ABC salary once a fortnight. For Special Projects he directed the classic drama adaptation of Henry Lawson's *The Drover's Wife* starring Clarissa Kaye, one of the finest productions of that or any other era.

The ABC was apparently untroubled by the salaries it paid for no output. Its inefficiencies were legend. Freelance writer and actor Michael Boddy wandered into the Forbes Street premises one day and picked himself out an empty office, from a selection of several. It contained a desk, a typewriter and a telephone. He spent the day bashing out one of his own scripts. No one asked any questions, so he came back the next day. Then the next, and the next. Eventually he settled in on a permanent basis. In no time he was on the tea list (the tea lady came round with her trolley and knew that you took milk, no sugar and handed you your tea and a Nice biscuit), then he was listed in the internal telephone directory, and one day the people from O&M arrived and said they were redecorating his office, and what colour would he like it painted.

The ABC was an easygoing employer in other ways, too. When I started working in Education in William Street, I learnt that if you wanted to get anything done, you had to do it in the morning.

After lunch people either returned to their desks around three o'clock in various states of inebriation, or went from lunch directly to the pub up the road and spent the afternoon arguing, debating and drinking. No one in management seemed to notice. This could have been because it didn't make much difference, as the pace of work meant that if you were the least bit industrious you could get a day's work done before strolling up Palmer Street to lunch. Here Franco's no-name restaurant was located upstairs in an undecorated shanty from the 1850s. Franco served cheap pasta, and with it you could order the "special Coca Cola" – red wine served in Coke bottles, because the restaurant was unlicensed.

John Worrall came up with a piece of nonsense called *Alfred, Lord Tennyson, Sings* for Special Projects. It was a studio piece, more suited to the BBC in the 1930s, a send-up of some of Tennyson's sillier poems which were set to music by the radio broadcaster and composer Richard Connolly, and performed by George Whaley with the assistance of Corinne Kirby. We had to record it in Melbourne, where there was studio space available. So John and I travelled to Melbourne where the ABC put us up at the temperance Victoria Coffee Palace. We got into trouble for getting drunk in John's room and singing late after the show had been recorded. In Melbourne I met John's mother, the charismatic radio personality Martha Gardener. John was a gentle, rather fragile soul and I got the feeling that he may have been overwhelmed by the large personality of his mother and the success of his father, who had been a businessman in Melbourne radio. *Alfred, Lord Tennyson, Sings* went to air in due course, unnoticed, and sank without a trace. I doubt anyone even bothered to telerecord it.

John retired early from the ABC and moved to Kangaroo Valley. In 1991, the same year Tom Haydon died, he drove his car off the road returning home late after a dinner party and was found dead a couple of days later. John was a sad case of a highly intelligent square peg who didn't even fit a square hole.

One day I came into the office at Special Projects to find Storry Walton occupying a desk. Storry had produced and co-directed, with Gil Brealey, the television adaptation of *My Brother Jack*, from the novel by George Johnston, with scripts by Johnston's wife, Charmian Clift. *My Brother Jack* was the most successful television drama the ABC had made until that time.

Storry had come to Special Projects to make a documentary about the artist Sidney Nolan. It was to be written by Nolan's old friend and Storry's recent colleague, George Johnston. Hal Missingham, director of the Art Gallery of NSW, had arranged the first major retrospective of Nolan's work to mark the artist's fiftieth birthday, and Nolan had agreed to the film being made, using the exhibition as the peg.

I asked Storry if he had a script assistant. He said no, would

You can tell how green I am because I'm the only one taking this seriously. Sid in the centre, grip Kinsey McDonald kneeling, Ron Lowe behind the camera, camera assistant Colin. *Riverbend* is behind us.

I be interested. Finally, I had something to work on which was worth doing.

This would be Nolan's first public exposure since he left Australia with his wife Cynthia in 1948. Although he had been back often and had painted the Australian landscape extensively, the stormy end to his relationship with his Melbourne patrons, John and Sunday Reed, meant that he had largely avoided publicity and, in particular, Melbourne.

The story of the Reeds' role in Sidney Nolan's emergence as an artist and his love affair with Sunday Reed are now well known. But it was a matter not discussed in 1968, and the story as it was told to me was that wicked Sunday Reed was hoarding all the Ned Kelly paintings and refusing to give them back to poor innocent Sid. There was a poisonous relationship between the Reeds and the Nolans; to complicate matters, Cynthia was John Reed's sister. Incredibly, the Reeds, pivotal characters in Nolan's career, were not seen or even *mentioned* in the first film about Nolan's life as a painter. Tragic really, as interviews with them would have been something for posterity. The *Ned Kelly* series, one of the most dynamic and iconic set of paintings ever created by an Australian artist, was not included in the retrospective – which otherwise was an enormous, dazzling display of genius, culminating in the mighty *Riverbend* panels.

I met Sid and the Johnstons, George and Charmian, on the first day's filming at the art gallery when crates of paintings were opened under the supervision of the ebullient Hal Missingham. Hal kept telling us he was on strike, due to an argument with the government about money for the gallery. This did not stop him being always around and available. I worked on the shoot in Sydney, but the ABC would not pay for me to travel with the crew to the locations in Victoria and Alice Springs. So I stayed behind, typing transcripts of the interview sound tapes as they were sent back. George accompanied Sid and the crew to Victoria where they filmed in Melbourne, the Wimmera and the Kelly country, but because his tuberculosis was at an advanced stage and he could not fly, Charmian went with Storry and Sid to Alice Springs and Ayer's Rock.

I found Nolan to be the nicest of men – amiable, charming and polite. He was great television talent, because once the camera rolled and Storry said "Action", he would talk until the film ran out. Nice as he was, I could see that there was a will of steel behind that friendly face, and a very complex personality – the details of which have been emerging ever since.

During the time that Charmian was away filming, George was at a loose end. He came to my house for lunch on weekends, when he would sit in a corner of the garden, long skinny legs crossed, a cigarette permanently in his hand, and yarn. One afternoon at their house in Raglan Street, Mosman, he read us the first chapter of his new novel, *Clean Straw For Nothing*, which was set in (although not identified as) the Paddington house of producer Jill Dempster, in Sutherland Street, just around the corner from my terrace. George could not walk more than ten steps without stopping to get his breath. We would stop with him, keep talking, and then when he was ready, without comment we would all move on, a sad little cavalcade. The side of him I saw on those occasions was gentle and funny, and I grew fond of him. He certainly did nothing to aid his health, being more or less never without a cigarette. We expected him to die before long. We took it for granted that he did, too.

I was in awe of Charmian. At forty-four, in spite of a life lived hard, the poverty during their time in Greece and all the drinking, she was charismatic and beautiful, with the greenest eyes I have ever seen and a clear, measured voice. She vibrated sensuality and intelligence. One evening when I called in to the house in Raglan Street while George was away, she said to me, "Everyone always says poor old George. No one ever says poor old Charm."

Her death by suicide two years later was shocking. It was George who was supposed to die, not Charmian! She was so young, forty-six, and so talented. But reading Nadia Wheatley's account of the last few years of her life (*The Life and Myth of Charmian Clift*, 2001), the wonder is that she lasted so long. And yet, anyone might have walked in on her that night. What would have happened if, as everyone expected, George had died before her? Relieved of the burden of that destructive relationship, would she have found a new future, or was the relationship so interdependent that she would have been unable to survive without him?

Being ahead of their time was the Johnstons' greatest tragedy. If they had been born just ten years later they would have built their careers as writers in a receptive Australia, with literary grants and subsidies, and reciprocal tax arrangements which would have enabled them to avoid the years of poverty in which lay the seeds of their and their family's destruction.

Their legacy to Australian literature lies in the novels *My Brother Jack*, *Clean Straw for Nothing* and *The Sponge Divers*, as well as Charmian's elegant and prescient pieces for the *Sydney Morning Herald*.

During the filming of the Nolan documentary, it began to emerge that there was bad feeling between Cynthia Nolan and Charmian. Cynthia, stick-thin, stern and tense, was the odd one out in the foursome of the Johnstons and Nolans. George, Charmian and Sid were warm, talkative and friendly, but Cynthia stayed very much in the background, out of the way of the filming. One night when I was having dinner with her while the crew was on location, she told me a story about Charmian's novel, *Peel Me a Lotus*. Sid and Cynthia had spent some time on the Greek island of Hydra when the Johnstons were living there, and Charmian had written them into the novel, so thinly disguised she might as well have named them. It was a particularly (and apparently calculatedly) cruel portrait of Cynthia, who was outraged on her own behalf and on behalf of Sid, who had been financially generous to George when they were at rock-bottom. She saw it as a betrayal; she did not enjoy those weeks sitting around in Sydney while Sid travelled the countryside with the film crew and the Johnstons.

The film was shot in colour – only mentioned because it was an oddity in the ABC at that time, when everything was made in black-and-white. It must have been due to Storry's and Ashbolt's determination, as it would not have bothered management in the slightest if a film about paintings was shot in monochrome. The film was eventually titled *This Dreaming, Spinning Thing* as a wry tribute to Nolan's ephemeral verbal style, after a comment he made as a result of watching thousands of parakeets swirling over a clay pan in the centre near Ayers Rock.

A few months after the Nolan film ended, Storry and I were involved in a debacle called *Over the Equator* which became known within the ABC as *Over the Navel*. It was a program to celebrate the first satellite link between Australia and Japan, and involved cutting live to air between segments in either country – very new and very revolutionary technology. The executive producer was Dr Peter Pockley, head of the Science Unit. Peter was a very sincere man but short on a sense of humour. Storry enjoyed playing tricks on him and sent him a memo saying that, as the show was so important and there was so much work to do, all the production staff would have to sleep at the studio, and would Peter provide camp beds, catering, showers and pyjamas. Peter went into a panic and Storry let him flap about for a bit, wondering how he could lay on all the items needed, before letting him in on the joke.

On the night of transmission, Japan contributed charmingly bland pieces such as a children's choir singing *Crick Go the Shears Boys, Crick Crick Crick*, while we filmed a message from the new Prime Minister, John Gorton at Kirribilli House to the Japanese Prime Minister, Mr Sato. Everything was going fine until we cut to the ABC studio in Hobart where, without warning, an overweight, very bad belly dancer gyrated in close-up, belly button unattractively prominent, across the link to Sydney and on to Japan. The horrified producers and vision switchers in the Sydney studio were unable to do anything but stare and say, "Christ! Where did that come from!"

A producer called Tom Manefield had been given the job of putting together the segment from Tasmania. At the rehearsal in the afternoon, all had gone smoothly, a soprano singing *Bless This House* or something. But some time between rehearsal and transmission, the singer took ill. Apparently it had not occurred to Tom to call Storry to warn him and get approval for a substitution ... The Japanese were not amused, and for a while everyone behaved as if diplomatic relations between Australia and Japan would be severed permanently as a result. Storry and Tom had to front senior management in Broadcast House to Explain.

There wasn't much happening in Special Projects when Ron Lowe, the cameraman on the Nolan film who had become a pal, mentioned to me that the TV series, *Skippy*, the adventures of an anthropomorphic kangaroo, was looking for a continuity girl for a few weeks to replace their regular girl while she took some time off. He had suggested me to his friend Jill Dempster, *Skippy*'s associate producer. There was the slight problem that I was employed by the ABC, whereas *Skippy* was produced by an independent company, Fauna Productions. But obstacles are there to overcome.

I met with Jill who, behind her elegant exterior, had a brain like a steel trap and the organising ability of a field marshal. She said, "Well, the job's yours if you can get away from the ABC."

So I trotted off to Broadcast House to see DProdNSW, who told me to take three months' leave without pay, clearly thinking one less mouth to feed.

Since the introduction of television there has always been a battle to keep Australian drama on Australian television screens. Drama is labour-intensive and expensive to make. Australia has a small population and there is limited potential for international sales.

Without the government-regulated quota system, there would be no Australian drama produced by the commercial networks, for the obvious reason that they are only interested in the bottom line, and foreign TV drama can be bought for a fraction of the cost of producing original material. But it has been demonstrated over and over again that when the quality and entertainment value are there, audiences love Australian drama and are keen to watch it. With the development of the internet, pay-TV and video on demand, the modern-day question of quotas continues to be a vexing one.

Hector Crawford had managed to start *Homicide* in 1964, and by the late sixties there were some independent drama series being shot in Sydney. These included *Riptide* and *Woobinda (Animal Doctor)*. The lead in *Riptide* was an American actor called Ty Hardin, known to the crew as Try Harder, who was famous for saying, "You can't expect me to act and say my lines at the same time".

In 1967 *Skippy* was created by the producer Lee Robinson, in partnership with actor John McCallum and a lawyer, Bob Austin; it was sold to the Nine Network. It is no secret that the original story lines were "adapted" from the American series, *Flipper*. An incredible ninety-one half-hour episodes plus a feature film were produced between 1967 and 1969. Unlike programs at the ABC, the series was shot in colour and it sold all over the world; it still continues to screen in the small hours in many countries. It provided the training ground for a generation of Australian film crews.

Lee Robinson was one of the pioneers of the post-war film industry. *Walk into Paradise*, which was made during his partnership with Chips Rafferty, was the first Australian film to be selected for competition at the Cannes Film Festival. While in partnership with Chips, Lee directed several feature films including *King of the Coral Sea* and *Dust in the Sun* (always referred to as *Lust in the Dust*), many of which made money. Lee's best directing days were behind him, but he still wrote scripts for *Skippy* which, when I arrived, was wrangled into production on a day-to-day basis by the other producer, Joy Cavill, and Jill Dempster.

The series had been in production for more than a year by the time I got there and it ran like a well-oiled machine. Everyone knew what they were doing except me.

Although I had been working in production of television programs for a while, I had had nothing to do with drama and I had only the vaguest notion of what continuity was. I can tell you now that the continuity girl is the editor's representative on the set, making sure that the action matches in the various shots which are filmed out of sequence so that it can all be edited together into one smooth scene. The continuity girl also records all the information, including the camera angles and details of shots covering the scene, to facilitate the editing process. She prompts the actors during rehearsal, watches the dialogue and notes if a piece of the script isn't playing well. She is the director's security blanket, taking care that they do not shoot themselves into a dramatic corner from which they cannot extricate themselves. If unsure about the performance in a take, the director will look at the continuity girl for a second opinion. If she pulls a face which means *mmm, not so good*, the director will call for another take. The continuity girl has to know everyone else's job while doing her own.

When I think now about turning up to a film shoot not knowing a thing and expecting to fit in, I feel ill. I was so ignorant, but game. I would have had to wait years at the ABC to get into the drama department, which was the job all the scriptos wanted. So this was my chance and I had to make it work. The ABC had a book called *The Five C's of Cinematography*, one C of which was Continuity. But I was not allowed to borrow the book, and I had to drive by the ABC at the end of each filming day so as to study the chapter. To make matters worse, *Skippy* producer Joy Cavill had been the doyen of continuity girls, with a deservedly formidable reputation.

I'm surprised that I was not sent home after my first hour. I had a truly terrible time those first days on the set of *Skippy*. The director, a coolly sardonic Englishman called Eric Fullilove, had no time for a beginner and treated me, correctly, as a hopeless incompetent. Some members of the crew were helpful, but some were quick to assign blame for their own mistakes at the feet of the new arrival. Survival of the fittest. Joy and Jill (who had also done continuity for a while at the ABC) must have known what a klutz they had on their hands, but to their great credit they kept quiet and let me find my feet. Which I did, after the first few ghastly days. I began to learn about eyelines, matching wardrobe, left to rights, camera setups and all the tiny details which have to be right for the editing.

Joy was prone to walk onto the set while I was hunched over, drawing my little diagrams and trying to figure out the camera angles in a complicated scene, and say, "You've crossed the line." Crossing the line is the cardinal sin of continuity, because it means that two shots will never edit together. She probably did it to show off, but it had the purpose of teaching me my craft in a way that was unforgettable.

After a while I began to think, well, this is fun. But I still had a long way to go before I became competent enough to relax at the job and enjoy it. It takes about five years to become a truly professional continuity girl, and it has to be learnt on the set, beside the camera. With digital cameras and the advent of the video split where details can be checked on replay whenever required, the job is not as demanding as it once was. When the only visual record on the set of what had taken place was a black-and-white polaroid photograph – more or less instantly superseded – the continuity girl was the eyes and ears of the crew and the editor.

When the regular continuity girl came back to work, I was kept on to help in the office because a feature film, *Skippy and the Intruders*, was about to go into production. This was my second break. I did a bit of everything, including interviewing actors who wanted to be considered for roles. On one interview report I wrote: "Jack Thompson – very handsome, could make a good leading man. Try in a small role." Every episode had a role for Helen Morse, who was the Cate Blanchett of her day, that is to say, beautiful and talented, with a face which could play pretty well any character. We constantly offered Helen the guest lead. And she regularly turned us down.

The lead human role in *Skippy* was played by Ed Devereaux, one of the generation of Australian actors which included John Meillon, Peter Finch, Bill Kerr, Bud Tingwell and Ray Barrett, who had been forced to leave Australia after the war because there was no work. Ed returned to Australia to create, most movingly, the eponymous role in Storry's *My Brother Jack*, and had been brought back again for *Skippy*. One of the remarkable and admirable things about this amazing little series was that no washed-up Yanks or superannuated Poms were imported for roles in *Skippy*. All the actors were Australian – although the directors, it has to be said, were English.

Unfortunately Ed found his role as Matt Hammond, head ranger, Waratah Park, undemanding and sometimes frustrating. It was rumoured that he drank to relieve the boredom. One afternoon in the production office I was talking to Jill at her desk in an anteroom outside Joy's office. We could hear Ed, his voice raised, giving Joy a hard time behind the closed door. Eventually he came out, red in the face, saying through clenched teeth, "This fucking country ... this fucking industry ... No one has any fucking idea what they're doing ..." He had worked himself into a state and, to lend emphasis to his already overstated position, he raised his fist and theatrically punched the wall. The wall, being a partition of cheap plasterboard, immediately gave way and Ed's arm disappeared up to the elbow into the cavity. The surprised look on his face was heaven as he sheepishly extracted his arm and, anger turned to foolishness, slid out of Jill's office, leaving a gaping hole which Joy left there for a while, just to remind him.

Fauna Productions offered three years of production school in three months. There I learnt everything about the mechanics of film production. As well as getting a grip on continuity, I learnt about schedules and call sheets, budgets and cost reports, directors and actors, cameras and film crews. Joy and Jill were great teachers. I returned to the ABC knowing a lot more than when I left. Not only that, I had had a whiff of independence.

—oono—

ABC TV was doing an adaptation of H. M. Brinsmead's award-winning novel for children, *Pastures of the Blue Crane*. Two weeks before production, the drama department's regular continuity girl had a family crisis and resigned. Back from *Skippy* and in the right place at the right time, I provided the solution to the problem and took over.

The novel was adapted for television by Eleanor Whitcombe, later the screenwriter of *My Brilliant Career* and *Careful, He Might Hear You*. The director was Tom Jeffrey. Tom had been working in various areas of the ABC, starting as a studio hand and rising to direct the innovative childrens' series *Crackerjack* which starred Michael Boddy and Reg Livermore, followed by the groundbreaking current affairs show, *This Day Tonight*. *Pastures* was a big break for him, his first chance to direct drama.

Pastures was designated a serial, the story being told in eight half-hour episodes. Today it would be told in four one-hour episodes and called a mini-series; it would also be shot in colour.

The biggest budget production of the drama department since *My Brother Jack*, it was to be shot in Sydney, Murwillumbah, Coolangatta and Brisbane – on the harbour, on ocean beaches and in the emerald cane fields and violet mountains around Mount Warning. Tom and the producer, Brett Porter, begged to be allowed to shoot on colour film, which required an increase in the budget of $8,000 – a piffle, even then. This time management won, ensuring the show would have no sales anywhere outside the ABC.

With Tom on the low loader between takes, on location for *Pastures of the Blue Crane.*

The lead actors in *Pastures* were Jeannie Drynan and Harold Hopkins, two of the most beautiful young people God ever put breath into. The story was about racial prejudice, and in a politically incorrect move which would never happen today, Harold played a boy who was part-Melanesian and turned out, in a Gilbertian twist, to be Jeannie's half-brother. (Casting white actors to play Aborigines in lead roles was the way it was done then. In an episode of *Delta* a couple of years later, Peter Sumner played a "part-Aborigine" in muddy black makeup, while the real blackfellas played supporting roles.)

A very young John Hargreaves played a porter with a couple of lines on a railway station. Not having been involved in the casting, I was not particularly interested in the actor playing this tiny part until I watched him work. "Who's that?" I asked Tom. John was still at NIDA and it was probably his first film role. Even in a walk-on, he stood out. Tony Buckley writes in his memoir, *Behind a Velvet Light Trap* (2009), that John was the Australian contender for the schoolteacher in *Wake in Fright*, the role that went, on the English financiers' say, to English actor Gary Bond. On such whims do actors' careers depend. John would have been

The *Pastures* crew

electrifying in that role and the film's success would have ensured him international stardom. As it was, Bond's accent is the weak link in *Wake in Fright*; he never became a big star and, outside Australia, neither did John Hargreaves.

Tom was a natural directing actors. Thoughtful and perceptive, he understood how to motivate them without dictating how they should create the performance. He was confident and competent directing the camera. Actors and crew liked and trusted him.

It was a magical experience. For me, everything I'd learnt since starting in TV Education came together, and now I was able to study the creative side of filmmaking, being perfectly placed to watch actors' performances, coverage and camera angles, and the translation of script into drama.

Things were afoot in the drama department. A series adapted from Tony Morphett's novel *Dynasty* about a newspaper family was in the pipeline. Tom was assigned as one of the directors and I went with him as his script assistant.

Dynasty was made in a format referred to as "integrated", meaning that the interior studio scenes were recorded on videotape with three cameras simultaneously, and the exteriors were shot on film on a single camera.

Videotape was a new innovation. It wasn't so many years since shows went live to air, and there were many stories of disasters either narrowly averted or worse, seen across the country. Tom had worked on a show where the set started to collapse around the actors, who frantically had to speed up their dialogue and, without appearing to hurry, race into the next room so as not be flattened in front of the evening prime-time audience.

There were no colour cameras in the studios so the series was made, once again, in black-and-white ... which, in this case, quite suited the story of skulduggery in boardrooms and family mansions. The stars were the drop-dead handsome and adorable Kevin Miles, Anne Haddy, spunky Nick Tate and Nick's grand old dad, John, as the patriarch. John Tate was a repatriated expatriate, another fine actor who had been working in England for most of his career.

Around this time, as work began to happen in Australia, many of our lost talent started coming home. Some, like John Meillon, Ray Barrett, Bill Kerr and Bud Tingwell, came home for good, now that they could earn a living. They all wanted to work in their own country. Unlike the actors of the modern era who get their careers started in the subsidised film industry in Australia, then go to Hollywood but mostly are able to choose to live at least partly in Australia, the actors of this earlier time had no choice but to leave and stay away. International travel was prohibitively expensive and slow.

Drama was on a roll, because quite soon after *Dynasty* we moved on to *Delta*, a series about environmental detectives played by John Gregg, Kirrily Nolan and again, Kevin Miles. Another old pal was in the directing team, Wolf Storch. *Delta* was to be shot all on film, but still not in colour. Black and white was king.

I feel it needs to be recorded somewhere, because I still feel the outrage, that it took three six-day weeks of twelve- to eighteen-hour

days – 250 hours – to shoot fifty minutes of black-and-white television for *Delta*, and that was without including the screen time
shot by an elaborate second unit. This was ABC inefficiency at
Olympic standard. An hour of television drama is normally shot
in two five-day weeks of ten-hour days – 100 hours, no overtime.
Delta was an ambitious show, often shot on location, but the real
problem was the director of photography, known around the ABC
as Captain Kilowatt. Instead of being employed as the ABC's
senior drama cameraman, he should have been given a bollocking
and told to get his act together or get out. But management was off
with the pixies somewhere. I became used to driving home from
the set at two in the morning and getting up at six to return to
work by seven. For what it cost to make two episodes of *Delta*, we

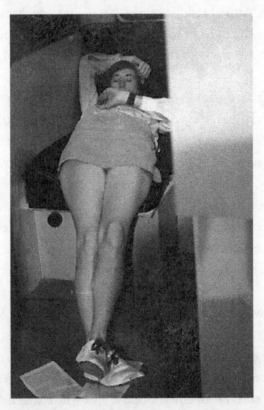

We made a collection of people falling asleep during their breaks, although
there may have been another reason for taking this shot.

could have shot another for no extra cost.

While we whinged a lot, no one thought to make an issue of the inhuman working hours. There was no ABC union and our basic pay was small, so the overtime was useful (although no one thanked the cameraman for that), and we were young and in love with what we were doing. We just worked, slept, got up and did it again. On Sundays I slept late, did my washing, cleaned the house, went to lunch, drank too much, went to bed early and got up on Monday morning to start all over.

One episode was about a mine collapse. A cave-in set where some miners were trapped underground was built in the studio, but the tunnels and the action prior to the mine collapse were shot at a colliery in the Hunter Valley. Dressed in miners' rig – overalls, hard-hat and safety light – we travelled two miles underground in open coal trucks.

You had only to walk a few metres away from the set, turn into another drive and turn off your safety light to find yourself in the blackest darkness imaginable. Not even the tiniest flicker of ambient light intruded and you could not see your hand raised right before your eyes. It was a dangerous exercise, disorienting and spooky, and you had to be very careful about remembering the way out. Miners only did six-hour shifts underground, but the ABC film crew did our regular ten hours, eating lunch in the windowless crib room. After a few hours underground, people began to behave oddly. Most of the girls at one time or another had a bit of a cry. One day, for no reason, I found myself bursting into tears. No one took much notice. We were always relieved to get into the coal trucks and travel to the surface, where we besieged the unit manager who knew to have everyone's cigarettes waiting as we flung ourselves from the trucks.

One day the *Delta* production manager said to me, "Hey Sue, we're sending a second unit out to Leigh Creek, would you like to go for the ride?" An episode called "Death Walk" was being directed by Wolf, who was filming John Gregg and Kirrily Nolan

Before and after ten hours down the mine.

dying of thirst on Lake Eyre. Unfortunately, it had been raining – a lot – and although the scenes were not completed, their time was up and they had to return to Sydney.

An RAAF Hercules was going out to pick up the crew and equipment, and while it was there, to act as a camera platform for second unit aerial shots. A cameraman from the camera pool called Dennis was assigned to film from the aircraft our heroes trudging across the burning salt lake. "There's plenty of room on the plane, and you're not doing anything," the production manager said. "Go out and give Dennis a hand, if you'd like to." The RAAF had been pressed into service to transport the crew and equipment out and back, for no charge to the ABC – unimaginable in these days of full accounting.

Denis and I drove to Richmond and boarded the giant plane which was empty, apart from a row of canvas seats along each wall of the aircraft. Once airborne, the noise of the engines was so loud that conversation was impossible. The flight took six hours, and the monotony was only relieved by visits to the cockpit and cups of tea brought to us by the load master.

When we started getting close to location, the aircraft circled about 500 feet above the ground, then began to lower its loading bay. The entire rear of the plane disappeared from view, leaving Dennis strapped into a harness with his camera hanging out the opening. I was strapped firmly into my seat, well away from the opening, taking no chances. By prearrangement, the film crew below were to make themselves scarce so that the camera could film two exhausted environmental scientists staggering through the heat haze, dragging their possessions and actor Wyn Roberts behind them in a makeshift sledge.

What greeted us, was a sea.

Lake Eyre, for the first time since racing car driver Donald Campbell had been rained out in his world land speed record attempt in 1963, was under water. Grey skies were reflected in grey water as far as the horizon. The crew and cast were bogged down in red mud, frantically trying to find a few square metres which looked vaguely dry in which to place the actors for the shots. It was hopeless. Dennis rolled a few feet of film and called out, "Bugger this. Let's go to Leigh Creek and land."

The aircrew, Dennis and I checked in at the Leigh Creek Hotel, a frontier establishment in the Joliffe style, and waited in the bar for the film crew. This was the original Leigh Creek, not the new, modern village a few kilometres south. The crew eventually arrived in the kind of funk that only a complete disaster can create. They were covered in red mud, exhausted and dispirited. Wolf was a nervous wreck.

It is a given in filming that the more expensive and difficult the situation, the more you can guarantee that the weather will do exactly the opposite of what you want it to do. And as filming always requires fine, sunny, consistent weather, this usually means rain, wind and freezing nights when actors have to behave nonchalantly as if it's the tropics.

In the case of "Death Walk", months had been spent arranging for these shots on Lake Eyre, an essential component of the episode because it was entirely written around our characters abandoned in this location. It was an enormous coup to find the resources and budget to film in such an exotic location so far from Sydney, and now the entire enterprise was, to use an apt term, a washout.

A very rowdy night was spent in the bar of the Leigh Creek Hotel. I was sound asleep in my small cell of a room above the bar some time after midnight when I was awoken by the blanket being lifted off me and a flannelette pyjama-clad leg inserting itself into the narrow single bed. I sat up, terrified, and gave a little scream.

"Shush, shush, it's only me," said Dennis, the cameraman. Dennis was, to put it as nicely as possible, past his best. He had been a news cameraman at the ABC for a long time, and was nearing the end of his career. He was overweight and balding, with a couple of chins and a florid Irish complexion which was the product of a lifetime of sun, cigarettes and beer. And on this occasion, no matter how you looked at it, in flannelette pyjamas he was no catch.

"For God's sake, Denis," I hissed at him, "get out of here!"

Undeterred, he continued to climb into bed. "I couldn't sleep; I'll be able to sleep better in here," he said.

I gave him a shove. "Get out! And get out now! Back to your own room!"

He started muttering to himself in a kind of wounded tone, removed the offending leg and disappeared out the door. I couldn't be angry. But I turned the key in the door before I turned over and went back to sleep.

The next morning a very hung-over crew flew back to Sydney. The missing scenes were subsequently rewritten for night and filmed in the studio at Gore Hill. For once, the black-and-white photography was an advantage, but the episode never made much sense.

───

Tom and I did an episode with the incomparable Frank Thring who, with Max Phipps, was required in the script to go native. Frank and Max spent most of the episode dressed in feathers – possibly they were in New Guinea. They adored their costumes and did their best to upstage each other. Frank lived up to his legendary reputation for flamboyance and wit. He told us the story

Max is thinking how to upstage Frank. He should have stayed in bed.

about starting the chariot race in *Ben Hur*, in his role as Pontius Pilate.

"I waved my arm and dropped the handkerchief," he said, in his exaggerated theatrical drawl. "The chariots thundered past ... and there, on my wrist, was my watch!"

I was assigned to do continuity for the second unit for an episode of *Delta* called "A Beautiful Burn", about bushfires. For several days, the camera boys and I sat around in the bush dropping matches into grass or leaves to get close-ups of fire starting. Then one day we were called to provide extra camera coverage alongside the main crew for a scene where a house burns down. A full-sized house had been built by the art department in an approved part of Frenchs Forest. There was much activity as several cameras were lined up to give multiple coverage of the once-only event. Rehearsals were held for the action which was to take place around the house once it caught fire.

Our camera was set up and ready; we were sitting under a tree having a cigarette, observing while the preparation continued. As I watched, a props man ran up to the house. He was holding a rolled-up newspaper in his hand and it was alight. He ran around the house, dipping the torch into the prearranged combustion points. None of the thirty or so people buzzing importantly about took any notice. Before I could transfer the surprise from my brain to my mouth to ask whether he should he be doing that, the house was an inferno.

It was as if you had poked a stick into a nest of bull ants. There was comprehensive panic as people raced everywhere, yelling to each other. Cameras were hastily pointed towards the building and the assistant director ran around screaming "Turn over! Turn over!"

In two minutes, the set was a pile of blackened ashes on the ground and the director had his head in his hands. It was the only time I ever saw anything happen quickly on *Delta*.

By the end of 1971, it was time for me and the ABC to part. My time on *Skippy* had shown me there was another world out there, and I had begun to run foul of the management of the Drama Department. Big mouth, couldn't keep it shut. And I had begun an affair with their star director, Tom Jeffrey. They didn't like that, either. So in September 1971 I filled in my last time sheet and set off into the world of freelance film production. I could hear them exhale as I departed.

In spite of the many things that were wrong with the ABC, I have much to be grateful for. It was an apprenticeship in which I got the opportunity to learn about creative storytelling on film. I learnt how to mix the creative and the organisational in a way which benefits the final result. Observing ABC management taught me one of the most profound lessons in life: you can learn as much by seeing things done badly – and therefore how *not* to do them – as when they are done well.

At the ABC there were many admirable, talented and generous people who were happy to create an opportunity if it was in their power. As people helped me, I have always tried to help others in this most difficult of businesses.

TWO

Incident at the Bon Gout

By the early 1970s I was freelancing, married to director Tom Jeffrey, and part-time stepmother to his two small children, Romola and Adam. I sold my little house and we bought a bigger terrace at the other end of Paddington.

Through my brother Robert, who was now a journalist at the *Sydney Morning Herald*, I met the Chief of Staff, the ebullient Irish-Australian Brian Johns and his short, hirsute deputy David White. And through them I was introduced to the world of journalism and politics.

Life began to include late-night parties and dinners, the dinners usually at Sandro's, an Italian restaurant at the top of William Street, Kings Cross; it was frequented at lunchtime by the ABC and at night by the Fairfax press. Conversation was loud and voluble and covered politics, books and theatre. Sandro's amiable eponymous host knew everyone by name and kept the doors open until whatever time the last rowdy table ran out of arguments and departed. On Sundays there was a regular lunch at the Taiping, a Chinese restaurant in an unprepossessing motel in Elizabeth Street which was the unofficial Sydney office for Labor supporters, where the food was cheap and sensationally good.

Through David and Brian I met their friends Lenore Nicklin, Mick Young and Eric Walsh, Richard Hall, George Negus and many of the people working for a Labor victory. After twenty years of Liberal Party rule, there was a feeling of confidence and optimism in the air. Under Gough Whitlam change was on its way – a new Australia was about to be born.

My family had always voted Country Party as it was the party for the bush. But the movement for change swept away my conservative allegiances. I have never joined a political party and I have occasionally swung my vote – frequently in State elections – but in 1972 there was only one person to vote for, and that was Gough, with the promise of a future for Australia which could make it a force in the world. It was indeed, Time.

Tom was already committing most of his spare time as (unpaid) secretary of the Producers' and Directors' Guild of Australia, working for government support for a feature film industry. Following lobbying by the PDGA and other groups and individuals, including editor turned producer Tony Buckley, writer/producer/ director Michael Thornhill and the politically well-connected duo of Phillip Adams and Barry Jones, Prime Minister John Gorton had set up the Australian Film Development Corporation in 1970 and it had begun to look as if an independent film industry might be possible. But now Gorton was gone, deposed by the flailing Billy McMahon, and it was clear that the only hope for continued support was Gough and the Labor Party.

No one could foresee the political disasters to come, many of them brought about by politicians of an earlier era who had been too long in opposition – a salutary lesson about never leaving one party in government for too many terms. But for all its shortcomings, the Whitlam Government marked the beginning of a new and ultimately better Australia. Tom and I bought a case of the "Victory Dozen", a selection of red wines which had Parliament House in red on the label, and a caption which said:

> *Specially selected for the Australian Labor Party to commemorate the Federal Election Victory on December 2nd, 1972. As this country flourishes in the exciting years ahead, so will the wine mature. Whenever it is tasted it will serve to remind us of the election victory in 1972 that reshaped our future.*

I still have a couple of bottles, undrinkable, kept for sentimental reasons and for the irony of the words.

—∞—

Meanwhile, the stirrings of a feature film industry had begun. Hazel Phillips shocked by getting her gear off in *The Set* in 1970 and everyone laughed; in 1971 Jim Sharman switched from theatre to film with *Shirley Thompson Versus the Aliens*, not exactly mainstream, but *Stork* by Tim Burstall was. Starring Bruce Spence as the eponymous misfit, *Stork* was funny and genuinely entertaining – the first Australian film to find a real audience. By 1972 other lasting talents of the industry were beginning to make their appearance – Peter Weir with *Office Picnic* and Bruce Beresford with *The Adventures of Barry McKenzie*. John Duigan's name appeared as one of the writers on Nigel Buesst's *Bonjour Balwyn*, while Brian Kavanagh's *A City's Child* was gentle and touching. *Alvin Purple* was launched on an unsuspecting audience in 1973; by 1974 the new Australian film industry had arrived with *Stone, The Cars that Ate Paris, Sunday Too Far Away*, Tom Cowan's *Promised Woman*

With the Big Mitchell. It might not look like work, but it was.

and Michael Thornhill's *Between Wars* – all in one year.

Being a freelance film technician in the 1970s was about the most fun you could have. You were working outside, often in gorgeous locations in great weather, because that was what looked good on film. At a time when everyone else dressed up for the office, you wore shorts or jeans and sneakers. Your workmates were young, attractive, clever and talented. There was a wonderful feeling of camaraderie. You were an important part of a team, your work was valued and respected, and you spent a lot of time laughing because laughter and a sense of the absurd are necessary to manage the long hours, the pressure and the often very silly things that are an inevitable part of making films. The atmosphere was relaxed but the work was highly disciplined.

And best of all, we were telling Australian stories.

Few Australians worked harder. A six-day week was the norm, outside as well as inside the ABC. An hour to watch rushes, part of the job but for which you were not paid, was added on to the ten-hour day. In the freelance world you often were not paid for overtime, either. When you left home in the morning you never knew what time you would get back. The rest of Australia was working a thirty-five-hour week, and "work" was a loose definition in many places, especially the public service.

Eventually, film crews grew tired of being exploited by production companies (who themselves often had to scramble to find the funding to keep going) and brought the union in to fix reasonable working conditions. These became five ten-hour days in the city, six ten-hour days away on location, meal breaks within five hours of starting work, overtime for work outside contracted hours and double time on Sundays. So years later, when the rest of Australia began to realise that it had to change its work habits to be competitive with the rest of the world, the film industry thought: about time.

My joy at working on a film crew was all the more intense because there wasn't a lot of it. When I started freelancing, there were already a couple of very good continuity girls well established in the market. So I spent a lot of time at home, waiting for the phone to ring.

Occasionally I would get work on a TV commercial or at Film Australia, the government documentary organisation, on its dramatised documentaries. Formerly known as the Commonwealth Film Unit, Film Australia was still living in the fifties. The staff played croquet on the lawn with the same enthusiasm as the men from O&M at the ABC played carpet bowls. Things happened slowly, but there was an upside. As with the ABC, penalty rates were paid for overtime beyond the eight-hour day. However, at Film Australia, everyone got paid from five minutes past nine in the morning, no matter what time you were called to work. I worked for three weeks on a film which consisted almost entirely of night shoots. We started work at about four in the afternoon and worked until dawn. Imagine my delight when I received my pay and discovered that I had been paid as if I had clocked on at nine in the morning, with all the commensurate overtime penalty payments! Sadly, this lucrative situation was not to last, and Film Australia was eventually brought into the 1970s.

I was hired to do some episodes of the TV series *Spyforce* when they ran two crews to keep up with their on-air date. There were two people behind *Spyforce* – producer Roger Mirams and writer Ron McLean. Ron, fortified by a steady supply of Scotch and cigarettes, wrote every episode, and there were over forty of them. That would be inconceivable today, when there are several writers plus story editors, script producers and script typists on a series. It's true, some of Ron's scripts were delivered on the set as he sat at a table near the camera in a halo of cigarette smoke, bashing the scene out on a portable typewriter one page ahead of the filming. But on the whole the quality of the show was remarkable and, like *Skippy*, it still screens in the small hours on networks around the world.

The stars of *Spyforce* were Jack Thompson – by now a dashing leading man – and Peter Sumner, abetted by Redmond Phillips and Katy Wild. The action took place in World War II New Guinea, played by the reserve at Deep Creek, Narrabeen. The Force Headquarters was a small set in a two-storey ramshackle block of flats on the estuary in Narrabeen which also held a mock-up of a spitfire hanging from the ceiling. The production office was upstairs where the clacking of typewriters had to stop when the studio bell was rung for a take.

Japanese baddies were played by whoever Roger could round up in the tourist traps of Sydney on the weekend. Japanese tourists (or indeed Indonesian, or Filipino – Roger wasn't fussy) found themselves bussed down to Narrabeen, thrown into very well-used Japanese khaki, given a wooden cut-out rifle and told to run around screaming. There was only one fully functional Japanese rifle with bayonet in the props department. A "Japanese" would be directed to run past the camera with bayonet waving, then hand it to the next son of Nippon who would repeat the action and so on.

Money was always in short supply. Money is always in short supply on films – there is never enough, no matter how much you have. It's the first rule of filmmaking. But *Spyforce* was a special case. Roger did the dance of the artful dodger throughout the series, always one step ahead of the bailiff, and a lot of people in the industry didn't like him because they didn't get paid. Perhaps because I was a freelance I always got my cheque, so I only have happy memories of the chaos that was *Spyforce*. But I do remember that, towards the end, when the network didn't really want any more episodes but Roger had talked them into it, a runner stood by to drive to the lab, take the day's rushes to Channel Nine, which would then give him a cheque which he would take to Kodak and buy the film stock for the next day's shooting.

I worked on and off on *Spyforce* whenever they needed an extra continuity. I remember fondly the days when I could leave my house in Paddington at 7 a.m., stop at the pie shop in Narrabeen for a meat pie for breakfast and be on the set and ready to shoot by 7.30. AND never get fat!

———⊗———

John Daniell, the manager of APA, a production company in Neutral Bay owned by the cigarette company WD & HO Wills, offered me the job of continuity on a US-financed TV series to be shot in Sydney. It was six months' work, exactly what I had hoped for when I left the ABC. But a week later he called me again. Another continuity girl knew someone who knew the producer and got them to un-hire me and hire her. John had to do the dirty work, telling me.

John Daniell was one of the gentlemen of the industry, and there has never been an oversupply of those. He had started his career as a cameraman; he had the distinction of being on the deck of the *Missouri* for the surrender of Japan at the end of World War II, and later covered the Korean War. Whenever he could, John gave me work on APA commercials, but after a while those dried up and I was seriously out of work.

I hung around the house for a while then, admitting defeat, slunk into a secretarial agency and registered as a shorthand typist. No problem getting work there. I was immediately booked for two weeks to a chemical factory in Botany to type invoices. On the first morning I arrived at a building of grey brick and lavatory glass in a treeless street of factories. I was inaccurately thumping my way through a large stack of invoices on an ancient typewriter in a Dickensian office, trying to hold back tears of self-pity (I should have put up with those creeps at the ABC, I kept thinking), when a telephone rang.

"Miss Milliken?" The senior invoice typist handed me the phone with a look which said: temp typists don't take personal calls in *our* time. "Call for you."

"Hello?" I said. The agency with another job?

"Miss Milliken?" asked a commanding male voice at the end of the phone.

"Yes ...?"

"Hector Crawford here. John Daniell gave me your number."
John Daniell ... what a guy. How had he tracked me down? "With
some difficulty," he later told me with a grin. But what was Hector
Crawford, the God of television drama, doing calling *me*?

"Miss Milliken, are you busy?" Hector Crawford enquired.

I looked at my surroundings. "No, Mr Crawford," I said.

"Could you come to Melbourne to do a job for us?"

"Yes, Mr Crawford."

"Could you come this afternoon?"

I hesitated for less than a second. "Yes, Mr Crawford."

"Good. We will book you on the four o'clock plane."

I put the phone down, picked up my handbag and walked into
the cubicle of the man who had, just an hour before, thought his
invoice typing problem had been solved.

"I'm really sorry," I said. "Something has come up and I have
to leave."

His startled look tugged at my conscience, but not for long.

"Oh, dear ..." he started to say, but I was gone.

That evening found me on my first trip south of the border, hur-
tling in the dark towards Phillip Island to take over the continuity
position on a movie for the Hallmark Hall of Fame on American
television. Hallmark had contracted Crawford Productions as the
most experienced television production company in Australia to
provide production services for a Movie of the Week called *The
Hands of Cormack Joyce*, a story of poverty on the west coast of
Ireland in the nineteenth century. The Australian dollar must have
been going through one of its intermittent slumps against the US
dollar. I can't imagine any other reason an American company
would have even known where Australia was, let alone want to
film here. Australian crews and facilities were nowhere near the
world-class level of the film industry today; I and various other
technicians from Sydney were gradually replacing the Crawfords
Homicide crew who, it was being discovered, did not have the

experience to handle a 35mm film shoot on location.

The film was directed by a rugged veteran of American television and holder of three Emmys, Fielder Cook. Fielder and I immediately took to each other, if for no other reason than we both knew our jobs, which was a relief for him, and it was pretty exciting for me to be working with such a professional.

The cast was a surprisingly distinguished one: the Belfast actor Stephen Boyd, Messala in *Ben Hur*, and Colleen Dewhurst, better known in American theatre but a greatly respected film and television actress as well, who was between marriages to George C. Scott. Colleen had a big smile and a whimsical sense of humour. "You can't get there from here," she was fond of saying in her lazy drawl, the Maine expression applied to Phillip Island. Also in the cast were the splendid Irish actor Cyril Cusack and the teenage Dominic Guard. This film came after Dominic Guard's dazzling debut in Joseph Losey's *The Go-Between*, with Julie Christie and Alan Bates. He was a beautiful boy, gentle and sensitive, and sadly, after such a promising beginning, his career never sustained its early success.

Enid Lorimer, then in her eighties, played Cyril Cusack's wife, which did seem a little silly since she was twenty years older than him and she looked like his elderly mother. Enid had started her career on the English stage at the turn of the twentieth century. She had a Lady Bracknell accent in which she was fond of telling an anecdote and then saying, "Of course, that was before the war."

"Which war, Edith?"

"The *First* War, darling!"

The first assistant director was a middle-aged American, a short man with a big gut who wore Bombay bloomers – those absurd baggy khaki shorts favoured by male members of the British Raj – and a digger's slouch hat with the side turned up which he had purchased in a souvenir store. He was very pleased with his outfit but if he had known the contempt he was held in by the Australians, he would not have been quite so cocky. He was an imposter, a crony of the American producer. The shooting day was chaotic until Jim McElroy arrived from Sydney, took over the role of second assistant director and quietly brought some order to the set.

Among other imports from Sydney was the standby props, Monte Fieguth. Monte was whippet-thin with a cloud of curly brown hair. His father had been one of Hitler's rocket scientists who, in a deal which must have bemused him, ended up in Australia after the war. One day on set I observed Monte filling Cyril Cusack's pipe. He put in some tobacco, then got a pouch out of his standby vest and mixed the tobacco with something else.

"Monte, you're not putting dope in Cyril's pipe!" I said, disapprovingly, the senior prefect.

Monte grinned. "Why not?" he said. "It'll relax the old bugger."

And indeed it appeared to do so. Cyril sat cheerfully through several takes, puffing away at his pipe, a contented smile on his face.

Today, Monte would probably go to jail.

Giving Cyril Cusack some continuity notes.

The locations for Cormac Joyce were the wild shingle beaches on the Antarctic side of Phillip Island, where the art department had built stone cottages and dry-stone fences – the effect was quite convincing. It was mostly freezing, and one day when we were filming a scene of Stephen Boyd in a prop-built coracle in one of the bays, the seas were so rough and the stones underfoot so slippery that my feet went out from under me. I sank under the choppy waves, frantically holding my script and stopwatch out of the water and paddling with my feet to prevent being washed out to sea. I would only have been noticed if I had begun to drown, because everyone else had their own problems remaining upright while the stony shore shifted beneath them. Stephen Boyd, no stranger to dangerous filming (you'd think nothing would faze him after the chariot race in *Ben Hur*), was terrified as he was flipped around in the small, unseaworthy little boat while the camera crew frantically tried to line up the shots.

Back in Sydney, I was offered a job by TV commercials director Bob Kersey, husband of my school friend Anna. Bob wanted to add other kinds of films to his repertoire and I was to help him run his commercials business and research other projects.

Work in television commercials was plentiful as all commercials shown on Australian television had to be made by Australians. Even commercials made by the big international companies in other countries had to be reshot in Australia in order to screen here. The Menzies government, when setting up television in 1956, included this requirement in the legislation. This surprising aberration to the government's indifference to Australian culture (perhaps because commercials weren't seen as culture) was to have a seminal effect. Cameramen (no women then), grips, electrics, makeup, costume, set designers and production people practised their craft making commercials and were able to support themselves while waiting for work in drama. Some of the first wave of film directors, most notably Fred Schepisi and Peter Weir, along with many television drama directors, developed their experience making commercials. The worth of these opportunities was immeasurable to the developing drama industry, until it all changed with the Free Trade Agreement with the USA in the 1990s. Now many of the more elaborate and expensive commercials are imported, and the gulf between drama and advertising allows little opportunity for crossover.

One of the ideas Bob had was to make a film about the Salvation Army. Our research included a memorable tour of The Glebe with a Salvation Army officer. The suburb of Glebe in Sydney, as its name suggests, was at that time still principally owned by the Church of England which was landlord to most of the people who lived there. The graceful Victorian suburb of today with its bookshops, cafés and grand terraces was, at the end of the 1960s, a slum of shocking poverty and degradation. The Salvos were helping some of the elderly whose plight was ignored by the Church. We visited bent old men and frail old women, living in rooms unpainted since the house was built, with walls covered in mildew and rising damp, the plaster coming away from the lathe base and with leaking roofs and rotting floor boards. Some had no electricity. Plumbing was almost non-existent; the lavatory was a filthy shack up the back. There was a story to tell, but Bob could never find a buyer. Not long after this, the Church began to sell off the suburb, the poor were sent packing and the houses cleaned up and renovated for the middle-class market.

George Negus, who was then working for the new Attorney General, Lionel Murphy, told us that some friends were coming up from Melbourne to open a restaurant and we had to go to it to help them get started.

The friends were Tony and Gay Bilson who opened Tony's Bon Gout in 1974 in the Mansion House, a faded rooming establishment on the corner of Liverpool and Elizabeth Street owned by property mogul Leon Fink. As it turned out, Tony and Gay didn't need our help, because the restaurant took off like a bunny out of a burrow. Suddenly here was modern French food, excitingly experimental, dazzlingly sophisticated, in a rowdy, cheerful, convivial environment overseen with Gallic panache by their maître d', Alain Chagny. There was a fixed price of $12.50 for three courses, including Gay's divine desserts, and bring your own wine.

We began to eat at the Bon Gout regularly. When Lenore Nicklin started her Friday lunch table, we ate there every Friday. The nucleus of regulars – David White, Brian Johns, Dick Hall and George Negus – was augmented with whoever was around and interesting at the time, including all the Labor staffers when they were in Sydney. Michael Thornhill was a regular – cashing his dole cheque with Alain to pay for lunch – as were Frank Moorhouse, Donald Horne, Don Anderson, Bruce Allan and Betty Roland, having a late revival with her play *A Touch of Silk*. If you went to the Bon Gout for lunch you didn't go back to work. It usually wound up around five o'clock, and occasionally we would rise tipsily from the lunch table and drive unsteadily down Elizabeth Street to the Taiping for dinner. Livers could take it, then.

———

After a couple of years of freelancing on films crews, I began to take an interest in the organisation which went on behind the daily filming. It had been part of my job at the ABC and in the freelance world, organisation often seemed to be second-rate with time and money wasted unnecessarily, resulting in frustration and creative compromise. I wondered if it might not be done better.

So when my friend from the ABC, Louise (now married to John Seale and working as production secretary on a kids' TV series called *Catch Kandy*), mentioned to me that she wanted to go on location with John on Fauna Productions' new TV series *Boney*, I said, "Can I have your job?" She looked at me with an expression which said, *here's how I can get out of this*, and she arranged for me to take over.

The forgettable *Catch Kandy*, a half-hour series based around the improbable adventures of a couple of kids around the zoo and the harbour in Neutral Bay, was produced by a highly decorated former World War II flying ace, C. W. Bewick Hack. It didn't take long to work out that God gave Bewick one talent, and that was to fly Spitfires. He never seemed to have much idea what was going on, and if it hadn't been for the sharp wits of his PA, a nineteen-year-old English girl called Pom Oliver, he might have been even more bemused.

Pom became a successful producer; she was much later to walk to both the North and South Poles with a group of female companions. She had a very speedy brain, an excellent attribute in a production person, but it sometimes led to cutting to the chase a bit *too* quickly. On a later film she was typing up the actors' pro forma contract when a slip of the IBM golf ball converted the boring phrase "The actor will perform (this and that) ... and all such acts as are heretofore required ..." to "... and all suck acts as are ..." Not only did no agent ever query this unusual demand, they all signed the contracts without demur. When I noticed it and pointed it out to Pom, she laughed. We decided to leave it there to see if anyone else would pick it up. No one did, and the error was perpetrated in the pro forma for some years by other busy production secretaries.

Pom gave a young man on his first job in film the best advice I ever heard for anyone starting in production: "Never sit down."

The production manager on *Catch Kandy* whom I was supposed to be assisting was running, I discovered, a sandwich shop on the side and rarely put in an appearance in the production office. There were two first assistant directors who worked the set on alternate weeks. One was an affable youth called Gerry Letts, the other a handsome blond English public school boy, Mark Egerton.

I didn't mind at all that the production manager was in absentia.

Once I got my head around the show I was quite happy to have the place to myself. I had no trouble running the day-to-day shooting and scheduling Gerry's episodes when he sat opposite me for just too long, unable to make a decision about whether to have the bad guys on Wednesday or Thursday. I quickly discovered that I didn't have to do anything for Mark; he was on top of his job and would often tip me off on some problem which he could see coming before it happened. I came to rely on him.

When *Catch Kandy* ended I went back to continuity, but I had enjoyed pulling the strings rather than being on the end of one of them and I was on the lookout for another opportunity.

———

A year and a half later I was at home, out of work again, when John Daniell rang.

"What are you doing?"

"Well … nothing."

"We've got a movie starting shooting on location in Scone [a town in the Hunter Valley] and we need someone to look after the Sydney office. Could you do it for us?"

This wasn't exactly the challenge I was looking for. "Looking after the Sydney office" meant cleaning up the messes the film crew left behind, doing their shopping and having nothing to do with the filming. Nevertheless, trying to sound helpful as John was such a nice guy, I said, "Probably".

When I arrived for the meeting with John at APA studios there was the chaos of a film crew moving out on location. Wardrobe racks and silver camera boxes were everywhere, trucks revving up out the back, baggage in piles, people rushing purposely about. I ran into someone I had known at *Skippy*, Sandra McKenzie. She gave me a quizzical look. "What are you doing here, Sue?" When I told her, she said enigmatically, "Oh well, we'll see."

The crew had been shooting for a week and I had been running around town picking up all the things they had forgotten for the daily runner to drive up to Scone. I was leaving the office at about

7 o'clock one evening, walking through the deserted APA lobby to my car, when the clients' phone in a corner started to ring. I looked around – the phone was night-switched and there was no one to pick up, so I did. On the other end an irascible English voice was screaming profanities. The profanities and aspersions on parentage were being directed at me, although I had no idea who this maniac was.

"Hang on a second," I said when the caller paused briefly to rummage around for fresh insults. "I just answered the phone. Who are you?"

"I'm Don fucking Chaffey and I'm trying to make a movie up here for you lot of useless bastards and I haven't seen a foot of fucking film since I got here. And I want to know what the fuck is going on!"

The profanities didn't bother me although they were coming rather thicker and faster than usual. The caller was the director of the film I was doing the shopping for, *Ride a Wild Pony*, a Walt Disney movie adapted from the James Aldridge novel *A Sporting Proposition* about a poor boy who is given a wild pony to ride to school. The film was being paid for by Walt Disney in the UK and produced by Jerome Courtland, a former Disney child star who had married Walt's daughter. Jerry was a producer in absentia most of the time, including now.

This director, Don Chaffey, a widely experienced director of television and film including several features for Walt Disney in the US, was typical of his generation of English directors – pragmatic, tough, cunning and great fun to work with once you got on his wavelength. Which at this point in our conversation, I had not. In fact, I had not even met him. I was, after all, just the Sydney office liaison, below even the bottom of the pecking order on the film.

Eventually I got enough information from the call to realise that the problem was an organisational stuff-up by someone employed by APA. So I told Don I'd see what I could do to sort it out.

"Okay, darling, but do it fuckin' quickly."

As the trouble seemed to be with the daily rushes, I called the lab. This was to be my first contact with the extraordinary Bill Gooley, the unseen force behind the wonderful images of the first generation of Australian feature films. Bill's title was Lab Liaison. His job was to oversee processing of the negative and to follow all stages of the film's life until the final print, on behalf of the lab, the director of photography and the producer. He was the cameraman's friend, and there is more than one Academy Award-winning Australian cinematographer who had his bacon saved in the early days by Bill's alert assessment of the daily negative. In the days before on-set monitors and digital recording, everyone on the shooting crew awaited Bill's call to the production manager at 8 a.m. after he had viewed the previous day's rushes to check for faults in focus, exposure and any problems with the film. His sharp eye never missed a scratch, a hair in the gate or an out of focus shot; he could tell you if a problem meant a reshoot or not, at a critical time in the planning of the next few days' shooting. You did not release an actor from the film before rushes clearance on their last day's shooting, in case a reshoot was necessary. So a miss-call from the lab could cost a lot of money. Once the production manager had received Bill's call – "Rushes are fine" – the unit would collectively exhale and get on with the day.

Bill would not only tell you whether you had a problem or not, he would cheerfully comment on performance: "I think Bobby is better in take three than take five," he'd say, and although he viewed the picture without sound, his instincts were amazing and he was usually right.

During this first conversation with Bill on *Ride a Wild Pony* I said to him, "I don't know what's going on up there, but the only way to sort it out is for you to go up and see them. So why don't we go up together and I'll help if I can."

The next day he and I set out to drive to Scone in Bill's old Holden and a friendship was born. He was funny, quick-witted and an experienced, professional expert on everything to do with the processing and developing of 35mm motion picture film. He could sort out the bullshit from the important stuff and was very unimpressed by pomposity and incompetence. We arrived at lunchtime so we could meet with Don and the production crew in the lunch break. We established the problem, worked out a solution, then drove back to Sydney. Don got his rushes on time every day after that.

After another week or so passed, I got a second phone call from Don Chaffey, this time directed to me. "The fucking production manager's leaving. And a good thing too. You'd better get up here and take over."

The production manager's *leaving*? Three weeks into a ten-week shoot? It turned out that someone had agreed to the production manager taking three weeks off in the middle of the shoot to organise a big game fishing film on the Great Barrier Reef for the American actor, Lee Marvin. Well, even for the film industry, this was pretty extraordinary. No thought, apparently, had been given to how *Ride a Wild Pony* might proceed without either a production manager or a producer, as Jerry Courtland was still nowhere to be seen.

There was more bad news. The film was about a boy and a horse. In the first week the boy had fallen off the horse and was terrified; he would not get back on again. The unit of fifty or so people was about to move from Scone in mid-western NSW to Albury, on the Victorian border.

And so I found myself arriving in Scone just as the crew was packing up to depart. There was no handover – my predecessor was already winging his way to Cairns. I was taking over as production manager on a film whose budget was today's equivalent of $15 million. I had never run anything remotely like this. When I ran into Sandra McKenzie she grinned and said, "What took you so long?"

There were some pluses. Don Chaffey, thanks to Bill Gooley,

thought I could do no wrong. The director of photography was a cinematic immortal, the Englishman Jack Cardiff who had photographed Ava Gardner and Marilyn Monroe, and filmed *The Red Shoes* and *The African Queen*. He was a quiet, introverted man who got on with the job, and he was a great support in getting through the overloaded schedule. The first assistant director was the clever one from *Katch Kandy*, Mark Egerton. The crew would have been happy with anyone who could get the organisation settled down so they could get on with their work. I had good backup, a useful lesson for the future – always get the best people in the business working under you. I just put my mind to the problems, worked seventeen-hour days for the first week and, with the help of the patient production coordinator Jenny Day, slowly sorted out the organisation of the film and got everyone working together.

I quickly worked out how to handle Don. "I'd schedule this and this on the same day but you'd never get through it."

"What do you mean, I'd never get through it? I could if I wanted to."

"Oh, I don't think even you could do that."

"Put it on and I'll do it."

And he would. But if I'd tried to boss him around and said he *had* to, he would have climbed onto the ceiling, screamed abuse at me and refused to try.

Whatever happened to my predecessor, he was not invited back. I stayed on for the rest of the shoot. We caught up the time lost and finished on schedule. We solved the boy riding the pony problem by firing the horse wrangler and having a double ride the horse in the wide shots, and shooting the close-ups on the back of a utility, with a bit of fake mane in the corner of frame.

On the last night of the shoot I went to dinner with the crew at a café in Albury. I was talking to the person next to me when they gave me a nudge. I looked up and twenty people around the table began to applaud. It was their way of saying: thanks for getting the show back on the rails. Spontaneous accolades are rare in this business. It was an amazing moment which I have never forgotten.

Don, who had come to Australia originally to direct the *Ben Hall* series for the ABC, stayed on after *Ride a Wild Pony* to direct a movie adaptation of the ABC program *The Fourth Wish*, in which John Meillon gave one of his most popular performances.

———

In 1975 I had another experience with television commercials. I knew Grahame Jennings through his wife, Peggy Carter, a makeup artist. Grahame asked me if I would come to work for him as production manager. The idea of a steady job, at least for a while, was appealing. His office was in a warehouse in Surry Hills, near The Clock Hotel. It was open plan with a lot of polished floors, works of art, antique tables and fresh-cut flowers. Advertising chic.

Grahame (I always wondered if the 'e' was on his birth certificate), an elegant, fastidious man who had been production manager on Nick Roeg's *Walkabout*, was a charmer, but he had a reputation for being very slow to pay his bills. In TV commercials the client took forever to pay the advertising agency, so the agency took even longer to pay the production house. As the shooting crews were freelance and paid on invoice, they had little ability to control prompt payment for their work. I knew the company's reputation, so I made sure that invoices were paid within the month of receipt, and I was ready to resign if the problem continued.

It takes a special kind of person to enjoy making television commercials. On the one hand, commercials are played over and over and over again, unlike drama which the audience only sees once. So every shot has to stand up to constant scrutiny by the audience. On the other hand, they are often promoting the worst excesses of the consumer society, and I could never reconcile my life being turned upside down and made a misery to achieve thirty seconds of film about Barbie Dolls, Surprise Peas, Hungry Jack's hamburgers or Napisan: "The *complete* nappy treatment". I soon discovered that in making commercials, no one ever knows what they want until they see it – and then they know that it's what they *don't* want. Usually until the hour the shoot begins, creative offerings are being rejected by the agency or the client, with everyone on the crew tearing their hair out. Then, once you start shooting, you have to go very, very slowly, or the client – sitting on the side of the set in a comfy director's chair, cups of coffee and a delicious lunch provided – thinks they are paying too much and that the shoot couldn't possibly be any good.

Most of our directors were very good at wasting time. But Henri Saffran, a taciturn French ex-ABC drama director, couldn't be bothered with the game. He would finish a shoot by lunchtime.

"Are you sure you've got it all covered, Henri?" I would ask anxiously, shuddering at the thought of complaints and reshoots once the client saw the footage.

"Fuck them, darling, it's all there," Henri would reply as he got into his car and disappeared. And it usually was. But you had to be careful what accounts you put Henri on, even though he could direct the socks off all the others.

We were asked to quote on a Marlboro commercial. This was very exciting as they were one of the big two of the time – big budgets, grand locations – the other being Benson & Hedges. Cigarette commercials had money to burn. The agency told me to ring a man called Heath Harris, who had the contract to do the horse work. I made the call, got Heath's price which was generic to all the companies quoting, put in the quote … we didn't get the job. But I filed Heath's name and number away. The horse work on *Ride a Wild Pony* had been a disaster. I knew I'd need a good horseman some time in the future. And that turned out to be sooner, rather than later.

Don Chaffey was scheduled to direct a telemovie for Walt Disney called *Harness Fever*, later released as *Born to Run*. It was another story about a boy and horses, this time harness racing, in which the boy overcomes all odds and wins the race. No doubt partly due to Don's urging, but also to my problem-solving on *Ride a Wild Pony*, Disney asked me to handle the filming.

Post-production was to be done in the UK and Jerry Courtland was again the producer, so my job was to be production manager and to provide an Australian company through which the film could be made. I knew I'd be the de facto producer as Jerry would not be around much. Today I would be called the line producer.

This was a chance for Tom and me to set up a production company. Tom came on as second unit director. That company, Samson Productions, is still going, possibly the longest-lasting independent company in the business.

We settled on the Hunter Valley for the locations and I prepared a budget. Disney said it was too high. Welcome to the world of film producing. We cut the schedule from six weeks to five, Disney said okay, and in November I resigned from Grahame Jennings Productions, relieved to get away from all the temper tantrums and childish behaviour on commercials, to start preparing for a shoot at the end of January.

Harness Fever was an entirely exterior picture; there was no "wet weather cover" (scenes located inside warm dry buildings) and it rained every day for five weeks. We were based in Muswellbrook, with filming at a grand but fading colonial mansion called Edinglassie on the Denman Road, and at various locations around Denman. It rained so much – 100 mm in one day, on top of all the other days – that sometimes the crew, based in Muswellbrook, were cut off from the horses, stabled at Denman. Vehicles frequently got bogged and we lost hours of shooting time digging them out. One day at the Denman showground I watched the grips truck sink up to its axles in mud while standing still. It felt as if I would never get it finished.

To his credit, Jerry was very supportive. Every day I would ring him in Los Angeles with some new disaster. "You can't change the weather, Sue," he'd say. "Just do your best." He gave me a great piece of advice for working with financiers, be they studios, banks, bond companies or government agencies: "No surprises." You will have support if you give warning of impending disasters; often the horror fails to eventuate, then it looks as if you have done a great job in averting it. When the worst happens, they are ready to be part of the solution. Everyone hates a disaster dropped on them out of the blue.

Some of the great names of the renaissance of the Australian film industry shared the mud with us on *Harness Fever*. Mark Egerton was back as first assistant director; Pom Oliver, now Mark's wife, was production secretary; Geoff Burton was director of photography with a camera crew of John Seale, David Burr and David Williamson – all now internationally successful directors of photography; Bill Grimmond was second unit cameraman; art director David Copping; gaffer Tony Tegg; continuity Lyn McEncroe. Heath Harris of the Marlboro commercials, with his wife Evanne, were in charge of the horses, although they are not credited as trainers. An American was imported to teach the horses to do tricks, as Disney would not trust our word that Heath

Not having fun here. Discussing the hopeless schedule with Mark Egerton.

Tom lines up a shot with Bill Grimmond. Evanne doubles for Bobby,
Tom Farley drives.

Production accountant Treisha Ghent had $20,000 in cash to pay the extras
in the Mickey Mouse briefcase.

and Evanne were able to do the work that was required. They were wrong.

The cast included John Meillon, Kit Taylor, Willy Fennell, and Wyn Roberts, and Bobby Bettles again played the child who overcomes all odds.

Having sent *Harness Fever* off to the UK for editing, and flush with funds from the job, Tom and I went to the Cannes Film Festival for the first time. The Cannes Festival was considered the best place to make contacts in international distribution and to sell independent films. *Sunday Too Far Away*, *Picnic at Hanging Rock*, *The Devil's Playground* and *Caddie* had been screened in the market place. People were beginning to notice that there was something new coming out of Australia. We wanted to see the festival and learn about what went on there. It was my first trip to Europe since 1964.

We stayed in a cheap flat in the old port where the noise of un-muffled two-stroke motorcycles and *deux chevaux* revved past our windows all night. We inveigled ourselves into whatever parties, receptions and meetings we could. We arranged meetings with uninterested studio executives from the US in busy hotel suites where assistants buzzed around bringing in bottled water and cancelling appointments. We quickly learnt the Cannes look – the person you were talking to staring past your shoulder to check out anyone more interesting who might be passing. We discovered lunch on the beach in the open air cafés which served exquisite Mediterranean *soupe de poisson avec rouille* and everyone dressed up in their smartest casual outfits. We learnt to sit on the Carlton Hotel terrace with a glass of wine and make it last for an hour, acting as if we were successful film moguls. We sent some washing to a laundry behind the markets and got it back with a bill which today would equate to eighty dollars.

Jill Dempster, now Robb, my friend and mentor from *Skippy*, was at Cannes as head of marketing for the newly established

South Australian Film Corporation. Jill had chummed up with a glamorous French sales agent, Jeannine Seawell. Jeannine had seen the Australian New Wave coming; she represented a lot of the early films. She was a helpful, friendly, wise source of advice on Cannes and the international sales arena, maintaining her support and connection with Australian film until her too early death from cancer in 1998. Jeannine gave us a fundamental piece of advice: "Don't try to second-guess what the Americans want; *be yourselves.*" That advice was timeless, although still often forgotten by funding agencies and sometimes by producers.

Not long after we returned from Cannes, I got a telephone call from Joan Long. Joan was a film historian, writer and producer of documentaries, with a distinguished and pioneering career in the industry in the fifties and sixties. She was the scriptwriter of the much acclaimed *Caddie*. I knew she was producing a film called *The Picture Show Man* which was her first feature film and for which she had written the script. She was calling me because she'd had a terminal row with the film's production manager and was looking for a replacement.

The Picture Show Man was a work of fiction, loosely based on the experiences of Lyle Penn, a travelling film exhibitor in country NSW in the silent era. Lyle Penn sent Joan his memoir when he saw her documentaries about the origins of the Australian industry, *The Pictures that Moved* and *The Passionate Industry*. Joan had chosen John Power to direct *The Picture Show Man*. John was a successful director of documentaries, some dramatised, for the ABC, and I had known him during my time there. I thought he'd be a good choice.

Writer/producer was an unusual combination but this film was very much Joan's vision, and with the wisdom of hindsight I feel sure that if she had been encouraged to direct the film herself she would have done so and the film might have been a lot better. But this was the seventies, the industry was young and still quite full of male prejudice at the distribution and government agency level, and Joan was seen as a middle-aged housewife with some writing and documentary credits. No one would have backed her with what was then a very big budget – $700,000. (You would need $10 million to make *The Picture Show Man* today.)

Joan had written the lead role for John Meillon and cast John Ewart as his pianist. She pulled off a coup by getting Rod Taylor, who had become a big star in Hollywood, to play Meillon's rival picture show man. She rewrote his part to adjust for Rod's brash American accent. The cast from *Pastures of the Blue Crane*, Jeannie Drynan and Harold Hopkins, had supporting roles. Garry McDonald, pre-Norman Gunston, was John's cranky first pianist.

The locations were set for Tamworth and Grafton. In the 1970s there was enough of old Australia left to film convincingly any period back to the 1880s, with a minimum removal of modern street furniture and some dirt laid down over bitumen. You can now fill in the period gaps with computer-generated images, but back then you had to find as much for real as possible.

Again, the crew was a rollcall of the best of the era – Geoff Burton as director of photography, Bill Grimmond and David Burr on camera, art director David Copping, Mark Egerton as first assistant director, with Mark Turnbull (*The Piano, Charlotte Gray*) and Steve Andrews (*Cold Mountain, The English Patient*) as assistants. The location manager, Betty Barnard, had already had another life in radio where she had worked with Bob Dyer. She had been married to the brother of poet Kenneth Slessor and to the trombone player Bob Barnard. And possibly to others. I remember her fondly: stick-thin, fine-boned, working her way through a packet of Camels and a flagon of rough red which sat on the floor under her desk from crew wrap till all hours of the night, making phone calls and lining up the next day's requirements.

The horses and horse-drawn vehicles were again provided by Heath and Evanne Harris, who had by now become friends. This time they needed no American boss to tell them how to set up a four-in-hand in front of a stagecoach. During filming they stayed in a caravan at the showground to be near the horses. One Sunday when I went out to see them and go for a ride, they showed me a newly acquired very cute red cattle dog pup, about eight weeks old. "Isn't she a little killer?" Evanne said.

Joan had commissioned composer Bruce Best to write the songs for the film, but they had to be rehearsed, recorded by the actors and filmed with playback, so although there were many shots of the actors, there was only one soundtrack. No thought had been given to how this was to be done.

I remembered my pal from *Ride a Wild Pony*, Sandra McKenzie, who was experienced at casting, and an accomplished pianist and musician, having frequently played piano for theatre. Sandra joined the production, rehearsed the two Johns and played the piano for the recordings so that John Ewart, who was possibly tone-deaf but disguised it artfully, could mime to them during the filming. She also doubled as extras casting and threw herself into making friends with hundreds of farmers and their families, persuading them to turn up for wardrobe at 5 a.m. and spend the day sitting around doing the same thing over and over, for a very small extra's wage and a good lunch.

The film was financed through the government agency of the day, the Australian Film Development Corporation, with involvement from Village Roadshow. Joan told me she had found a contact who promised to bring $50,000 of independent funds to complete the budget. She would not say who the contact was.

Joan was very excited about getting Rod Taylor in the film. There are many Australian actors with international reputations now, but in the seventies Rod was about as big as it got, a genuine star and an international heart-throb. Joan wanted to take him to dinner at Tony's Bon Gout the night he arrived from Los Angeles. I suggested maybe a day or two later, after he had recovered from jet lag, but Joan insisted it had to be that night. The Bon Gout was by now the trendiest restaurant in town, booked out weeks ahead. She knew I was a regular there, but she went off and tried to book a table herself, without success. So then, undeterred, she asked me to see if I could get us in. Alain the maître d' and I were fond of each other; I loved his wicked sense of humour and his stage Gallic maître d' act, and he always seemed specially pleased to see me. "Good evening, Miss Sue," he would say with a cosy twinkle. So I called him, mentioned Rod's name, and he arranged a table for five – Rod, Joan, John Power, me and Rod's travelling companion, Terry.

Joan, John and I were punctual, and as we waited for Rod it wasn't long before the entire restaurant knew, via Alain who was bursting with ill-concealed anticipation, that a celebrity was expected. The anticipation built as the star's arrival continued to be delayed. We sat around. Eventually Rod made his entrance accompanied by Terry, a burly middle-aged American. They were accompanied by two ladies. We squeezed up and Alain fitted in two extra chairs.

The Bon Gout was a very small restaurant and as usual it was crowded. The other diners made no pretence of minding their own business. All eyes were trained on us.

It quickly became obvious that Rod was very, very drunk. Joan looked disapproving. Conversation was awkward as Joan, John and I tried to find common ground with a drunk actor, his monosyllabic travelling companion and their two lady friends. Rod ignored John, told me I was okay (I had done his arrangements to travel to Australia) and appeared to be feeling some hostility towards Joan, for (a) persuading him to return to Australia with which he had an ambivalent relationship, and (b) securing his services cheaply.

With thirty pairs of eyes on us and Alain hovering excitedly nearby, Rod leant across the table and said to Joan, with an actor's clarity of enunciation, "Darlin', you're a chintzy –" and he dropped the four-letter word starting with C.

I heard the full exchange and, although it took me by surprise, I somehow immediately knew that what he meant was: you did a good job getting me so cheap and I don't like you for it, but I kind of respect you.

Looking back on our association, I now think that Joan may have suffered from deafness which she took pains to hide. In any event, at this moment the only word which appeared to get through to her loud and clear was the one with the four letters. "OH!!" she exclaimed loudly, burst into tears, stood up and stormed out of the restaurant. Thirty pairs of eyes followed her, and when the door slammed behind her, like a tennis match they swivelled back to us.

"What'd I say?" Rod turned to me. "What'd I say? What's wrong with her?"

Well, you've just called your producer the most offensive four-letter word in the English language, and you haven't even started work yet. I looked at John.

"You've upset her," he said, in his mild way. "Perhaps it would be a good idea if you went out and apologised, and asked her to come back."

"Jesus Christ," Rod said, contrite now. "Do you think so?"

He lurched to his feet and, accompanied by John, left the restaurant. That left me with Terry the companion, the lady friends and thirty pairs of eyes. I couldn't see Alain's, they were rolled back in his head. I looked at Terry.

"He's had a shit of a day," he said. "The press have been onto him ever since he got off the plane, attacking him for leaving Australia. He was supposed to go and see his mother in her old people's home in Randwick but he never made it. He knows he should have, she was expecting him."

After a few minutes, Rod and John returned to the restaurant. "She won't come back," John said. "She's going home."

Now I was cross. Joan mightn't have liked it, but she was the *producer*. She had insisted that Rod have dinner the night he arrived, his first trip home in years. Confrontation never works with actors. They hold all the cards.

"Well, fuck her, darlin'," Rod said to me. "I'm going back to my hotel and I'm flying back to LA in the mornin'."

Disaster! The film would not collapse without him, but we would have to recast a major role, there wasn't any time, and a lot of very bad publicity would result.

Rod, Terry and the girls departed. John and I continued to sit at the large empty table and looked at each other glumly. "Let's get out of here," I said.

John thought for a minute, and then said, "We'd better go to his hotel, grovel a bit and see if we can turn him round."

We spent several hours in Rod's hotel suite doing a lot of grovelling, lying and saying Joan didn't mean it, she was just upset, etc., etc. There was no sign of the hookers and Terry was useless, just sitting in a corner, staying out of it. He'd agreed to come on the trip as company for Rod, not to act as his agent. Rod became more and more morose and vengeful. He was adamant he would be getting the first flight out the next day. Eventually, around three in the morning, we left, asking him to sleep on it and reconsider.

When John rang him the next morning, he had decided that it was more trouble to leave than to stay. But his relationship with Joan never recovered. They were polite to each other but I knew that they were always just one careless word away from tearing each other's eyes out.

Many years later, I saw Rod at the Cannes Film Festival in a crowd leaving a screening. He asked, "How's Joan?" and gave me a look and a twinkle that said he had not forgotten a thing, neither his bad behaviour nor hers.

Rod Taylor, John Meillon and John Ewart were contemporaries. They had started out together as boys, acting in radio after World War II, eking out a living and doing a lot of hard drinking, until Rod left for Hollywood and Meillon for London. They were friends but also rivals, and the dynamics between them on *The Picture Show Man* were complex. John Meillon was the star, but Rod was the *star* and Meillon was jealous. Johnny Ewart was

Meillon's mate, but he had also been Rod's mate and he attached himself to Rod during the filming, like a little kid to a more glamorous older brother. This made Meillon more jealous, and Ewart nervous and furtive. They were all drinking like fiends. Meillon was never far from his Qantas bag of VB cans, and the smell of rum and pineapple juice in Rod's trailer would make my stomach turn on the unavoidable occasions that I had to go in there to talk to him.

They were all of the generation where hard drinking was a way of living. In a profession which is insecure and frequently demeaning, alcohol can substitute for self-esteem. Both the Johns died too young. Rod got his life under control and is still working.

During pre-production, Joan told me that she had promised a job on the film to a woman who had made the introduction to the mystery person who would be contributing the $50,000. I wasn't pleased about this. Although it looks to outsiders that film crews are a lot of scantily clad young people standing around doing nothing, in fact the composition of a crew is critical and they have to be skilled, in tune with the creative requirements of the film and able to work as a team. A film shoot is a pressure cooker in which a lot of money is spent very quickly and a lot of vital decisions are made in a hurry which affect the eventual outcome. One person who doesn't fit with the rest can cause the same trouble as a boil on your backside.

I tried to get out of employing this woman by doing nothing about it, but Joan was persistent. Eventually I was cornered, by which time all the positions were filled – no accident. The only job left was Rod's driver. A car and driver were part of his contract. I said to Joan that I had better meet the woman and check her out.

The young lady duly turned up in my office, exuding confidence, and assured me that she was an experienced driver and that her driver's licence was current. With considerable misgivings, I hired her and arranged for her to travel with me when I drove to location in Tamworth so I could check her out at greater length.

The conversation, once we hit the highway heading north, was not what I was expecting. She spent a lot of time talking about Jack Rooklyn, the poker machine king, whom she appeared to know well, and a lot of the stories involved Lodge 44, a motel of dubious reputation on New South Head Road in Edgecliff. She let slip that Joan had attended a meeting with Abe Saffron, and it didn't take Einstein to figure out that he was the mysterious investor of the $50,000. I hid my surprise, not to mention my disapproval, thinking of how we needed the fifty grand and that what Joan did was none of my business.

When I let her take the wheel she drove too fast so I quickly relieved her, lecturing her about driving safely and the care of the actor. I had a bad feeling but decided to see how she went on the first day of shoot.

The first location was about forty minutes out of Tamworth. I arrived on set at crew call. As I got out of my car, someone said to me, "You'd better take a look at Rod's driver."

She came tottering toward me across the grass in five-inch heels, striped long socks and hot pants which barely covered her behind. I went to find Rod.

"Mornin' darlin'," he said. "I think you'd better find me another driver."

She left that night. Joan did not demur and the matter was never mentioned again. The $50,000 never materialised, although I doubt that had anything to do with the young lady's departure. The Australian Film Development Corporation quietly kicked the can for the budget shortfall.

I had learnt a big lesson: always trust your instinct, especially where safety is concerned. I had got off lightly, and I shudder now to think about it.

We had another heart-in-the-mouth moment during a visit to the set by the then Premier of NSW, Neville Wran, accompanied by the usual press crowd. Rod, showing off, insisted on taking the Premier for a drive in his picture show van. Drawn by four black horses, it had a high driver's seat like a stagecoach. Neville Wran was game – he climbed up beside Rod who took off, whipped the horses into a gallop and headed straight for a river crossing. The van flew through the water, spray everywhere, the horses' mouths right on the bit and, to everyone's relief, pulled up safely without depositing the NSW film industry's hopes of financial support in the river. Rod had driven stagecoaches in American westerns, and he had Heath Harris curled up under the seat, terrified but with a hand on a safety rein and the brake. Even so, I still can't believe they weren't all killed. It looked great and made all the next day's papers, no doubt to the Premier's satisfaction.

My favourite scene in the film is a two-hander between John Ewart and Jeannie Drynan. Beautifully written by Joan and played with masterly timing by the actors, it is an arch and clever double entendre on the art of piano tuning.

In spite of its shortcomings, the film is a worthy record of the industry in that innocent time in the 1970s when it was still possible to make films about Australian life without the interference

John Ewart and John Meillon open the traditional bottle of champagne on completion of the wrap shot. Note the tinnies in the foreground, probably Meillon's.

and demands of American financiers or the dead hand of the film bureaucracy.

Something happened in the 1970s which has never been repeated. Take a look at the following titles:

Stork; The Chant of Jimmy Blacksmith; Newsfront; Mad Max; My Brilliant Career; Breaker Morant; The Adventures of Barry McKenzie; Alvin Purple; Stone; The Cars that Ate Paris; Sunday Too Far Away; The Odd Angry Shot; Picnic at Hanging Rock; The Devil's Playground; Caddie; The Last Wave; Don's Party; Storm Boy; The Getting of Wisdom ...

Every one of these films was either a creative or commercial success, or both. Two-thirds of them, if made today, would cost between ten and twenty million dollars each. In order to achieve their budgets and the requisite distribution, they would require "marquee" names in at least one of the lead roles. Only three of the above films had marquee actors – Richard Chamberlain in *The Last Wave*, Rachel Roberts in *Picnic at Hanging Rock* and Edward Woodward in *Breaker Morant*.

In addition to the above titles, the seventies produced at least another twenty well-made, well-received films of the second rank, in which I would place *The Picture Show Man*.

The untrammelled creative energy which poured out of Australian filmmakers in the seventies after a generation of repression, and the generally supportive, non-interventionist financial support of the government film agencies, together with the esprit de corps which enabled producers to cut through rules and regulations to keep costs down, all had something to do with the success.

But that does not explain it entirely. The films were fresh, filmmakers could tackle big subjects and they could look at Australia's history in a way which is next to impossible today on the budgets available. Today, film bureaucrats inject their taste and their opinions into what gets made. They hold the purse strings and they exercise their power. And the pressure to make films for ever cheaper budgets is unending. Consider all the low budget, angst-ridden drug and teenage dysfunction stories of the last ten years.

A world away from the grand vision of the 1970s.

THREE

Indie Prod and a Guarantee

IN 1977, THE VIETNAM WAR had been over for only three years. I was against the war and against Australia's involvement from the beginning. The moral issue seemed a no-brainer. The Vietnamese did not threaten us, we had no business threatening them. I believe all wars are immoral and no one has the right to attack and take life, unless attacked first. The same with George W. Bush's Iraq War. Both were politically motivated aggressions with no regard for morality or humanity.

When I read Bill Nagle's novella, *The Odd Angry Shot*, about a Special Air Service patrol in Vietnam, I wondered if it would make a film. Although it was told from the soldier's point of view, at the time unfashionable, it seemed to portray a sardonic view of the futility of war. It was darkly funny, which we thought might help to attract investors and audiences at a time when most were wary of such a controversial issue.

We acquired the rights and Tom adapted the novel into a screenplay. Greg Coote at Village Roadshow gave us a distribution advance, and the NSW Film Corporation came in as co-investor with the new Federal film subsidy agency, the Australian Film Commission.

The NSWFC, run by a political mate of Neville Wran's, Paul Riomfalvy, and ably managed by Jenny Woods, was a cowboy kind of outfit which worked. If Paul and Jenny liked the project, they backed you all the way. This was empowering for producers, and the NSWFC supported some great films. An unusual feature of working with them was to be offered a Scotch by Paul at ten o'clock in the morning. Usually, by the look of him, he had already had several. To close the shortfall in the budget, our lawyer, Richard Toltz, came up with a tax structure which enabled us to attract private investors.

Graham Kennedy was the biggest star in Australia, hovering above all other show business names. Bruce Beresford had cast him successfully in *Don's Party* and he was keen to do more straight acting. Tom had the idea of casting him as Harry, the patrol leader, a world-weary SAS sergeant. Everyone else thought this was a slightly bizarre idea but Tom was determined. We sent the script to Graham via his agent, Harry M. Miller.

The word came back that Graham was interested. A lunch was arranged. We were both charmed by Graham's manners and deferential attitude to filmmakers (not an act) and his enthusiasm for the film. As we ate, I was surreptitiously checking him out to see if he was too flabby or unfit to play a hardened soldier, but in his tailored jacket and trousers he seemed trim and pink and healthy. He didn't flinch at the mention of boot camp, which we had arranged with the army to turn the actors into soldiers. He would certainly get us the publicity we needed to sell the film in Australia.

Harry Miller was also charm itself over lunch, when he was in Graham's presence. It was another matter when I had to call him to negotiate Graham's deal. I later became used to screaming agents, particularly in Hollywood. But Harry was my first experience. He was as rude and offensive as possible and carried on as if we wanted Graham to sleep in a tent on location and provide his own toilet. Whereas we had budgeted for him to have the best accommodation on the Gold Coast and to be looked after like the star he was. Harry was so busy being unpleasant that he

Graham Kennedy

forgot to ask for some standard perks for Graham, which I would happily have provided. Saved a bit of money there, I thought with satisfaction.

Graham, like most great performers, was easy to deal with, provided you could do your job as well as he could do his and you accorded him the respect due to his status, but didn't make a fuss about it. He was always on time for his call and always knew his lines. He worked hard and conscientiously, and he could be as funny off screen as he was famous for being on television.

The other members of the patrol were the hot young actors of the day, John Jarrett, John Hargreaves and Graeme Blundell, and a little-known but dynamic young actor, Bryan Brown.

Graham didn't enjoy boot camp quite as much as he thought he would. Once stripped of his elegant tailoring, he was unfit with a bit of a paunch. He was a heavy smoker. However, he loved being an actor, in an ensemble with what he called "real" actors who in their turn treated him with awe. So things got off to a good start. We asked the costume designer, Anna Senior, to do her best to make him look like a digger, and you either believed him or you didn't. But his performance was credible. We doubled him in one scene where he had to run across a bridge and throw a hand grenade into a nest of Viet Cong. He looked pretty realistic in the wide shot because it was an army sergeant doing the action.

While doing research for the film I went to Canberra to the Film Archive to look at stock footage of the war for visual reference. The Archive was crammed into a few cheaply partitioned offices among other public service departments. Cardboard cartons filled with film cans lined the corridors, stacked one on top of another, some broken, with cans spilling out. You had to be careful not to trip over them. The staff were enthusiastic and helpful, but despairing at their lack of resources. On the same trip I visited the War Memorial, as it had a film collection. Here the storage was better, but I was shown a windowless brick room, stacked floor to ceiling with cans of nitrate film, records from World War I. Many of the cans had liquid oozing out of them. Some cans were

John Hargreaves

Bryan Brown

labelled, many were not. "We have no idea what's in most of them," the Memorial assistant told me.

This was Australia's visual heritage, rotting away. In the years since, this has been rectified. The Archive now has its own building in Canberra and a realistic budget. Its staff are highly trained and dedicated to the preservation of the nation's visual history. But one wonders how much was lost.

The budget of *The Odd Angry Shot* would not stretch to filming in Asia, and in any event, filming in Vietnam itself was out of the question, so soon after the war's end. We therefore needed to get the cooperation of the army to provide equipment and personnel and to allow us to film at the Land Warfare Centre at Canungra, in the hinterland behind the Gold Coast in Queensland.

At first, the army didn't want to know us. The government had recently declined to assist Francis Ford Coppola with helicopters for *Apocalypse Now*, possibly because Coppola wanted the entire RAAF fleet of helicopters for a year. To make matters worse, there were several war films, mostly World War II, being mooted at the time, and the army feared that if it helped one, it would have to help them all. So what? There were no wars on, it would have given them something to do. Not surprisingly, they didn't see it that way.

As it happened, none of the other projected films raised their money; I persisted with the army brass and brought a little pressure to bear through my political contacts, until they reluctantly agreed to help. We had to pay for everything they supplied, but it was cheaper than starting from scratch and it meant we could use trained soldiers as extras, important for authenticity. The union wasn't happy about us using soldiers instead of civilian extras to play soldiers, but they grudgingly gave permission when the logic became inescapable, even to them.

We quickly learnt that if you wanted anything done by army administration, you had to avoid Wednesday. Wednesday was sports day in the defence forces and no one, but no one, answered their phones. Had anyone wanted to attack Australia, Wednesday was the day. A foreign power could have had the invasion done and dusted by dinner time.

Once we got past the top brass, our liaison officers were wonderful. Most were Vietnam veterans, keen to see a film made about the war. The officer assigned to advise us on matters military had been in the SAS in Vietnam, and badly wounded. Although sometimes we found him a bit too much of a stickler for accuracy, we knew that he would be in trouble if the film portrayed sloppy soldiering. Part of the film's enduring success has been the realism with which the fighting scenes are portrayed, and we owe that to Major Phil Thompson.

At Canungra, two young captains smoothed our way and provided everything we needed. They also found ways around the bureaucratic restrictions of our contract, getting us lots of stuff for no charge. The contract specified that if we used soldiers as extras for a full day, we had to pay the army an amount equivalent to their salary, but for some reason, if they were only used for half a day, they came free. So we quickly learnt to ask for half-day soldiers in the morning and half-day soldiers in the afternoon, thus getting the extras for a full day for no charge. The soldiers, of course, queued up to work in the film; it was a lot more fun than guard duty and film catering was much better than army food.

One thing we could not get the army to agree to was to put us up in army accommodation at Canungra, which would have been

Blundell & Kennedy doing it for real.

time-saving and cheap. So the crew and cast stayed on the Gold Coast and drove up to location, about an hour's drive each way, every day. The road was lethal. About half of it was a dirt country back road, with creek crossings and some very nasty bends. Soldiers regularly killed themselves returning home from a night out in the bars of Surfers Paradise. We restricted the crew to a couple of beers after work watching rushes, to avoid any mishaps on the way down the mountain. What happened when they got back to Surfers, though, was something we couldn't do anything about. Graham was a good boy and went back to his hotel to study his lines for the next day, but the other actors made the most of the night life.

The lovely and talented John Hargreaves was the ringleader. John didn't waste a minute of his short life. He partied so hard it became impossible for the assistant directors to get him up in the morning and off to work. After consistent complaints from first assistant director Mark Egerton that John was holding up shooting every morning, and that talking sternly to him, while eliciting a convincing performance of contrition, didn't make any difference whatsoever, I tried a different tack. One morning after I'd sent the other actors off, Tom and I knocked on John's door at call time. No response. Knocked again. Several times.

Finally, "Yeaaaahh?"

"It's Sue and Tom, John. We've come to take you to work."

There were grunts, groans and scuffles from inside the room. The door opened a crack and a bloodshot eye appeared.

"Shit!" The eye disappeared and the sound of someone frantically dragging on clothes followed. It was unheard of for the producer and director to pick up an actor for work in the morning. That was the production department's job. Wicked as he was, John was a professional actor and he knew what it meant. There was no small talk in the car as we drove up to location, and he was more or less on time after that.

The hinterland around Canungra made a realistic backdrop for the film, and the army and designer Bernard Hides created convincing sets. The biggest problem we had was helicopters. Vietnam was a chopper war, and we were charged full rate for flying time for helicopters from Amberley Air Base. We were no Francis Ford Coppola. The number of choppers we could afford was never enough. Today it would be a simple matter to use computer generated images (CGI) to add more in post production – hundreds, as many as could be fitted on the screen. But then, what you had was what you saw.

One day we were doing a scene which needed a lot of choppers. The script said: A stream of helicopters flew overhead. We could afford only two, circling the camera to look like more than two (Roger Mirams and the Japanese). Then our Captains learnt that a Chinook was travelling to Amberley and would be flying near Canungra. They hopped on the radio and ask the pilot to do a couple of flyovers for us. That made three in the scene, where there should have been fifty.

The *Odd Angry Shot* was the first time I came across drugs on

Watching our three helicopters with production designer Bernard Hides.

films. Till that time, alcohol was the relaxant of choice. As Mark Egerton said, you knew where you stood with the drinkers. They were hung over and sullen in the morning and they got better through the day. But with drugs, you never knew what was going on. About halfway through the shoot we had an agitated call from the proprietor of the motel where a number of the supporting actors and some stuntmen were staying. "*Get them out of here! They are smoking marijuana in their rooms! I will not have drugs in my place!*" A severe talking-to followed from the head prefect, and we had to find them alternative accommodation. Unfortunately, all the cheap motels were already booked, and the culprits ended up sharing one of those huge marble-and-gold luxury Gold Coast apartments, which wasn't punishment at all.

When the shooting went over schedule by a few days, we had nowhere to stay as we overlapped school holidays, and all our Gold Coast accommodation was booked out to holiday-makers.

Tom directs the patrol.

Although the army had declined our original request to stay at the base for the whole shoot, by now we were all friends, and the Canungra commandant agreed to help out. So we arranged to move up to the barracks.

The only snag was Graham. His contract specified first-class accommodation, which no amount of imagining could be extended to cover the spartan army quarters. I broached the subject with him.

"Graham, would you care to move up to Canungra with us? It would save you that awful drive."

Politely, "No, Sue."

A driver had to be despatched each morning to drive down to Surfers to pick Graham up, and again in the evening to deliver him back to his hotel. I tried again on the last day, when a big wrap party was planned in the officers' mess following completion of shooting.

"Graham, it's going to be a bit of a wild night tonight. I don't want you going down that road in the middle of the night, it's so dangerous. And I'd like all the crew to be able to have a few drinks and let their hair down. Would you like to stay up with us? We'll get you a nice room."

Again, politely, "No thank you, Sue."

This meant that one of the assistant directors had to stay sober to drive Graham home whenever he chose to leave the party. A cruel blow. After six-day weeks, fourteen-hour days on their feet, they were entitled to some fun.

One of Mark Egerton's assistants had not worked out. He was my choice, but I'd made a mistake. He did his job only just well enough to prevent him being fired, but nobody liked him much. The actors detested him. So I thought I'd kill two birds with one stone. If someone had to miss out on the fun it would be Tony. And if Graham wanted to be difficult, he could travel in the company of someone he couldn't stand. I told Tony he was to drive Graham home whenever he was ready to leave the party, and he was not to drink alcohol until he got back to Canungra after delivering Graham to his hotel. I said nothing to Graham. I asked Su Armstrong, the production coordinator, to hold a spare room just in case.

The party was a humdinger. All the army people who had helped us, the film crew and our naughty party animal actors let it rip. By midnight the mess had run out of beer and was selling spirits by the bottle. The party was still in full swing. Graham, I observed, was the centre of an admiring group of soldiers, knocking back Scotch and enjoying himself.

About two a.m. one of the crew came to me and said, "Sue, Graham is ready to go home."

"Find Tony and tell him," I said. I went to find Graham.

"Graham, are you sure you wouldn't like to stay the night? It's so late. We have a room for you if you want it."

Like a broken record: "No thank you, Sue."

I was beaten. "Okay, Tony will take you when you're ready."

A look from Graham which in a nanosecond said, Check.

"I think I'll stay."

And when I left the party some time around four, he was still happily drinking Scotch and entertaining the army boys, the star with his audience. He got his revenge, though.

Many weeks later, back in Sydney, I had to ask him to approve some stills which, under his contract, he had the right to reject. The Roadshow publicist wanted to use some shots from the proof sheets which had a big felt pen X across them. I rang him and made an appointment to see him around five one evening. Then I went out and bought a bottle of vintage Perrier Jouet champagne, the one with the art deco painting on the side. We can drink this together on his terrace overlooking the harbour as the sun goes down, I thought happily, and then I'll ask him about the stills.

I arrived at Graham's Hunters Hill mansion with the still shots and the bottle of chilled champagne under my arm. He answered my knock with a smile and a kiss. "Sue, how lovely to see you."

We went into his kitchen and I handed him the champagne. "I brought you this," I said.

"How lovely," he said. He opened the fridge door and put the bottle inside, then turning to me, still smiling, asked, "Would you like a beer?"

He then proceeded to agree to all the shots I needed.

Just back from Vietnam? "No."

Our working relationship with Graham endured into a lasting friendship. He was genuinely fond of Tom and me, and we loved him. We were not as good friends to him as Noeline Brown and Tony Sattler, who became his family; in the years he was living in the Southern Highlands our contact was limited to the occasional fax and Christmas card. I last saw him in his nursing home in Bowral. You could talk about anything from the old days and his memory was sharp. But the present was a place he had no intention of inhabiting.

The Odd Angry Shot did well at the Australian box office, sold well internationally, made money and continues to sell into the DVD market today. It is invited to festivals to screen in retrospectives, and Tom maintains a correspondence with war veterans around the world who see in the film something which resonates with their own experience.

Shortly after completion of *The Odd Angry Shot*, the Treasurer of the day, John Howard, retrospectively disallowed the tax scheme under which our investors – and those in other films – had given us their money. They lost their tax deduction and had to pay tax at an elevated level. Needless to say, they never returned to film investment. The scheme was legal, had been approved by the government funding agencies and was controlled because it did not work without the involvement of those agencies. So the loss to revenue was quantifiable and limited by the amount of available government funds. Our investors had made their commitment in good faith – they did not deserve to be punished by a mean-spirited politician.

My farming Uncle Bob died just after *The Odd Angry Shot* was finished, and with my brother Robert, Tom and I took a small farm he had owned in the hinterland behind the Pacific Highway south of Taree as our share of his estate. The farm had been acquired by my father's older brothers around 1920 and the land had been cleared with bullocks, this backbreaking work attested to by the stack of heavy wooden yokes in the dairy, and by the death from a heart attack of one of the brothers, Tim, at the age of sixty.

The land is on the north-eastern slope of Mount Talawahl, the highest hill in the area, with views across twenty miles of plains and forest to the sea and on to Forster and Cape Hawke. The upper half of the mountain is covered in subtropical rainforest, and the bottom half in kikuyu and clover. Cabbage tree palms dot the grassland, and back then ancient fences lay in various states of disrepair across the paddocks.

In the last years of Uncle Bob's life the farm had been neglected, the cattle had gone feral and the paddocks were overrun with lantana, that pretty little pink-flowered shrub brought to Australia by

Lady Macquarie. The house, a one-room shelter built from timber hand-cut on the land before the turn of the 20th century and added to after the war, had no electricity, no running water and, by the time we got there, it was overgrown by an enormous lantana bush which reached its thorny limbs across the roof and into every room. The cows had been making themselves at home in the house and the floors were covered with a carpet of dried cow shit.

We set about to clean up the house and the land and made the house habitable in the way a well-set-up tent is habitable. We have continued to enjoy the peace and beauty of "The Mountain" ever since. The house is as basic as ever; it recently survived a mini-cyclone which took off half the roof.

After Christmas 1979 we spent a couple of weeks at The Mountain, then finished our break by driving up to Nowendoc to visit Heath and Evanne Harris who had moved from Sydney to a farm on the windswept plateau between Nowendoc and Walcha.

On a wintry hillside they had built a house and stables and a round yard so that they could better service films requiring horses and other animals. They ran several camels in the paddocks which gave the locals something to talk about. Evanne's mare,

The house at The Mountain

The Mountain

Blacksmoke, had special quarters to herself near the house. This horse had crossed over. A coal-black thoroughbred, she stood sixteen hands high. She and Evanne had such empathy and mutual understanding that they were wonderful to watch together. Blackie basically did anything Evanne asked her, and Evanne did pretty much everything Blackie wanted. When we went for a ride up into the open forest Blackie would come with us, like a dog, cantering alongside the group of riders, no bridle or lead rope, no instructions necessary, waiting patiently with everyone else while gates were opened and closed, and keeping pace with the group. She would rear, lie down, play dead, pick up your hat, anything you could think of, and she loved it all as a game.

It was wise to keep on the right side of Evanne, as she had an unusual way of recording her relationships with people – she would name an animal after them. She had an unerring instinct about the personality traits of animals and people, so it wasn't always something to be sought after. When she worked on a US movie of the week starring Racquel Welch, she never said what she thought of the ageing sex symbol but she named a small piglet after her.

91

The piglet grew into a six-foot sow. In response to Evanne's call across the paddock, "Racquel, Racquel!" it would run to her and roll over for its enormous pink belly to be rubbed.

Killer, the red cattle dog pup which had arrived during the filming of *The Picture Show Man*, had grown up and shown exceptional aptitude for film acting. Now she had had a litter of pups of her own and on this visit, unexpectedly, Heath picked up one of them and said, "This is for you."

I had grown up with dogs and Tom and I had often discussed wanting one, but our lifestyle and the house in Paddington were not suited to an animal, so we had given up on the idea. But now, handed this seven-week-old gorgeous thing, we put up no resistance and just accepted her into our life. Into the car she went, a bit of string tied to her collar, and home to Sydney with us.

Cattle dogs are born white and gradually take on their colour – red or blue. Our pup became a delicate strawberry blonde with a pure white tail. We called her Rita, after Rita Hayworth, because she had red hair and her mother was a film star. There was a significant amount of dingo in this line, and both Killer and

Rita liked to be up with the action.

Rita had intelligence and a streak of cunning which made them entrancing companions and willing workers with a film crew.

The timing was right. We had moved into a phase of our working lives which gave us enough independence to incorporate a dog, so Rita came with us to the office and to film locations. She adored going to The Mountain. In the creek on the boundary of our land there was a mud hole, and while I was opening the gate into the neighbour's paddock, Rita would disappear; when I was ready to ride on, she would bound back, a dark, chocolate-brown from her nose to the tip of her beautiful tail, eyes glittering, as happy as a dog ever gets.

In the late seventies a group of independent producers got together to form IFFPA – the Independent Feature Film Producers' Association. There were a growing number of issues to deal with. The unions were picking us off one at a time, so a group approach was called for. It was also a more effective way to lobby the government for continued subsidy to the industry and to deal with the film agencies with a united voice.

The unions were particularly militant throughout this period.

They made producers' lives a misery through the seventies and into the nineties. Most producers were single operators without capital, battling to survive and to run businesses on their quite small fees. Generally they earned less over a year than many of their employees. Most film crew were independent contractors, working through their service companies. Films were well supervised financially due to the involvement of the government agencies and well run by responsible and capable production managers. But this didn't bother the unions. On *The Picture Show Man*, the technicians' union ordered its members at the laboratory not to process the negative because the crew was not 100 per cent unionised. Instead of talking to individual crew members, the union had a jackal-like policy of attacking the weakest link, usually the producer. (Bill Gooley, God love him, processed anyway and called us each morning until the dispute was resolved to give us a detailed report on the negative.) I always took the view that union membership was a matter for the individual and the union, and not the responsibility of the employer.

The situation was not helped by the fact that the NSW Film Corporation was set up by a state Labor Government which had appointed the union secretary to the Corporation's board. You could not get any money out of the NSWFC unless the crew were 100 per cent union members. For years, producers were forced to send crew lists to the union and to submit to standover tactics and verbal abuse from small-time Hitlers drunk with their own power.

The IFFPA group included Tony Buckley, the McElroy brothers – Hal and Jim – David Elfick, Matt Carroll, Patricia Lovell, David Hannay, Michael Thornhill, Margaret Fink, Joan Long, Tom and me. We met and plotted regularly.

Before long, the Film & Television Production Association of Australia, F&TPAA, got wind of our activities and invited us to join. F&TPAA was an employers' organisation run for the benefit of the film studios – APA, Porters, Artransa etc. – all of whom survived on the production of television commercials. F&TPAA was the registered employers' representative for arbitration purposes. When we had approached it for help in our conflicts with the unions, F&TPAA had breezily flicked us off as gnats who were too unimportant for the big boys to bother with. But once IFFPA started making its presence felt, F&TPAA decided it was time to get in on the act. Considerable pressure was put on the members of IFFPA to join F&TPAA.

As you would expect from a bunch of self-driven individuals, the decision about whether to join or not divided the members. Eventually it was agreed to join. A Feature Film Division of F&TPAA was created, and to cut a long story short, it eventually gobbled up the association and took it over as the drama production industry grew and the importance of the old studios declined. Later the name was changed to the Screen Production Association of Australia – SPAA – and it continues today as the formal employers' representative for all of the production industry.

In one capacity or another, I spent ten years on the council of F&TPAA/SPAA and it was never dull. The membership was volatile, opinionated and outspoken. There were constant staff problems. The unions were better funded and spent much of their time dreaming up ways to outsmart us. Usually, they succeeded. A bunch of volunteers who were frantically busy just staying afloat were no match for dedicated full-time union employees.

In the middle of April 1980 I got a telephone call which once again sent my life in an interesting direction. Richard Soames was the head of Film Finances, the UK completion guarantee company. We had met briefly when Tom and I were in Europe in 1976. We had noticed the Film Finances listing in the trade magazines and thought, aha! – another source of money for films. When we met, however, it was politely pointed out by Richard that Film Finances didn't actually *finance* films, it guaranteed to the investors that the film would be completed and delivered, for which service it charged a fee. When we had asked him if he was interested in working in Australia he rolled his eyes and said, not at all, we know nothing about Australia.

Now I was invited to have lunch with Richard and his finance manager at the Sebel Town House, the hotel in Elizabeth Bay much loved by show business people. It transpired that Film Finances had put a toe in the Australian water after all, albeit very cautiously, on a Hollywood picture. The company had bonded a William Holden film which had filmed on location in NSW. Now they had agreed to bond *Roadgames*, a thriller starring Stacy Keach and Jamie Lee Curtis. *Roadgames* was an Australian film which producer/director Richard Franklin had financed in the US. Film Finances was less certain about this film and wanted to have a representative on the picture. John Daniell, now head of Production and Development at the Australian Film Commission, had suggested me.

Richard Soames is a tall, diffident Englishman with a sharp sense of humour and a brilliant business mind. He suffered from myopia and at that time wore glasses with thick, almost impenetrable, lenses. He was the master of the awkward pause, into which many a guilty producer dropped information they had been planning to keep to themselves, just to break the silence. Richard ran the world's most successful completion guarantee company for more than thirty years and it was no accident that he remained on top in what has to be one of the planet's riskier businesses.

Characteristically, he didn't tell me much about what he wanted from me; I just figured out that Film Finances wanted to avoid *Roadgames* going over budget and I was to do what I could to see that that happened. Also characteristically, he didn't quibble about my fee or my expenses.

Shortly after our meeting I flew to Melbourne to meet the *Roadgames* production crew.

"Of course you realise it can't be shot in the time," was the first assistant director Tom Burstall's opening remark to me. The time allowed in the budget was eight weeks. Trying not to panic, I

Richard Soames on the set of *Les Patterson Saves the World*, 1986.

asked, "How long, then?"

"Well, I've scheduled it in twelve weeks," he said with finality. Tom soon resigned. And then it got worse. His replacement, who had never been to the locations, scheduled two big scenes 150 kilometres apart on the one day.

The film was about a truck driver travelling to Perth from Melbourne with his pet dingo, and a murder mystery along the way. It is now no secret that Stacy Keach's recreational drug of choice at the time was cocaine, and on *Roadgames* I guess he was warming up to his later jail sentence. Unfortunately he became a bit too friendly with the stunt coordinator who at the time was also having a romance with funny substances. Jamie Lee Curtis was a nice girl, professional and straightforward. She was also very young. She did her job and stayed out of trouble.

The dingo was played with panache by Killer, and Heath was on the crew as Killer's handler. More than once he was to alert me to looming disasters.

Richard Franklin was a talented director, but his bedside manner left a lot to be desired and the crew didn't like him. The producer, Barbi Taylor, was a capable and experienced production manager but she was out of her depth trying to control Richard, who had a cavalier attitude to the budget and who had learnt all the tricks during his apprenticeship in Hollywood, which had included working with Alfred Hitchcock. In any event, it was Richard's film and he had brought Barbi in to deal with the physical producing, so he was never going to take much notice of her attempts to restrain him.

I spent a lot of time on location, flying in and out and each time finding a worse situation than the one I'd left, in spite of all the promises that everything would be fixed. I spoke to Richard Soames in London a lot, some of the more interesting calls being made from a party line on the Nullarbor late at night. I would clear the production office so I could tell Richard what was going on and get his advice, but I knew that we had several interested locals listening in as the line hummed between Madura, Perth and London.

The completion guarantor is responsible to the investors for delivering the film, preferably for the amount budgeted, but in any event the film that the investors had been expecting. So if this result can't be had for the money available, the guarantor has to provide the extra funds. While the contractual power it has over the production is total, it nevertheless has to be exercised carefully, because investors do not want a film which has come in on budget but which has expensive elements missing, just to save money. As an example, think about *Picnic at Hanging Rock* without the girls climbing the rock and disappearing. "Oh well, we had to save two days' shooting to save money. The film can end with the picnic before they climb the rock."

Fortunately, most producers are competent and capable and see that their films are made for the budget, or guarantors would be out of business very quickly. Many producers are better than competent; they ensure that the best result is squeezed out of every penny. But every now and again a combination of circumstances brings about very bad behaviour, and then the guarantor has to step between the doggy doo to try to get to an end result which satisfies everyone. When things go wrong on a movie, the seeds of disaster have been there from day one. It is a matter of sniffing them out and then trying to make changes or build a support structure which can resist the attempts of the participants to wreck the whole edifice.

The director holds all the cards. Changing directors is almost never an option, as the time and money involved is counterproductive even before the quality of the result is taken into consideration. So if a director wants to kick over the traces, manipulation, pressure and threats are about the only weapons of control when reasoning no longer works. But a director has to be very, very good and consistently successful at the box office to survive a reputation as "difficult".

One thing I have observed in thirty years of watching the making of other people's movies is that while a smooth shoot does not guarantee a successful film, a troubled production pretty much guarantees a flop. Perhaps this is because too much effort goes into the fights, ego trips and cover-ups, and not enough into considering what is the best way to tell the story.

Roadgames had a difficult director and a producer without the right amount of authority. The lead actor and the stunt coordinator were frequently high as a kite. The director's Film School student attachment learnt that it was best not to find herself and the director alone in his trailer. I was trying to keep the show on the rails while figuring out how far, as the completion guarantor, I could go to achieve the best result. It was a blooding, and in spite of my efforts the film went over budget, but I'd like to think not as much as if I hadn't been there. Richard Soames was stoic, didn't blame me and paid the overage, as he was to do many times in the future, without demur.

Later that year I was assigned another film for Film Finances. Hemdale, the UK company which was a partnership between

David Hemmings and John Daly, was making a film in New Zealand called *Race to the Yankee Zephyr*. Melbourne producer Tony Ginnane was also involved. David Hemmings, the beautiful actor from *Blow Up*, was the director. It turned out he was a much better actor than director.

The film was to be shot near Queenstown. Again I spent a lot of time on location, doing my ineffective best to control David Hemmings. It was like trying to hold on to frogspawn; he made Richard Franklin seem easy to handle. The film went merrily over budget. Richard Soames paid a visit during the filming, but even he wasn't up for controlling David and, short of removing him (which as mentioned was an action which usually only made things worse), all we could do was damage control.

The trip home from that visit was notable because we hitched a lift with the financier and entrepreneur Peter Fox in his private Lear Jet. The eighties had begun.

In May 1981 the Fraser Government enacted legislation which for the first time gave dedicated tax incentives to investors in Australian films. The attraction was a 150 per cent deduction on investment, and a 50 per cent rebate on returns. The fairy god-mother to the industry was the Minister for the Arts of the day, Senator Robert Ellicott. I believe that the Treasurer, John Howard, consistently negative, voted against the legislation in cabinet.

The legislation was the result of a concerted lobbying effort by the film industry, with all the traditional enemies – producers, unions, government funding agencies – hopping into bed together for as long as it took to pressure the government. It was said that inviting the Minister to visit the Cannes Film Festival was the coup de grâce – a few days at the industry's most glamorous and hedonistic gathering and he was won over. I doubt that was the case, but Senator Ellicott was such a nice bloke and such a friend to the industry, I'd like to think he enjoyed himself.

Because of Howard's action in retrospectively disallowing the informal scheme which had been working quite nicely, and at a limited level, to finance films, production had been in the doldrums. Development of scripts, however, had continued because the government film agencies had enough money to pay for scripts to be written, but not enough to fully finance the making of films. The industry, therefore, was bursting with unproduced scripts. With the introduction of the new legislation, known as 10BA from the division of the Taxation Act under which it was listed, production took off like a bushfire in a westerly wind.

Until this time the Australian Film Commission had made provision within its investment allocation on each film to cover the possibility of the film going over budget. Now, with so much more production happening, the amount required to be put in escrow would have sent the AFC broke. But funds to complete a film if it got into difficulties were an essential protection in the financing process. So, with barely a conversation about it, I found myself representing Film Finances on all the new 10BA films.

One of the requirements of the new legislation was that the film had to be completed within twelve months of the year in which the investor claimed the tax deduction. As investors were only interested in writing a cheque as close to the end of the tax year as possible – that is, at the last possible minute so that they could get their tax deduction immediately – that meant that all the 10BA films had to be completed by the following June 30. The normal length of the production process – at least for modest Australian films – from the start of pre-production to delivery of the final print, is about forty weeks. This meant that all the films financed at 30 June 1981 had to rush into production immediately so they could be delivered before the end of the following tax year.

All of a sudden, twenty feature films went into production. They included *The Man from Snowy River*, *Monkey Grip*, *Squizzy*, *Starstruck*, *We of the Never Never*, *The Killing of Angel Street*, *Winter of our Dreams* and *Puberty Blues*.

There were, at the time, no more than three experienced feature film crews across the country. The bunching of production naturally brought out the worst in people as they tried to steal crew from each other or persuade themselves that someone who had been a runner on his last film could be competent to be first assistant director on his next. Inflation was rife as experienced technicians played one production off against another to see how much they could increase their salaries. Chaos ensued. I was never off a plane.

In the midst of all this, Tom and I grabbed a winter weekend at The Mountain. We were shut up in the kitchen on a cold wet night, the fire stoked up and rain battering the iron roof. Around 10 o'clock, just as we were thinking about going to bed, there was a shout and a flashing light outside. We looked at each other, eyes wide. Axe murderers? Rita awoke from her dream under the table and her hackles rose. We looked around for a weapon but nothing came to hand. We cautiously opened the door. I bravely let Tom go first, waving a torch. Voices came out of the darkness. Rita barked the kind of bark which dogs make when they are scared too, to tell the intruder to back off or they'll go for the throat.

Slowly, out of the rain, two figures emerged. We let Rita make as much noise as she liked until we heard, "It's John and Leigh."

Su Armstrong, my coordinator on *The Odd Angry Shot*, was working in my office, helping out with the Film Finances load. We had no phone at The Mountain, so the arrangement was that I would call her each morning from the telephone box in the village to check how things were going (mobile phones being a thing of the future). As there was no way for her to contact us directly, the only person I could think of for her to ring in an emergency was John Vaughan, my uncle's solicitor who lived in Forster, so I had given Su his number and then forgotten about it.

We had been asked to guarantee the adaptation of the classic Australian novel *We of the Never Never* at the last minute. It was financed by Adams Packer, a film venture between Kerry Packer and Phillip Adams, and rushed into production to meet the tax deadline. It was to shoot near the property in the real story, Elsey

Station, out of Katherine in the Northern Territory. I should have gone to location to vet it before they started, but it took off in such a rush there was no time; I was assured that everything was under control and there was no need for me to get in their way. Not the last time verbal assurances weren't worth the paper they were written on, to quote Sam Goldwyn.

Now, Su had received a desperate call that the film had hit trouble. Urgent action was needed. John and Leigh took Su's message of being urgent as being *urgent*, and jumped in their car to drive the fifty kilometres late at night, in the rain, from their house at One Mile Beach on the other side of Forster, to give us the message: call Su Armstrong. They missed the track across the house paddock in the dark and their car had slid down the hill and become bogged. They were wet and very muddy when they arrived at the house, to be greeted by a furiously barking dog and two very unwelcoming people. Appalled by our inhospitable greeting, we dragged them into the house, stoked up the fire, opened a new bottle of wine and gave them towels to dry themselves off.

Early next morning after we had dug out the Vaughans' car, I drove down to the phone box and rang Su. The filming had ground to a halt. The production manager had already departed ahead of a lynching by the crew, and the producer had resigned and was on his way to Darwin airport, never to be seen again. In a way which I was to learn was a hallmark of dysfunctional management, they had sat on the problems, futilely hoping they could fix them, before calling the guarantor. This always has the effect of creating a big explosion, exactly the opposite of the outcome they want.

The director of *We of the Never Never*, Igor Auzins, was a television director from the Crawford stable. His one previous feature film was *High Rolling*, distinguished for the arrival on screen of a very feisty Judy Davis. Igor was a handful (another one) and although he must have toed the line shooting *Homicide*, when he got on to a movie set he seemed to think he was John Ford. The book, one of the jewels of Australian classic literature, deserved better than this heavy-handed attempt to transfer it to the screen. But that was not my problem or my responsibility. My job was to get the movie shot.

By the time I arrived on location, filming was still suspended because there was nothing ready to shoot. The crew were sullen and uncooperative, having been given too much false information or no information at all. Igor was keeping a low profile on the basis that these were *production* problems, nothing to do with him.

I scratched my head.

In my years as a film guarantor I saw many dysfunctional productions and a litany of bad behaviour, but I have never, before or since, seen a film which had ground to halt because there was *nothing* ready to shoot. We got the production back on track and oversaw completion of the film, but the damage was done.

Some years later Tom and I drove from Darwin to Alice Springs, stopping at Katherine on the way. The homestead set

Production Designer Jo Ford's cry of frustration on *We of the Never Never*.

from the film had become a tourist attraction. A few miles away was the site of the real Elsey homestead, now just a patch of bare ground on a rise overlooking a dry creek bed. We visited the hot springs, deep malachite water surrounded by palm trees and tropical growth, described so vividly by Jeannie Gunn when a droving party stopped there for a swim. Now, the pools were solid with half-naked tourists and the nearby carpark filled with vans and four-wheel drives.

Other memorable experiences that year included *Dead Easy*, produced by John Weiley and directed by Bert Deling, director of the avant-garde seventies films *Pure Shit* and *Dalmas*. Bert was used to doing things his way and John, always a lovely guy with sometimes wonderful ideas, proved not to include tough line-producing skills as one of his key strengths. Film Finances made a payout to complete the film. Then there was *Burning Man*, nicknamed Burning Budget. Another overage.

By the end of 1981 it was obvious we could no longer run the business with just ourselves, Rita and occasional help from friendly production managers. We set about looking for someone to run the office and, after a couple of false starts, we hired a shy twenty-six-year-old secretary, Christine Gordon. Chris remained with us, with a short break, for more than twenty years. She was the rock around which the business was built, she knew everyone and where to find everything. For information or help, "Call Chris at Samson" became a byword in the industry.

FOUR

Lawyers, Accountants and their Well-Heeled Clients, or an Excuse for Bad Behaviour

THE FINANCIAL BOOM of the eighties brought both money and rodeo riders to the film industry. The tax scheme attracted a lot of peripheral hangers-on who hoovered up their profits and added hundreds of thousands to the cost of production. On the other hand, the incentive was an important development in the evolution of the modern Australian film industry. It took the business into a bigger, more sophisticated financing environment, and the sheer turnover ensured that some of the great money makers of all time were produced – *Crocodile Dundee, The Man from Snowy River, Mad Max II* and *Beyond Thunderdome*. The great mini-series dramas – *All the Rivers Run, Harp in the South, Bodyline, Vietnam* – took Australian television drama to a new level and won massive audiences who were thrilled to be entertained with Australian stories.

Building on the successes of the seventies, a powerhouse of talent evolved from a tiny film industry. It is hard to believe now that as recently as thirty years ago Australia was an international backwater; many people, if they thought about it at all, believed people spoke German there. It was Australian films which first reached out to the rest of the world and made it take notice.

The Australian taxpayers got their investment back in spades.

—∞—

For completion guarantor Film Finances, having the business all to ourselves was, of course, too good to last. The first of a succession of competition completion guarantors entered the Australian industry in 1983, with varying success. One of the early films bonded by the new competition was *Midnite Spares*, a film about car racing.

Film production can on occasion be physically dangerous. Crews work very long hours, under pressure to get things done as quickly and as cheaply as possible. Action filming is inherently risky. Until 1983, there were no specific safety regulations in the Australian film industry. Safety was a matter for the combined common sense of the producer, director, production staff and on-set heads of department. Mostly, this worked pretty well. So when a talented young camera assistant, David Brostoff, was killed during filming on the set of *Midnite Spares*, the industry was in shock. It was an accident, but one which should never have happened.

I had a conversation soon afterwards with Heath Harris about the tragedy. Heath and Evanne were extremely safety conscious; it was one of the things I liked about working with them. Heath said, "There should be an industry safety code which all productions and crews have to abide by." It was one of those statements which, once you've heard it, seems obvious.

I took Heath's idea to the F&TPAA council who agreed that we should design a safety code and that it had to involve the unions as representatives of the actors and film crews. We wanted to get an industry consensus on a set of standards and procedures which would work both upwards and downwards. Producers and production managers would have obligations in setting up and running a production. Film crews and actors would have rules which would encourage them to speak up when pressures of time and money made it difficult for them to object to doing something which in their view was dangerous. In today's world of over-regulation, it seems weird to think that this was ever the case. But it was.

It was also one of the rare occasions – apart from lobbying the government for more money – when we found ourselves on the same side as the unions. They took on the work of drafting the code, working with a committee of representatives of all the interested parties. Out of this came a small but comprehensive handbook titled *The Film Industry Safety Code* which was issued to every working member of the industry. It instituted, among other things, a compulsory safety report on every film, prepared by a qualified person, which outlined all potentially hazardous activities proposed by the script and/or the locations, and actions to be taken to prepare for the risks. Although the code has now been superseded by government Occupational Health and Safety regulations, the safety report continues as an integral part of the preparation of every film.

Among the films we guaranteed in the early eighties was *Careful He Might Hear You*, produced by Jill Robb. Jill set up her production office in one of the buildings in the Sydney Show Ground at Moore Park, a popular location for short-term rentals as production offices. One morning when I dropped in to see how they were going, she said, "I've seen people riding horses around here. I think I'll check it out and see if we can get a ride."

She introduced herself to John Leckie, a Centennial Park ranger who ran a boarding service on the side in the showground stables. John offered us a couple of horses and, for the duration of pre-production on *Careful*, Jill and I would ride out in the early morning a couple of times a week, with Rita ecstatically trotting along at heel, and we would discuss life, gossip and cost reports as we cantered round the leafy riding track in Centennial Park. At the horse trough, two-thirds of the way round, Rita would race ahead, jump up and dive into the trough, tunnel through the water and jump out again, shaking out a cascade of fine spray before resuming her position beside my horse's nearside back leg, radiating joy.

Centennial Park, early morning

I continued to exercise horses for John, riding three or four mornings a week before work. No one much used Centennial Park then, and soon I got bolder – I would leave the track in the dawn mist and gallop through the trees, up the slopes and down through the long grass to the lake on the outer perimeter, with Rita beside me. We all enjoyed the exhilaration and the freedom of the morning. Once in a while we would cross paths with John the park ranger on horseback. He would say sternly, "Now, girlie, back on the track," and we would head for the horse track until he was out of sight, knowing that he knew that what he didn't see he didn't know.

A lot of my time was being spent with F&TPAA lobbying the government to try to iron out some of the practical problems with the 10BA legislation. After Bob Ellicott moved on we had a surprisingly good relationship with the new minister, Tom McVeigh, a National Party dairy farmer from Queensland who took to the Arts portfolio with zest. However, our love affair did not last long.

In March of 1983 the Hawke Government was elected and Barry Cohen took over as Arts Minister.

Ministers of the Crown, in my experience, come in two varieties: self-important egotists, and hard workers who listen to their constituents, get to know their portfolio and do their best to make a success of it. Of the ministers I've dealt with, the latter include Bob Ellicott, Tom McVeigh, Bob McMullen and Michael Lee – equally divided by politics.

In 1983 the ATO changed the timing ruling, allowing two years instead of one to complete the film following the year in which the tax deduction was claimed. This eased the bunching of production, which made a big difference to the way films were planned and managed.

A year later Igor Auzins was back, directing a film produced by John Weiley about a mythical ironman race called *The Coolangatta Gold*. The film was being made for Hoyts Edgely, a partnership between Terry Jackman, the youthful and dynamic head of Hoyts Cinemas, and Michael Edgley, the diminutive scion of the circus family. They had formed a partnership to finance and make Australian films. Set on the Gold Coast, the budget for *The Coolangatta Gold* was over $5 million. In today's depressed film industry, $5 million is a lot of money. In 1983 it was huge.

John assured me he could handle Igor; the film, on the face of it, was not such a big deal logistically – two brothers pitched against each other in a quest to win a fabled race. How hard could that be? Very, as it turned out.

First of all, it rained a lot. The film was mostly composed of exteriors, meaning little wet weather cover. Sequences were never completed, and trying to match the weather at a later date to the part of the scene already shot became like an ingrown toenail where you can never quite get that last little bit out. Then there was "The Race". John had pulled off a promotional coup to have a real race sponsored by Kelloggs, with a large cash prize, to be run on a specific date. The actors had to be integrated into the actual event.

I was up and down to the Gold Coast like a yoyo. John was always reassuring; when Igor was confronted he would respond with a look from his ice-blue Baltic eyes which focused itself somewhere far behind you. Because of all the weather problems, it was difficult to keep track of what coverage was essential and what constituted Igor going for his Academy Award. Gradually, it dawned on me that it was possible that the whole film was being shot *twice*.

Film Finances made a contribution to the final cost, the film did no business and the Coolangatta Gold race went into limbo for several years. However the race has since made a reappearance, and every time I see publicity about it I shudder.

The Coolangatta Gold was Igor's last Australian film as director. John went on to have an interesting career, making the groundbreaking and profitable documentary *Antarctica* and the large-format documentary features *The Edge* (about the Blue Mountains) and *Solarmax* (about the sun). An innovative thinker, he was a valuable member of the F&TPAA council for several years.

In October, the Labor Government reduced the tax incentive from 150%/50% to 133%/33%. It got harder to attract investors.

In November, Rita gave birth to ten pups. It was a planned pregnancy. The father was a well-bred red heeler we had met in Centennial Park. Although he lived at the Albury, the gay pub in Paddington, he was an uncomplicated heterosexual and proved a happy volunteer. The pups were perfectly marked, five red and four blue. We had nine little dependents to find homes for.

The South Australian Film Corporation undertook a mega production of Rolf Boldrewood's Australian classic, *Robbery Under Arms*. SAFC financed it with the support of Robert Holmes à Court under the 10BA legislation. It was an ambitious undertaking which was to be a six-part mini-series shot on 35mm film with a feature film to be edited out of the mini-series material. Sam Neill played Captain Starlight. The production was well run, on budget, the producer and directors dedicated. The feature film was released first, only to nosedive at the box office. This put a dampener on the mini-series, which was good entertainment for its genre. Robert Holmes à Court quickly lost interest in the film industry.

—◦◦◦—

David Roe had come to Sydney as the executive director of the Australian Film Institute in the late seventies. In 1984 he became a producer for the Yugoslavian director Dusan Makavejev. Makavejev was famous for his film *WR: Mysteries of the Organism*, which had created a controversial stir at European film festivals. His most recent film, *Montenegro*, had screened at Cannes. Now he was in Australia to make a screen adaptation of Frank Moorhouse's novella, *The Coca Cola Kid*, which was eagerly anticipated by the people chosen to work on the film – some of Australia's best. No one was prepared for what was to come.

Makavejev and the Australian crew went together like fish and sausages. The crew were the Australian A list, including future Academy Award winner director of photography Dean Semler, production designer Grace Walker, and costume designer Terry Ryan. They just wanted to make a great film for this famous director, but nothing they did seemed to please him. Production was chaotic and before long the crew were shattered and demoralised.

Eric Roberts and Greta Scacchi played the leads in the film. Eric was high-flying on another well-documented Hollywood cocaine habit, and Greta couldn't stand him. The shoot was made bearable for her by meeting Tim Finn, who composed the score and with whom she spent a number of years subsequently.

A lasting image from the film is of David Roe making an appearance as a quarantine inspector, in the manner of the day – skinny pale legs in short shorts and long socks, striding through a newly-landed Qantas jet, spraying the overseas visitors with insecticide.

Makavejev and Australia parted company without regret.

—◦∞◦—

Hoyts Edgely financed another epic, this time about those iconic stumblebums, Burke and Wills.

John Sexton, an ex-ABC journalist/producer, had become an independent film producer. He had produced two indifferent adaptations of comic strips, *Ginger Meggs* and *Fatty Finn*, followed by the successful *Phar Lap*. Now he was on board this new Hoyts Edgley production as producer, with a script written by Englishman, Michael Thomas, about the disastrous journey of the explorers Burke and Wills from Melbourne to the Gulf of Carpentaria.

John knew his limitations and did not pretend to be a hands-on producer. He engaged a top line producer, Greg Ricketson, and two of the best production people in the business, Carolynne Cunningham (later to become Peter Jackson's first assistant director on *Lord of the Rings* and nominated for an Academy Award as producer of *District 9*) and Lynda House (later producer of *Muriel's Wedding*) as production manager and production coordinator. Mark Turnbull was first assistant director. This made for a production team which could punch above its weight on any film anywhere in the world. The cinematographer was Russell Boyd (*Picnic at Hanging Rock, Gallipoli* and to win an Academy Award for *Master and Commander*). Evanne was in charge of the animals, which included twenty camels.

Jack Thompson was engaged to play the Irishman Robert O'Hara Burke, and the English star Nigel Havers played William John Wills. Greta Scacchi appeared briefly as Burke's love interest, and actors such as Chris Haywood, Arthur Dignam and Redmond Phillips made appearances.

The production was scheduled to shoot on Cooper's Creek, not far from where the real explorers came to grief in 1861.

All very good, so far. Very promising. But the director was

Graeme Clifford.

Clifford, an Australian film editor working in Hollywood, had directed the well-received *Frances* in 1982. A perfectly nice man to meet socially, even likeable, he turned into Mr Hyde on the set. Once production started, it seemed to me that he wasn't going to be bound by any rules, budgets, producers or pesky completion guarantors.

In no time at all, the film was over schedule, over budget and bogged down in confusion. I flew to location for a showdown with Clifford and the producers.

The production had set up mining camp accommodation on the bank of the Cooper, a couple of miles from Innamincka. I flew to Adelaide, then to Moomba in a commuter jet where I was met by John Sexton who drove me to the camp, filling me in on the latest problems. The road was just tracks in the bulldust, nothing but desert and spinifex to the steel-blue horizon. Carolynne Cunningham had an adventure on that road halfway through the shoot – probably due to a moment's inattention caused by the weighty problems of the schedule and lack of sleep, she rolled her Hertz station wagon. Unhurt, but unable to get back on the road, she was rescued by a handsome mining engineer who just happened to be passing. He drove her to Moomba for a checkup, drove her back to Innamincka, then for quite a long time after, flew in from all around the world to visit her wherever she happened to be filming. How romantic is *that*!

Romance was in the air for Evanne, too. Going through the break-up of her marriage to Heath and very unhappy, she met a tall blond wildlife ranger who she referred to as The Bird Man; he stayed in her life for several years.

After I arrived at location I walked over to the camel camp. Evanne said, "I'm just going to the set – can you give me a hand?" So I rode out with her to the set a couple of miles away on a bay horse called Mouse, leading a camel. I was told later that Clifford was very tense about the arrival of the completion guarantor. What he wasn't expecting was that she would arrive on a horse leading one of his camels. After a startled introduction, he studiously ignored me.

Terry Jackman and Michael Edgely flew in the next day in their own jet. No bouncing up the bulldust track for them. They were both wearing neat bush shirts and very tiny pink shorts. If they had not both been so overwhelmingly heterosexual, one would have wondered. Meetings were held about script cuts. Terry and Michael strode off to Clifford's demountable quarters, brown legs and muscular bottoms flexing, to have it out with him.

They emerged with success. "He's agreed, yeah, it'll be fine," Terry said. As if, what was the problem, guys, and why did we have to come all the way out here to fix it?

They took off in their jet and disappeared.

I relaxed and went for a ride with Evanne into Innamincka at the end of the day. We tethered the horses like something out of a western, had a beer in the pub, then set out in the pale evening light to ride back to camp. On the way we passed the airstrip, just a length of gravel beside the road, where a small plane had just landed. We said goodday to the three adventurers who had secured their aircraft and were opening a bottle of wine.

"Like a drink, girls?" they asked. Why not?

Sitting on our horses, reins loose, we enjoyed a glass of wine with three men we had never seen before and would never see again, before riding off down the dusty road to the camp as the sun turned the desert a deep pink and gold.

The next morning Graeme Clifford took a car, drove into Moomba, rang Terry Jackman and said thanks for the visit. Then he drove back to the camp, walked into the production office, tore a strip off Greg Ricketson and yelled, "No fucking cuts!"

Camp life was, in its own way, equally bizarre. After a month on location the caterer, a reliable and capable professional and veteran of many films, had developed some undisclosed problem and was drinking heavily. Food continued to appear, but by the end of the day he was swaying and incoherent, lost in his own alcoholic miasma. A shipment of drinking water was salty, the supplier had not flushed out the tanks prior to delivery. The camp manager complained that the septic wasn't working properly because, he claimed, too many of the crew were on antibiotics.

At night, people congregated around a huge campfire in the desert. The nights were magnificent, cool and still, the stars sharp and close. Jack Thompson was channelling the Irish explorer, reality and history merging. He would sit at the campfire in the evening, talking in a stream of consciousness monologue to which the crew listened politely. One by one they would quietly leave, to be replaced by someone else with nowhere else to go. Jack talked on without pause, staring into the fire, occasionally turning to address the person closest to him. Although I had known him since *Spyforce*, he didn't like me in my new role which he saw as interfering with the masterpiece, and I didn't like that he didn't like me.

I was happy, many years later, to be able to cast him in a miniseries and to re-establish a mutual fondness. Jack is a true hero of the industry, and his commitment and quiet work for Aboriginal people is one of the greatest things about him.

Nigel Havers was having a miserable time. In a conversation over lunch he revealed that he loathed Graeme Clifford and the sooner the film was shot and finished, the happier he'd be.

After Clifford's little tantrum in the production office, I visited him on set to ask him to change his mind and agree to the time- and money-saving script cuts. He made no commitment. But shortly after, he told Greg Ricketson that he had agreed. Caro wasted no time publishing the script deletions on the daily call sheet. That set them in stone.

There was much champagne, from someone's secret stash, drunk at dinner and late into the night.

In amongst the stress of trying to get the production back on budget and schedule, there was always a lot of waiting around; I found time to absorb the atmosphere of the doomed expedition.

I had read widely about what was a monumental bungle in the Australian tradition of politics and grand ideas, starting with Alan Moorehead's 1963 work, *Coopers Creek*. The incompetence of Burke didn't make the achievement of walking to the Gulf and back in summer, and the irony of returning to the creek twelve hours after the rescue party had left after waiting six months, any less amazing. The season that Burke and Wills spent on Coopers Creek, after finding that they were stranded, was similar to the one the film crew was experiencing. The creek was full of water. Fish and large freshwater mussels abounded in the wide pools among the sandbars. On these alone they could have flourished for many months. The Aborigines offered them plants and game. How could anyone die of malnutrition amid such abundance? Only the ignorance of the white upper classes could have caused such an outcome. King, the third member of the party to make it back to the creek, lived with the Aborigines, survived and was rescued.

I drove to the DIG tree, about ten miles from the film camp. It stood in isolation, battered and gnarled but still strong. It looked over the creek with nothing on the horizon in any direction, the vital information still clear, deep in the bark of the trunk, after 120 years. I was alone, no

Nigel Havers, up Coopers Creek

one within fifty miles. A moment to be treasured, so close to history.

Graeme Clifford was solicitous in his farewell when I left for Adelaide. I interpreted this as pleasure that he would not have to look at my sombre face on set every day, and could return to taking his own sweet time as he had before.

I was right. A grand opportunity, a once in a lifetime chance to tell an episode in Australian history filled with more dramatic turns than a Dickens novel, lost in a vision which somehow went awry much as the original expedition went awry.

And perhaps it was this which defined the difference between the great films of the 1970s and the many wasted opportunities of the 10BA 1980s. Money and ego were at the heart of things. The innocence was gone.

———

Tom was shooting a pilot for a TV series in Gunnedah. Rita and her mother, Killer, both had roles in the film as working dogs. Like a number of actors, Killer's social skills were not highly developed. On the other hand, Rita was a real little PR operator and was loved by everyone on the crew. One day when Rita was, as usual, the centre of attention, Killer could stand it no longer. In a fit of jealousy, she attacked her own daughter. There was a flurry of fur and skin, growling and screeching, and Rita emerged with a badly bitten ear. The vet had to be called, but like a trooper she stayed on the job. Her relationship with her mother, though, was over.

Killer had form. On another film which I was visiting as the guarantor, I was sitting with Evanne while she waited for Killer to be called on set. Killer sat quietly beside her, and next to the dog the grip was standing by with a smoke machine. He was a big man, at least six feet five (196 cm) and powerfully built. He was minding his own business, keeping the smoke machine humming.

"Killer can't stand that machine," Evanne said to me. Obviously this was dog communication, because Killer showed no outward sign of even knowing the machine was there. However, a minute later, without warning and with the speed of a crocodile, she dived at the grip and buried her teeth in his leg. Like me, he never saw it coming. He screamed and let fly with a kick which landed Killer some feet away. "My leg!" He was almost crying which, for a big, tough grip was a sight to see.

The dog, unhurt but keeping well clear, was looking distinctly satisfied. Evanne was dancing about, placating the grip, who was dancing about holding his leg. "She tore my jeans!" This eventually proved to be the main bone (!) of contention, once the unit nurse was called to administer first aid and he realised that the dog hadn't actually caused any physical damage. A new pair of jeans was provided by the production office. But Evanne kept Killer well away from smoke machines from then on.

I visited Tom on location in Gunnedah. I had been born there but left when I was seven months old; I was interested to see the town in which my parents had, from all their accounts, been happy young marrieds. As both of them were dead, I had only memories of conversations and a few small Kodak snaps to help me try to find the house we had lived in. While Tom was on set with the crew, I drove around the town trying to find the house. I had a photograph of my mother sitting on the front step holding a barefoot baby. The same baby was in my father's arms in front of the garden fence, a road and paddocks behind. There were shots of my father in army shorts and a pith helmet, attempting to turn dirt into a front garden. It was obvious the house had just been completed, and I seemed to recall being told that we were the first tenants.

Here I was forty-five years later, driving around the edge of town, unable to find any street with houses resembling the one in the photographs. I was ready to give up when, late in the afternoon on my way back to our motel, I noticed a thirties-looking cottage. The street was in a built-up area, houses on both sides with well-developed gardens and a lot of trees. I parked the car and walked. And there I found it. Details had changed, but the architecture was unmistakable. And of course, the paddocks across the road no longer existed. All houses now. It was a spooky feeling. I sat for a while, thinking about my parents. I thought about their simple life in this pleasant country town, and how I wished I could tell them that I had found their house, and how pleased they would have been. Then I took some photographs, and drove away.

FIVE

Bruce and Barry

By now I was feeling like a change from being a full-time completion guarantor. Although you have to be sensitive to the creativity of others, there is no opportunity to be creative yourself. The work is all about people management, logistics and pressure. I persuaded Su Armstrong to come and work full-time with me, and she took on the day-to-day monitoring of productions.

I received a call from the director, Bruce Beresford. He was coming back from Hollywood to make a film called *The Fringe Dwellers*, a story about Aborigines, and he was looking for a producer. I had met him only once on a brief visit to the set of *The Money Movers*, when he had said a polite hello and then returned to his crew. But I admired his work as the most polished of the Australian directors. The costume designer Anna Senior, a friend of Bruce and his wife Rhoisin, had already mentioned to me that Bruce wanted to make *The Fringe Dwellers* and he might be looking for a producer. I was keen to meet him.

During a meeting over lunch in a restaurant in Chatswood, he told me about the film. My only experience of working with Aborigines had been on the *Delta* series at the ABC. I had liked their ready friendliness and their cheerful nature; the opportunity in this film to tell an Aboriginal story appealed to me. Bruce gave me a copy of the script and a bit of background about the financing.

During the course of the lunch he also told me that his marriage was breaking up and that he had met someone else. At that moment I was more interested in the film than his domestic situation, and it was not until some time later that I discovered that his new relationship was with one of Australia's finest journalists, Virginia Duigan who, as it happened, was a good friend of my brother since they had been colleagues on *The National Times* in Melbourne. Robert often talked about Virginia but we had never met. Now, she and Bruce were destined to become my friends and Bruce a colleague and integral part of my future in the film industry.

The Fringe Dwellers was to be financed by the UK distribution company, Virgin Films, together with 10BA tax finance from Australia. Hilary Heath, the actress, producer and partner with her husband Duncan Heath in their UK talent agency, was executive producer. The financing was well advanced, and it was my job to tie up all the ends, negotiate a path between the lawyers, the Australian Film Commission, Virgin and the 10BA investors' representatives, and get my hands on the cash flow. Hilary could not have been nicer. She was friendly and helpful, which made finalising the deal with Virgin reasonably straightforward.

The thing about film financing is that no one ever actually wants to write a cheque. No matter how enthusiastically they carry on about making the movie, getting your hands on the money is *always* like getting blood out of a stone. The lawyers for the various parties, often following their clients' instructions but sometimes just because they can, will obfuscate, bully, nitpick and use any tactics they can to prolong the process. The producer is stuck in the middle between the director, the actors and crew on the one hand, all wanting to go make the film, and the financiers on the other, like donkeys in those old cartoons where the man is hauling on the reins and the donkey has its four feet firmly anchored in the dirt, not going anywhere. *The Fringe Dwellers* was no different. Between the bureaucrats at the AFC and the representatives of the 10BA investors, there were many cross words before the contracts were all in place and they could avoid writing cheques no longer.

Meanwhile, Bruce and I worked on the locations and the casting. Nene Gare's novel about an Aboriginal girl who wants to better her life was set in the 1960s in Geraldton, Western Australia, where Nene's husband Frank had been an enlightened district officer. It was inspired by stories she had heard through her close friendships with the Aboriginal people of the area. As we did not have the budget to film in WA we set about looking for an appropriate location on the east coast. Bruce had heard about Cherbourg, the Aboriginal settlement close to the town of Murgon in Queensland, so we flew up to take a look.

Murgon was a small country town ideal for our purposes, as it was the right size to fit the story, its look would fit an earlier period and it had a ready supply of Aboriginal extras available in Cherbourg, just three miles down the road. One of the many disgraceful blots on the settlement of white Australia, Cherbourg was the dumping ground for Aboriginal people forcibly removed from their tribal lands all over Queensland in the first half of the twentieth century, where their culture, their language and their self-esteem were destroyed. In 1985 it had a population of 1000, most of whom had no jobs and no purpose.

I find it quite difficult to write about the relationship between Aboriginal and white society twenty-five years ago because in some ways it has changed remarkably, and in other ways, sadly not at all. Indigenous people will never recover from the impact of white settlement and there is so very much still wrong with the way they are treated today. That said, awareness and interest in Aboriginal culture and respect for Indigenous people have all improved.

Murgon was just a few miles from Kingaroy, the family seat of Joh Bjelke-Petersen, the right-wing Premier of Queensland who was still in office. In 1985, in spite of the proximity of Cherbourg, there appeared to be no Aboriginal employment in Murgon, and no integration. There were two pubs, the "white" pub and the "black" pub, and no one crossed the divide. When they realised this, the film crew took to drinking in the black pub, and we made the actors welcome to join us in the white pub. I'm sure that this caused consternation to the white burghers of the town but no one dared show it. I was invited to dinner by a very nice woman who had grown up with my mother in Wingham, and whose family I knew well. She told me that she had lived in Murgon for twenty years and had never spoken to an Aborigine. How could this be so? Her husband was a manager in the town and there were Aboriginals in the main street every day. I doubt she had even considered the subject until the arrival of the film crew, when the coincidence of our Wingham connection brought it home to her. The two societies lived in a parallel universe, one behind the glass, the other looking sadly in.

There had been very few Aboriginal drama films to that time – notably *Backroads* by Phillip Noyce and *The Chant of Jimmy Blacksmith* by Fred Schepisi. These were groundbreaking films but they both had a mixed cast of white and black actors. *Fringe Dwellers* had only two white roles, both of them minor. For a number of our cast, this would be their first experience of acting in a film. Bruce cast Justine Saunders, the most experienced and talented Aboriginal actor then working, in the leading role of Mollie Comeaway, and laidback actor and writer Bob Maza as her husband Joe. Kylie Belling, whose first acting role was as Trilby's sister Noonah, was a stolen generation girl, and the film was her first proper contact with her people. (Recently she was seen, touchingly, as the mother in *The Sapphires*, with reference to the tragedy of children being taken from their families.)

Michelle Torres, who was to become a successful filmmaker herself, and Michelle Sandy, a girl with a fabulous singing voice, played the cousins. The key role of Trilby, the daughter who yearns for a better life, was the most difficult to fill. There was not the depth of Aboriginal talent that there is now, for the obvious reason that there had been few opportunities. After all, it was not that long since it had been acceptable to cast white actors in black face to play Aborigines. Bruce decided to cast dancer Kristina Nehm in the role. Ernie Dingo agreed to play Trilby's boyfriend, Phil.

Seven-year-old Denis Walker, son of the Aboriginal activist Denis Walker, was cast as Bartie, the youngest Comeaway family member. Denis' grandma was Kath Walker, activist, writer, poet and artist, who later changed to her tribal name, Oodgeroo Noonuccal. Young Denis was living with Kath due to some family malfunction at his parents' level. Kath decided to come with Denis as his minder, so Bruce cast her in a small speaking role. Before filming started I flew up to meet her at her home on Stradbroke Island. Called Moongalpa, "sitting down place", it was a serene patch of grass and bushland close to the sea. Kath greeted me politely but not warmly. I was shy; it's possible she was, too. But one of the

With Michelle Torres, Bruce Beresford, Ben Sandy, cinematographer Don McAlpine, Denis Walker, Justine Saunders and Bob Maza. Rita beside the clapper board. Mollie Comeaway's hat is now in the National Film & Sound Archive.

things I came to admire about her was that you had to earn her respect. I don't know if I ever did. We spent a couple of hours talking about the film and I asked her advice about a number of matters. I continued to rely on her wisdom throughout the filming. It was one of the great privileges of my life to have known her.

While it was obvious we brought to Murgon a different approach to Aboriginal people, the locals kept their resentment, if any, hidden. In making the film we encountered overt prejudice only once and that was in Kingaroy. We had booked some of the crew and some actors into a Kingaroy motel. When production manager Helen Watts and I visited the motel to confirm the booking, it emerged in conversation that some of the prospective guests were Aboriginal. The motel proprietor turned nasty immediately and made it clear he wasn't having any blacks staying at his establishment. We could have made an issue out of it, but that would have caused embarrassment to our actors and made it very unpleasant for them to stay there. So it gave us considerable satisfaction to cancel the entire booking, and to make it very clear why. There was a sizeable amount of money involved, leaving the motel without our custom at short notice. We rearranged things in Murgon and managed to fit everyone into the motels there, which were friendly and welcoming.

Then on the first Saturday night, Alan Dargin, a boy of twenty, had too much to drink and threw a brick through his motel window in the small hours. Helen was called by the proprietor, not pleased, early next morning. Oh dear, we thought. So we went to Kath and asked her what she thought we should do. "You leave 'im to me," she said. "You mob been good to us. We don't need this kind of stuff. I'll fix 'im." Whatever she said, we had no more trouble out of Alan, and he went on to become one of Australia's finest didgeridoo players, playing with musicians and orchestras all over the world. He died too young, at forty-nine, like so many of his people.

We used extras from Cherbourg most days during filming. It

was wonderful on the one hand, and on the other, heartbreaking, to see how quickly they came to enjoy coming to work, and how much pleasure they got from having a focus, payment for their work and respect from the film crew. It was pretty obvious that after we departed, things would go back to the way they were before.

There was criticism of *The Fringe Dwellers* from young Aboriginal activists who disapproved of white filmmakers telling a story about Aboriginal people, and of the story itself which was written by a white writer and portrayed a situation from the recent past. They probably had a point. But the film gave work to a lot of actors, profile to some, and it touched the lives of everyone who worked on it, making us all better friends to Indigenous people. In my case, I gained an understanding of their character and their difficulties, and immense admiration and respect for their courage and their sense of closeness and family. I have, ever since, actively supported opportunities for Indigenous filmmakers to tell their own stories, as the logical progression from others interpreting their culture. This has now come to dazzling fruition with films like Warwick Thornton's *Samson and Delilah*, Rachel Perkins' *Bran Nue Dae* and Wayne Blair's *The Sapphires*. *Redfern Now*, the anthology series by Rachel Perkins and Darren Dale's company for ABC television, is some of the finest drama ever seen on our screens. We have begun to see an original vision of Australia, told on film through Indigenous eyes.

The Fringe Dwellers was Mark Egerton's last film in Australia; he left for a new life in his old country, England, the morning after a rowdy and celebratory wrap-combined farewell party. He went on to a successful career as a first assistant director in international films, including *Mosquito Coast* for Peter Weir, and he returned to Australia briefly to First for Bruce once more on *Mao's Last Dancer*. Mark was a brilliant first assistant, the best I ever worked with.

Don McAlpine photographed *The Fringe Dwellers* and also *The Odd Angry Shot*. Don is one of Australia's greatest cinematographers, with credits like *Mrs Doubtfire* and *Clear and Present Danger*. At the time of writing he is still shooting movies at the age of nearly eighty.

As a footnote to *The Fringe Dwellers*, Bruce cast Rita to play the Comeaway family dog. Since she was travelling with me anyway, she was not a heavy expense to the production. She generously allowed the production office to drink her fee, a bottle of good champagne. Bruce liked Rita so much her role kept growing, perhaps beyond the status of a dog in such a family. I loved Bob Maza forever for keeping a firm but subtle grip on her during the

progression of the truck from the camp through town to the new house. It was Rita's proudest moment, up top with Bob and all the furniture, lording it over all the dogs below.

More than twenty years later I was amused to see the truck scene reproduced in Baz Lurhmann's *Australia*. The difference was that the dog was now inside the cabin, sitting between Jack Thompson and Hugh Jackman. That dog was a descendant in spirit of Rita, as she was played by a golden kelpie called Jedda who was bred and trained by Evanne and her partner Bruce Gleeson.

Bruce gives Rita some last minute instructions. Bobby Maza gets his makeup checked. Kylie Belling wouldn't mind some attention from the director.

An early cut of *The Fringe Dwellers* was viewed by Pierre Rissient, the scout for the Cannes Film Festival. He recommended that we send a print of the finished film to Paris for consideration for selections for the official Competition. At the end of March we received a telex from the President of the Festival, Gilles Jacob, confirming that the film had been selected. This resulted in a flurry of activity, a marketing plan, a translation of the dialogue into French for subtitling, and a budget to send actors and me to Cannes for the festival. Bruce by now was filming *Crimes of the Heart* in the US, so could not attend. This was a drawback, as Cannes is a directors' festival and films are not quite so well loved by the jury if the director is not there to present them. Nevertheless, he could not be in two places at once, so the rest of us did our best. Bruce's now ex-wife, Rhoisin, who had done some work on the screenplay adaptation and was credited as co-writer, agreed to attend. This was helpful because she spoke fluent French.

Having attended the Cannes Festival with films which were not in Official Competition but battling with hundreds of others to find buyers in the marketplace, I now discovered that being in Competition was definitely the way to go. We were accommodated at the best hotel in Cannes, the Gray d'Albion, and our every minute was taken up with functions, drinks, dinners and press. One night at dinner I sat next to Tony Curtis, a fabulous old charmer who had everyone laughing. Justine and Kristina were flown over for the screening. Justine was working in the TV series *Prisoner*, but the producers kindly rescheduled to give her two days off, just long enough to fly in, do some press, attend the screening and the official dinner, party all night then fly home. Both girls had a great time and looked absolutely ravishing in their formal dresses on the red carpet at the Palais.

Justine Saunders, me, Rhoisin Beresford and Kristina Nehm on the steps of the Palais. Executive Producer Damien Nolan and his wife behind us.

The week after I returned from France, my brother Robert's first book was published. *No Conceivable Injury*, a report on the Royal Commission into the British atomic weapon tests at Maralinga in the 1950s, is regarded as the definitive account of these tests and their effect on the environment and the local Indigenous people.

Su Armstrong was kept busy through her second year with Film Finances. She was overseeing thirty features in production, a record, along with many still in post-production.

Among them was *Time Guardian*, a kind of futuristic horror movie. In spite of its $8 million budget, it managed to go over budget, and a comment on the film's IMDb website pretty well sums it up: "John Baxter (the scriptwriter) is an absolutely brilliant short story writer and apparently a life-long student of films, so I was very interested to see what his only screenplay was like. I simply could not believe that he came up with such a piece of total crap."

A bigger nightmare was *Melba*, a television mini-series about the diva, produced by Pom Oliver and Errol Sullivan, and directed by the theatre director Rodney Fisher. When given a movie camera, Fisher joined the ranks of Igor Auzins and Graeme Clifford, and drove everyone nuts with his obstinacy. In addition, the film was caught in a disastrous currency situation as it had extended sequences filmed in Europe, at exactly the wrong time for the Australian dollar.

Bruce Beresford and I got along well during the making of *The Fringe Dwellers*. I first and foremost admired his filmmaking skill, but I also delighted in his sense of humour and his intellect, which challenged everyone to an extra level to keep up with him. Creatively he always knew what he wanted, but he would listen to other ideas. When what he wanted was in conflict with the funds available, he would either find a way to get the same result for less money, or alternatively find a way to save money elsewhere to compensate. Crews and actors adored him. Everyone wants to work with Bruce.

One of Bruce's closest friends, perhaps his closest, is Barry Humphries. In their peripatetic lives they meet whenever they can. During post-production of *Fringe Dwellers,* hilariously they arranged to meet at a Chinese restaurant in Chatswood for lunch but inadvertently each attended a different restaurant. Chris Gordon in my office was the recipient of several increasingly irate phone calls demanding to know where the other one was, and why they had not arrived.

Around this time I had a call from Barry. He and his wife, the artist Diane Milstead, were making a film about Sir Les Patterson. Would I be interested in producing it? Bruce had obviously said nice things about me. "Don't do it," Bruce said, when I told him. "I love Barry, but the script is *terrible.*" Barry had asked him to direct it, but he declined.

Bruce was right about the script, but when I met with Diane she brushed all my concerns aside. It was an early draft, Barry knew there was work to be done and he would do the rewrites. The opportunity to work with the funniest man in Australia, a comic genius whom I had admired since I first saw Edna on stage, was irresistible. So, ignoring Bruce's advice, I agreed to produce *Les Patterson Saves the World.* Paul Morgan & Co, the Brisbane stockbroking firm which had underwritten and financed *Crocodile Dundee* to the great joy of its investors, was keen to do the same for Barry and Sir Les.

Barry and Diane hired George Miller to direct – *The Man from Snowy River* George, not the *Mad Max* Dr George. *Snowy River* had been a huge success, and George had done a great job of bringing in a logistically difficult film on time and on budget. Prior to *Snowy River* he had a successful career directing television drama in Melbourne. He was clever, a bit unpredictable, with a sharp, off-beat sense of humour. He seemed like the right person and I was happy with the choice.

There continued to be a problem, though, with the script. The rewrites failed to appear. I constantly asked Diane when the new work would be done, and the responses changed from "Barry will do it" to "I will do the rewrites tonight, you'll have them in the morning." But still nothing showed up. Having got the film off the ground by persuading Paul Morgan to underwrite it and raise the money, Barry handed over the preparation to Diane.

George just barrelled on, in love with Barry and thrilled to be working on a film about Sir Les and Dame Edna, all of which blinded him to the fact that the script was a tasteless exercise in which the vulgar comedy of Barry's characters, so successful and insightful on stage, would fail to translate to the big screen.

There is a parallel with Roy Rene "Mo" who, like Barry, was a megastar of his day and whose racist, vulgar comedy was side-splitting on stage, but whose films failed to entertain.

George and I were not the only ones attracted to the film because it meant an opportunity to work with Barry. Pamela Stephenson, Tim Finn, Graham Kennedy and Joan Rivers all were happy to make appearances. Unfortunately, George proved to have little flair for directing comedy, and although nothing could have saved the film, without some of the heavier-handed moments it might have been funnier.

What we began slowly to realise during production was that the Humphries marriage was in trouble. Too late, we began to think that the film might have been a way for Barry to keep Diane happy, and therefore out of his hair. As shooting loomed and the rewrites to the script continued to fail to appear, I became more and more worried. But how do you tell the funniest man in Australia that he's not funny? At the last minute, in a response to my nagging, Barry made a few changes. But by now it was too late, the train had left the station and we were on board for the ride.

To make matters worse, Diane and I quickly grew to loathe each other. At the same time, Barry couldn't have been nicer. Unfailingly polite, he was usually punctual and helpful. "Barry is always the same," Bruce had said, and this was pretty much true. And reassuring. It was rare to see the cocktail of characters he lived with pop out of the urbane Humphries persona. It did happen a couple of times. We arrived at his Point Piper house one morning for a meeting. Barry was out on the verandah overlooking the sun-speckled harbour, elegantly dressed as usual in a tailored suit with handkerchief in breast pocket and perfectly complementing shirt and tie. As we walked out to join him, he turned to us and told three really quite filthy jokes, roared a Sir Les laugh, and then switched to polite, courteous Barry.

Another morning I was at home getting ready to go to work, after a couple of bad days with Diane. The phone rang. Dame Edna was on the other end, screaming at me about something Diane had told him I'd done. Later when I saw him on set, Barry said, "Sorry about this morning."

Before production started, Barry wanted to shoot a still shot for the cover of the prospectus, a legal requirement for raising money from the public. It was decided to shoot Sir Les riding a camel. On a sunny afternoon, Evanne delivered a very laid-back camel called Adam to the sandhills at Kurnell, and in due course the stills photographer pulled up in his Porsche, followed by a Honda Accord driven by Sir Les Patterson in full costume and makeup. A vision occurred to me of what would have happened if they had had a traffic accident on the way: "Agitated member of the public gets out of his dented Camry ready to punch the other driver, Sir Les climbs out of the dented Honda ..." Luckily this did not happen, and Barry was very brave, perching and leering on a camel which was trying to maintain its balance on a steep sandhill as directed by the stills man.

The main location for the film *Les Patterson Saves the World* was a disused tannery at Botany, quite close to Sydney airport. It had lots of large, empty, dilapidated old buildings, some palm trees and a lot of open space. Designer Grace Walker created elaborate interiors and exteriors for Abu Niveah, the fictional country in the film. (Barry had an unexplained fixation for the cosmetic product, Nivea Creme. We had to get permission from the company to use the name. "Oh, Barry is always on about this, no idea why," the man said.)

Pamela Stephenson takes a ride with Sir Les.

Whenever the Sydney airport flight path was east-west you couldn't hear yourself think and the place stank, a powerfully putrid smell of blood and bone. We should have taken this as an omen.

The final sequence filmed in Sydney was a revolving restaurant in New York where Dame Edna is dining with the Possums for Peace. The bad guys arrive, there is a chase, Colin the koala gets into the control room and pulls the lever which speeds up the revolve, and chaos, naturally, ensues. We built the set in a warehouse in Homebush – an amazing piece of work. The restaurant was full size, and many times bigger than that intimate room at Tony's Bon Gout. Outside the windows there was a cyclorama of the New York night sky, and the restaurant revolved at varying speeds up to thirty kilometres per hour. I stood on it when they were testing it and there was no way you could keep your balance at full speed. Gradually your feet loosened from the floor and you spun out towards the walls, ending up stuck like a fly to the carpet.

The union decided to give us a hard time on *Les*. Or rather, a newly appointed Acting Federal Officer (Poo-Bah), based in Melbourne, decided. I continued to be of the view that, unless the

Two of the greatest talents Australian show business has ever produced.

production had done something wrong, the relationship should be between the union and its members, not between the union and the production. Having worked on crews I understood their needs; I tried to be a good employer and a fair one. No one ever had cause to go to the union to get a problem resolved on my films. I refused to be intimidated by bullying and I enjoyed a fight, unless it wasted time which should have been spent on more productive matters.

This jumped-up megalomaniac started ringing me with ludicrous demands and threats. After several unpleasant conversations, I told the office not to put him through to me for a while. I said they should always be polite and say I was out, or in a meeting, or ... anything they could think up, and that I would call him back. He rang every day, sometimes twice, for a couple of weeks. I was never available and I never, ever, returned his calls. This drove him crazy, which was very satisfying. Finally, when I decided to speak to him and get it over with, he threatened to take us to court and to prevent the film ever being screened in Australia. He thought the film was going to be a high-profile hit and could be held up as an example of the power of the union and, no doubt, himself. The irony was that the audience took care of his threat – no one went to see the film. Even the union eventually realised what a fool it had employed, and moved him off to lick stamps in some corner somewhere.

There were two overseas locations, the first some sequences in the US with scenes of the President in the Oval Office, and exteriors of New York. These were all filmed in Los Angeles, and we had a pleasant week driving around in rented limousines, filming downtown as New York, and in a small studio in Culver City which owned an Oval Office set – one of about twenty in Hollywood. Joan Rivers had fun playing the President of the United States and in return invited Dame Edna onto her weekly show after filming was finished. Back then, Americans just didn't get heterosexual men in drag and Dame Edna was a flop. It looked as if Barry's attempts to establish himself in the USA would be unsuccessful. But he persisted and eventually became nearly as big a star in America as he is in the UK and Australia – a truly phenomenal talent.

On the evening of the last day of filming, I booked a table at

Joan Rivers as the President of the United States.

Spago on Sunset Boulevard, then Hollywood's trendiest restaurant, to take the Australians who had come with us for the US shoot to dinner. As I was reaching for the bill at the end of the meal (the production would pay as a way of saying thank you) Barry leaned over and said, with emphasis, so that everyone at the table could hear, "I'll take it, Sue." As it came to around $1,000, everyone was impressed by his generosity and thanked him profusely. I smelled a rat. Sure enough, the bill turned up in the film's accounts department a few weeks later. Barry had paid on his credit card. I that if we neglected to reimburse him, he wouldn't have the nerve to ask for the money. This proved to be the case. So he earned the crew's thanks, after all.

The final shooting was for second unit location exteriors in Morocco. This was a challenge, as none of us had ever been to Morocco. We eventually located a film company in Marrakesh to set up the shoot for George and the camera crew. This company insisted on full prepayment of all costs prior to commencement, around $30,000, which we duly telegraphed to them. Wouldn't you know it, the money just never arrived. There was consternation as George and the boys landed in Marrakesh to be told that nothing

With Evanne on the set of *Les Patterson Saves the World.*

could be done, because we hadn't paid. So off went the funds again, the shooting proceeded, and after a frantic taxi ride to the airport followed by gesticulating locals who objected to something – life mirroring art – the crew returned in one piece, with the film. We wrote the first payment off. We mightn't have been smart enough to figure it out in advance, but we were certainly smart enough to quit while we were ahead.

By the end of filming, it was out in the open that the Humphries marriage was on the rocks, and rumours were circulating about certain extracurricular activities in relation to Barry. The girls in the production office, with their sharp eyes and their ears to the ground, had known about this mischief for some time. Eventually Diane found out what everyone else knew and hell descended. One Saturday morning there was a screening at the laboratory of a work in progress of the film. Barry was late. A taxi pulled up outside and a dishevelled figure emerged, fumbling with change to pay the fare. He was unshaven, long hair awry and dressed in a pair of striped flannelette pyjamas. "Bloody Diane cut up all my clothes!"

A few years later I ran into Barry at Bruce's house. By now he was divorced from Diane and married to Lizzie Spender, the daughter of the former English Poet Laureate – another blonde, but statuesque, quiet and fey, the antithesis of Diane. When we found ourselves together Barry leaned over to me and said, "Sue, I want you to know I'm very happy." He gave me a look which meant: we both know what I'm talking about.

I smiled and replied, "I'm really pleased for you, Barry." And I was.

Hoyts were so excited about the prospect of the film's success that they rushed the opening, which meant we had to rush completion of the post-production, which meant there was no time for audience testing – or for anyone to have a proper look at the film before it hopped out, more naked than Barry in his pyjamas, to screen for the first-night audience. I always hate rushing the opening; a film, like a good roast, needs time to settle between completion and public exhibition. Time to plan a campaign, time to get the trailer right, time to see how audiences who know nothing about it react to the film. Time, perhaps, to do some re-editing, even some re-shooting. This is important for any film and something that the Americans do all the time. It has never, unfortunately, been considered important for Australian films by those experts, the government funding agencies. In the case of comedy, it is incredibly important, and in the case of Les, more time and some re-editing might have helped the comedy.

Who knows if it would have made any difference? To my horror, Barry decided in 2008 to allow the film to be released on DVD. It has never appeared on my CV …

Diane, George, Barry and me.

SIX

Any News? The Dino Experience

BRUCE HAD COME ACROSS the true story of Mario Varischetti, a miner who was entombed in a flooded mine in Coolgardie in 1908. It was a boys' own adventure about how a deep-sea diver was transported by special train from Fremantle to Kalgoorlie, setting a speed record on the way, was lowered into the flooded mine in an old-fashioned diving suit and helmet, located the miner who had been trapped in an air bubble in total darkness and silence for two weeks, and brought him out alive. The project was called *The End of the Line*, and Bruce was very keen to make it, if we could raise the money.

Then in 1986, Dino de Laurentiis came to town. The legendary and controversial producer of such famous and diverse films as *Bitter Rice*, *Nights of Cabiria*, *La Strada*, *Barbarella*, *Serpico*, and *King Kong* (No. 2) was one of the great survivors of the international film industry. He had produced his first film in 1940. He moved to the USA in the early 1970s and in 1983, taking advantage of the money sloshing around the economy, bought the distribution company Embassy Pictures, turning it into De Laurentiis Entertainment Group (DEG), which he floated on the stock market in 1986, raising nearly $270 million. He set about making a slate of movies which he planned to distribute through the Embassy structure. Then, lured by the 10BA film incentives, he devised a similar plan to take advantage of the stock market boom in Australia. He arrived in Sydney with much fanfare, announcing that he was going to build us a film studio. He was welcomed with circumspection by the politicians in NSW, but he and Joh Bjelke-Petersen were made for each other. Joh offered him seven and half acres on the Gold Coast and a ten-year lease. The fact that there was no film industry to service a studio in Queensland did not deter Dino. He got a bargain, and that was that.

He formed a subsidiary of DEG, De Laurentiis Entertainment Limited (DEL) and Terry Jackman (who had departed Hoyts at the end of 1985) was hired as Executive Chairman. Then the company floated, and raised $27 million on the Australian stock market. Dino immediately made a big splash by purchasing the film rights to Robert Hughes' best seller *The Fatal Shore* for one million dollars.

Bruce and Dino met when Bruce was directing *Crimes of the Heart*. They became, and remained to the end of Dino's life, great friends. It was an unlikely friendship – the tiny, domineering Italian producer/entrepreneur and the burly, intellectual Australian director. But they loved each other.

Throughout the making of *Les Patterson*, I had been working with Bruce on the development of *The End of the Line*. When Dino arrived in Sydney he agreed to finance the film. DEG would provide a distribution guarantee of 65 per cent of the budget, a group of stockbrokers would underwrite the total budget and they would raise the funds – $12 million – from the public by way of a prospectus under the 10BA tax incentives, which had now been reduced to a 120% write-off plus 20% rebate on returns. The investors would be guaranteed 65 per cent of their money back within a year of the release of the film. It was a great deal for the investors and a great deal for Bruce and me. We had excellent fees and an arrangement which gave us an escalating share of gross receipts once the film had recouped its negative cost. We had a real chance of getting some very attractive back end, even if the film was not a blockbuster.

The prospectus to raise the public money for *The End of the Line* took several months to finalise. Everything was ready for signing when production manager Helen Watts and I flew to Kalgoorlie to look for locations for the film in early February. We hoped to shoot the exteriors where the story actually took place, in the tiny town of Coolgardie.

Helen and I spent a pleasant couple of days driving around Coolgardie and Kalgoorlie, researching locations and infrastructure. Then we flew back to Perth. The following morning I was in a deep sleep in my hotel room when the phone rang. Groggily I picked it up. It was six a.m.

"Sue! It's-a Dino." He didn't pause for me to say hello. Well, that was normal. "I talk-a to Bruce. He agree with me. We no make-a *End of the Line*. We make-a *Total Recall*."

It may sound rude to depict Dino's speech thus, but he had such a stage Italian accent, that was how he talked.

"But Dino ..." I had never heard of *Total Recall*. I was trying to wake up, collect my thoughts and explain to him that we were seconds away from production of *End of the Line*. We had spent months preparing it. It made no sense to drop it now. But Dino wasn't listening. "No. We make-a *Total Recall*. We do it in the studios. You come-a to Los Angeles with Bruce. We talk." I already knew better than to try to argue with him, especially over the phone. He was not a man for small talk, probably because his English was so bad. It was said he had scripts translated into Italian before he read them which, we later theorised, may have helped to explain some of the awful films DEG financed.

As I hung up, I saw disaster looming. Bloody Bruce, I thought. He knows what I'll say, which is why he has not mentioned this hare-brained idea to me. I dialled his number. "Bruce, what is going on?" A sheepish pause at the other end.

"*Total Recall* is a great idea. All those special effects. We can do it now, and *End of the Line* next."

"But *End of the Line* is financed. And you and I *own* it. Let's make it now, and then you can do *Total Recall*." *Total Recall* was owned by Dino, we would be working for fees and, if we were lucky, a few points at the back end of a distribution deal which would ensure there were never any net profits.

Bruce hates confrontation. Although I did my best to point out the craziness of the situation, there was no dissuading him. He wanted to please Dino and, like a very bright kid with a new, very challenging toy, he was intrigued by the visual effects, more complicated than anything he had done. To be fair to him, which I didn't feel like being at that moment, he actually had little choice. If Bruce objected, Dino could just pull the plug on *End of the Line*, and he was ruthless enough to do so. Dino wanted *Total Recall* because he wanted a big splash in the new Gold Coast studios, and *End of the Line* had few studio sets. *Total Recall* would be 100 per cent shot in the studio, apart from the background plates. *And it was an American picture.*

After I put the phone down from Bruce, I remembered Helen, asleep in a nearby room. She had spent months planning, budgeting, crewing *End of the Line*. Now, all for nothing.

Nor, indeed, Coolgardie. Helen Watts with me on another location.

We were booked on an early flight back to Sydney. Still in shock, I couldn't think how to break it to her. After we'd checked in, we were sitting with a coffee in the lounge. I have to do it now, I thought. "I've got some news," I said.

Like all good production managers, she was alert to trouble in an instant. She gave me a penetrating look. "What's happened?"

She took it well. The life of a freelance film worker is at best unpredictable. But, like me, she could see how insane the turn of events was.

"Oh, dear," she said.

The screenplay for *Total Recall* was adapted from a novelette by the famous science fiction writer, Phillip K. Dick, titled *We Can Remember It For You Wholesale*. A small gem, it is set in 2040 and tells the story of a man who feels the need to take a holiday on Mars. As he can't afford to go there, he visits a centre where they implant a false memory of a holiday of your choice in your brain, so that when you wake up, you remember it as if you'd actually been there.

However, in the case of our hero, the implant awakens something disturbing. It turns out he has actually been to Mars on some kind of mission, and the memory has been erased by the bad guys who are still watching him. It all goes berserk from there.

The original short story covered the first two acts of the film script, and they worked very well as prose. The third act was added by scriptwriters Ron Shusett and Dan O'Bannon and it was, to me at least, very obvious that the film did not resolve as well as the short novel. Bruce, as always, planned to do some rewrites.

We flew to Los Angeles a few days after the Kalgoorlie trip for meetings with Dino and his staff. On the night we arrived, Bruce and I went for dinner at the Beverly Hills home of Bruce's friend producer, Marty Elfand. When we arrived a housekeeper let us in. We sat around for a while until Marty, cheerful, short and heavily overweight, appeared up the stairs dripping with sweat, mopping himself with a towel. "Jesus Christ, I've got a new trainer. That guy really gave me a workout." And a potential heart attack, I thought to myself.

Later Tess Harper, actor from *Crimes of the Heart*, Bruce's most recent Hollywood film, turned up, followed by Richard Gere. Richard Gere was as nice off screen as his persona on screen, and let me tell you, just as attractive. We sat around talking while Marty made us a steak and a salad.

The next morning I tried once again, nervously but desperately, to persuade Bruce and Dino to postpone *Total Recall* until we'd made the other picture, but they were two alpha males and they weren't listening to me. Realising that I could either go along with them or find something else to do, I surrendered to the task at hand.

In 1987, creating visual effects was a primitive undertaking compared to the ever-evolving digital world of today. You could not create scenes in a computer and then render them out to film at cinema quality. Visual effects had to be done either on set in the camera, or in the laboratory, much as they had been done for the previous one hundred years. *Total Recall* was about 60 per cent visual effects, in a futuristic earth and on Mars. We had no idea how to do it. The Australian production designer, John Stoddart, who was Bruce's choice to design the film, joined us in Los Angeles. John had heard of a small company called Introvision who created special effects with their own patented combination of models, mirrors and front projection. Their most notable cinema work at that time was the train sequence in the successful film, *Stand By Me*. They had achieved amazing results for a TV show called *Inside the Third Reich*, where they placed the actors within actual rooms in the Reich Chancellery, which was demolished by Allied bombing in 1944. The sets were achieved using four fifty-year-old black-and-white photographs, and the scenes – in colour – were completely convincing as the actors moved around within the rooms. Introvision billed itself as "the film production technique of the future". Well, that was then …

I spent a lot of time at the DEG headquarters, working with the lawyers on the financing of the film. I wanted to be sure that if we committed to this path, the money would be there to achieve it. Everyone was terribly nice and friendly and reassuring. What are you worried about, you backwater Australian? seemed to be the polite message.

Dino's office was in a corner of the building which was the old Embassy headquarters on Wilshire Boulevard. He sat behind the largest desk I have ever seen, a small presence behind an acre of teak. In the corner opposite the desk was a black leather sofa and armchairs, where I sometimes had time to read through all the daily trades while waiting for him to finish a phone call. In an adjoining office resided a man called Fred Sidewater, who had been with Dino since his arrival in the USA. Softly spoken and rarely in evidence, he would appear when money was being discussed and then quietly vanish. But Dino did not do anything without him.

Outside Dino's office sat his secretary, a middle-aged woman. Dino never got up from his desk, and he didn't use an intercom. When he wanted something, he hollered. The secretary was usually on the telephone, eternally rearranging his travel plans, which seemed to change on the half hour.

"If he takes the three o'clock to St Louis and goes from there to Charleston, can he be in Chicago by seven …?"

"Mindy," Dino would call. She was the only person in the building who didn't jump when Dino called. "Mindy!" he would call again. "MINDY!!!" Eventually, in her own good time, she would hang up the phone, roll her eyes, grab her notebook and head for his office. "Yes, Dino," she would say patiently. I had plenty of opportunity to observe this performance as I spent a lot of time sitting outside Dino's office, waiting to be summoned. That was before the time on the black sofa waiting for him to finish a telephone call.

We had a couple of working dinners at Dino's house in the Hollywood Hills – a long, white two-storeyed bungalow perched on a plateau with emerald lawns and a view across the swimming pool through the blue haze above the city to the wide Pacific Ocean. His personal chef prepared perfect Italian cuisine as we sat at a long table and talked through the script with the writers.

We had a meeting with Rafaella de Laurentiis, Dino's daughter, whose mother was Silvana Mangano. Rafaella was president of production at DEG. She had recently produced *Dune*, the groundbreaking special effects movie, and we wanted to hear her thoughts on *Total Recall*. After fifteen minutes an assistant came in and signalled to Rafaella. "I'll have to end it now," she said. "I can't keep Leonard Nimoy waiting."

The Australians trooped out.

Not long after, Dino paid another visit to Australia. He stayed in the presidential suite at the Regent Hotel, which has floor to ceiling windows with spectacular views up and down the harbour. Sydney turned on torrential rain for the duration of Dino's visit, and as he sat at the gold-leaf desk gloomily staring out, the windows were an opaque sheet of dark grey water.

While planning was proceeding for the studios, Dino was determined that we would all move to the Gold Coast for the duration of the production.

"We build-a three houses at the studio," he announced. "One-a for me, one-a for Bruce, and (dismissively) one-a for you others."

Oh, yeah, I thought. Not for me, thank you. Bruce didn't want to go to Queensland, either. So we quietly made plans to do the early preparation and model construction at the Sydney Showground. We told Dino that we would save money – always a winning argument – by doing pre-production in Sydney, and we would move to Queensland when the studios were ready. He wasn't pleased, but as he was already telling me to cut-a-the-budget, the logic was inescapable.

So in May we opened a production office at the Sydney Showground, in a comfortable Federation cottage tucked away in a corner behind the cricket ground and across from the dog pavilion

Bruce and designer John Stoddart, viewed across my desk.

where we had filmed the Saigon street for *The Odd Angry Shot* ten years before. The house had, until recently, been a residence, and it had a working kitchen and a nice green lawn with camphor laurel trees and a picket fence. Helen Watts was now back on the payroll as production manager. John Stoddart was hiring model makers, so we took space in one of the biggest show pavilions for construction of the models.

The Introvision team arrived from LA for meetings and planning, along with Mentor Huebner, a "concept artist" and story boarder who started working with John Stoddart and Bruce, making elaborate drawings in the style of a 1950s comic.

Bruce's regular cinematographers were unavailable for this film, so we were looking for someone new. I suggested Peter James who had photographed *Caddie* and a number of other early Australian revival films. Bruce and Peter met, liked each other, and Peter has continued to photograph Bruce's films ever since, including *Black Robe*, *Driving Miss Daisy* and *Mao's Last Dancer*.

Bruce, John Stoddart, Peter James and I flew to Western Australia to look at location possibilities for Mars. Bruce is always the most reliable of people to travel with. Some directors like to play the role of disorganised artiste, but Bruce likes his ducks in a row at all times and he is never late. When John and I arrived at the airport he was already there, reading the *New York Times Book Review*. Peter James overslept and missed the flight.

We needed to find red desert which could be filmed for background plates for the special effects, and it is surprising that when you get specific, there is not as much real "desert" in Australia as you would think. Our destination in WA was the Pinnacles. We drove out at dawn to photograph this extraordinary location and wandered around freely amongst the thousands of pillars in every size up to ten feet tall. On the way back to town, we stopped to watch two old-man kangaroos having a boxing match, silhouetted against the forest by the early morning sun. The female they were fighting over waited demurely nearby until the winner came to claim her favours. The boys were going at it hammer and tongs. She must have had a lot of pheromones.

Casting began. As with all films, this one would not proceed unless lead actors who were both commercial drawcards and appropriate for the roles were hired. Interminable conversations took place between Bruce, Dino and the people at DEG about acceptable names for the lead. Mark Harmon, Jeff Bridges, Richard Gere, Christoph Lambert, Sting, Mickey Rourke, Richard Dreyfuss and Tom Berenger were all mooted. If Bruce liked the name, DEG didn't. Eventually Mark Harmon was agreed on. A script went to him, but he wouldn't say yes or no.

Dino raised Arnold Schwarzenegger. Bruce was horrified. His film was to be a light, spoofy treatment of the subject with a lot of elegant dialogue. Arnie was a very big star, but subtlety was not his middle name. The search went on.

In July Helen and I flew up to Queensland to check on progress at the studios which were under construction. Much like Australian public buildings of the nineteenth century which were built from plans designed for edifices in Manchester, the Queensland studios were being built off the plans of Dino's studios in North Carolina.

When we arrived the site was a mud hole. It had been raining for weeks and construction was behind schedule. The service areas around the stages seemed all wrong. There were simple ways they could be rearranged to make integration with the stages much more efficient. However, it was useless trying to make suggestions. What worked in North Carolina was going to work in Oxenford, Queensland.

In July Evanne married again. The new man in her life was a handsome horseman who looked like the Marlboro Man. The wedding was at Smoky Dawson's ranch, and the bride arrived at a gallop in a horse-drawn sulky driven by her son Cody. There was a moment of tension when Killer and Rita, sniffing around under the chairs, thought they might reprise their fight in Gunnedah. But they were quickly and forcibly separated and failed to upstage the stars of the show.

By now, Tony and Gay Bilson had moved from the Bon Gout to the Glen Murcutt-designed restaurant on the water at Berowra, an hour's drive from Sydney. Their fans made the transition willingly and now the ambience was spectacular and the food even better, if that were possible, than in the city. Bookings were just as hard to obtain.

One Sunday, Tom and I were sitting at lunch with a group of friends. We watched a seaplane land on the river, as it did from time to time, to deliver the wealthy or overseas visitors for lunch. This time, there was a little flurry as Anders Ousbach, the maître d', hurried down to the wharf to greet the group which disengaged itself from the seaplane. A conversation went on for a few minutes. Then the group got back in the seaplane, which taxied away along the river and took off. Anders returned to the restaurant. "What was that about?" we asked Gay when she walked past.

"They didn't confirm their booking," she said.

At the end of July, producer Tony Buckley turned fifty and threw a lunch for about fifty of his friends at the Berowra Waters

Inn. The restaurant was closed for the winter, but Tony and Gay opened up for one of the nicest and most generous people in the film industry, and it was a fitting way to celebrate with him. No problem with Buckley confirming his booking.

Meanwhile back on *Total Recall*, along with the interminable casting problems as pre-production proceeded, the expansive financial environment in which we had begun the adventure began to change. In Hollywood, DEG posted a first-quarter loss; its slate of movies started opening and ominously, one after the other, died at the box office. Disastrous flops.

There began a weekly battle over cashflow to make sure we had enough funds to meet the payroll. We had huge outgoings with production staff, model makers, art department staff, construction staff, visual effects staff, rent and travel. DEG began taking its time to send us drawdowns.

Mark Harmon indicated he was interested in doing the film. At the end of July, Dino faxed that he had made a pay or play offer to Harmon, and that everything was on track for a January start to filming.

Then Mark Harmon told Bruce, "I'd really like to work with you but it may not be on this one."

Rafaella resigned from DEG.

We asked Dino if we could screen test Sam Neill, who was perfect for the role. Dino said no. The same day, Dino told Bruce's agent that "the financial difficulties were behind him, and he was ready to proceed." But the green light kept going on and off.

At the end of each working day we would gather in my office, open a bottle of wine and glumly discuss the possibilities of actually getting the film made.

After waiting weeks for a response from Tom Berenger, next on the list, Bruce called him. Berenger told Bruce he had not received the script – sent from DEG to his agent. So he had not even read it. But, Berenger said, I have a script of my own which I'd like you to direct ... He informed Bruce that he had three more pictures to do before he would be needed for *Total Recall* and "I might be tired by then."

Mickey Rourke passed. Jeff Bridges passed. Richard Dreyfuss was in Brazil for two months. Dino sent him a script but there wasn't much likelihood of an answer. Dino agreed for us to test Sam Neill.

Meanwhile, the production was like a runner with his feet on the blocks, and the starting gun keeps getting raised, cocked … then dropped. Everyone was going nuts. We had a crew T-shirt printed which said "Any News?" on the front, and "No News" on the back.

Dino arrived in Sydney for a DEL Board meeting in September. Bruce screened the Sam Neill test to the board, who liked it, but Dino would not give the okay. To be fair, Sam was at that time a big name in Australia and on television internationally due to the TV series *Reilly, Ace of Spies*, but he was not a star of the standing to carry a large film like *Total Recall*. Braver people would have taken the risk and *made* him a star, but with DEG in financial trouble, Dino had other problems.

The next morning, on Dino's way to the airport to fly back to LA, we screened, courtesy of Dr George Miller, ten minutes of Sam's new film *Dead Calm* at the lab in Camperdown. We hoped that his performance and the likelihood that the film would become a hit would persuade Dino to say yes to him. Terry Jackman had hired a large black limousine to drive Dino to the airport as soon as the screening was over.

After the screening as we were walking out to the carpark, Dino asked me to start making a deal with Sam. Oh, the relief! On this decision hung the next year of my life – and everyone else's involved with the film.

Since his return from living in America, Bruce had persisted in driving a 1961 Holden which he had had garaged during his absence. It was an old wreck of a car, the duco fading, the uphol-stery coming apart, but he could not be parted from it. It often broke down and we'd get a call to pick him up and have the car towed to the repair shop. Now, as Terry hovered anxiously beside the uniformed driver of the limousine, Bruce said to Dino, "Come on Dino, I'll drive you to the airport."

Ignoring Terry, Dino climbed into the old Holden and off they trundled, a burst of exhaust smoke and a clang or two as they left the carpark. Terry was left with the limo and, not untypical of Dino, not even a goodbye or a thank you. Helen and I went back to the office. We had an actor and work to do.

When Dino arrived back in LA he was still keen on Sam, but a couple of days later, when I phoned him to get approval for Sam's deal before signing off on it, he was non-committal. "I discuss it with Bruce when he comes here." He then admitted to me that "they" at DEG – unspecified but suddenly powerful, as the other films lost money – did not want to use Sam in the movie. I passed the news on to Bruce. The line had been crossed. He called Dino.

"No Sam, no director," he told him.

Stalemate. Picture back on hold again.

Bruce eventually agreed to replacing Sam if the actor was right for the role and made the money people more amenable. The script was sent to Willem Dafoe and Richard Dreyfuss, now back from Brazil. Both passed. The latest suggestion was Chris Cooper. Chris Cooper? Not exactly a household name even now.

It got worse. They started insisting that every role in the film be played by Americans. The film was being shot in Australia and we had budgeted to cast all the supporting roles, and hopefully a lead or two, locally. The union, no surprise, was breathing down our necks, fangs bared, just waiting for an opportunity to cause trouble. No film, then or since, imports every actor, as it is a crazy waste of money when there are fine local actors available.

Meantime DEG approved a down payment to Introvision to send their technicians to Sydney to work with the model makers, so now we had a special effects company but no cast.

The script went to Tom Selleck. He passed. Bruce came up

with the idea of Patrick Swayze, then very hot from *Dirty Dancing*. Swayze said yes! A breakthrough! But by then, DEG was in worse shape than ever. The full commitment to funding the picture was still withheld, even with a star who was acceptable to everyone. Howard Koch Jnr, a producer with extensive hands-on production experience, was brought in as Head of Production at DEG and he assumed financial control of expenditure for *Total Recall*. He was a tough, second-generation Hollywood type who could turn from charming to threatening in the time it took you to say "I disagree with you".

Fed up with the indecision, Bruce told Dino to cancel the whole thing. Howard Koch agreed. It was time to bail out. But Dino begged Bruce to stay with it. He told Bruce that everyone loved the script (even though Bruce had serious concerns about it, and the third act wasn't working at all). Dino said that his new Steve Martin film had just collapsed because David Lynch had pulled out as director. If *Total Recall* went down, it might finish him. The house of cards was tottering.

Bruce, against all common sense but out of loyalty to Dino, agreed to stay with it for a bit longer. So we stayed too. It was my job to tell the fifty or so employees we already had on the payroll, that even though there were problems with the financing, it *might* be okay. The film crew were worried but philosophical; the model makers were a species unused to the unpredictability of the film industry, and their anxious little faces would look at me for hope whenever I visited the model shop.

In the midst of all this, Tom and I had been house hunting. Inner city life had begun to get crowded. New parking restrictions at nearby St Vincent's Hospital drove workers' vehicles up to Liverpool Street. The old immigrant couple who had run the corner shop next door since the fifties had sold to a couple of nightclub owners who closed the shop. They came home at three in the morning, dropped some illegal substance and turned the sound system up loud enough to be heard on the other side of the harbour. It was time to move from Paddington.

In fact, we had missed our chance. By the time we started looking, it was the middle of the 1987 Sydney property boom. The crazy rise in housing prices meant that anything we thought was right and affordable turned out, on auction day, to be out of reach. In October, dispirited by events at work, I did another trail around houses for sale. One of the houses I looked at was a run-down Federation house on the hill in Bondi, close to Bondi Road. I walked in – I'd seen around 200 houses by now, so I could size one up in seconds. Too small. I was about to walk out when I realised there was something odd about this one. When I went out and round the side, I found the door to the other half. It had been walled-up down the hall, during the sixties by the look of the décor, dividing it into two flats. It had gracious proportions and some excellent original Federation features which had survived the partition, including cedar doors and woodwork, and a front door with hand-painted glass panels of waratahs and flannel flowers. The building was actually *three* flats, as I discovered when I walked down to the back and looked under the house. Flat three had been constructed around the piers, where the land dropped away. There was a large back garden with a palm tree and a little concrete fish pond, and from the top of the old rear steps you could see the sea, if you looked carefully between the blocks of flats which took up most of the view. Maybe, I thought, we could afford this one. The next morning I took Tom down for a look. The auction was that night. We decided to bid.

Tom had been developing a TV series for entrepreneur Gene Scott. Called *Stock Squad*, the series was about country police investigating the theft of cattle in the bush. It was a good premise for a series, and promised to be something different from the usual city cop shows.

In the late afternoon of auction day I joined Tom for drinks at the opening of Gene Scott's elaborate new offices, where twenty desks carried twenty brand-new computers, and all the furniture was new. Pretty impressive, really, for the film industry, where everything was always second-hand and the cheapest available, and the IBM golf ball typewriter was still king. The food and drink flowed, and Gene was in expansive mood, announcing all the work he planned for the next year.

At seven o'clock we were at Richardson & Wrench in Bondi Junction, ready to bid on 26 Imperial Avenue, Bondi. The room was packed and we were crammed into a corner at the back, almost out the front door. But the auctioneer didn't miss Tom's hand as he entered the bidding. Up went the bids, and up. Tom kept going. I looked at him and the look on his face told me that he was just going to keep bidding till we got it. It was the only way. The room burst into applause when the house was knocked down to us. We opened a bottle of champagne and put 44 Liverpool Street, Paddington, on the market. We'd have to borrow half the purchase price even if we got a good price for Liverpool Street. And then we'd have to borrow more to turn it from flats back to a house again. But finally we had an escape from the midnight rockers.

Meanwhile, we were *still* casting *Total Recall*. The female lead, a character called Melinda, was the next role to be approved by DEG. Bruce wanted a young actress called Nicole Kidman who had starred opposite Sam Neill in *Dead Calm*. She had done a couple of Australian films and a lot of television, but she was unknown outside Australia. We were still fighting about the number of Americans in the cast, the studio having ignored Bruce's suggestion of Jack Thompson – who, as he said, was better known internationally than most of the names they were putting up – for the head of the bad guys. Dino was completely uninterested in Nicole but wary of upsetting Bruce again so soon. He allowed us to screen test her. Off went the screen test to LA.

A DEG movie called *Million Dollar Mystery* opened in the US. The premise was, watch the film, follow the clues, guess where the money is hidden and win a million dollars. A woman from Bakersfield, California, guessed the answer in the first week and collected the money. The film died stone dead. And with it, the DEG empire.

Our house at 44 Liverpool Street opened for inspection prior to auction. Two days later, the stock market crashed. Property prices followed.

"We no use Nicole Kidman," Dino told Bruce. Howard Koch Jr called me. "We're never going to approve Nicole Kidman. We want an American in the role." They wanted Alexandra Paul to play Melina.

We were told that DEG was being sold and they might not proceed with *Total Recall*, but that we – that was, DEL and I – should look at other means of financing, such as a raising under the Australian tax legislation, 10BA. Not possible, I told them. You want an all-American cast. The film is American, it won't qualify for the tax incentives. They hated hearing that. "But if creative control is in the hands of Australians …?"

Terry called Bruce to say that Dino was leaving DEG. We got another call from Dino and Howard Koch, threatening that either all the cast were to be American, or they would move the film to Dino's studios in North Carolina. I told them that not only would the union close the picture down if we tried to import all the cast, the film's budget would never cover the extra expense. Bruce, very angry now, said he would agree to the Australians using American accents, if they insisted. But he would not work with an all-American cast.

We waited for the axe to fall.

Bruce spoke to Howard Koch who told him that Dino had left the company. Fred Sidewater had gone too. But the new financiers – whoever they were – seemed to be happy to keep *Total Recall* in production. Bruce's assurance about American accents had calmed everyone down, Koch said.

The owner of Introvision rang to say his cheque had not arrived from DEG. He threatened to pull his special effects team out of Australia if he was not paid by the end of the week.

I rang DEG. "If you ask me if things are good, I'd say no. If you ask me if things are bad, I'd say no. We should know by the end of the week," a production executive told me.

Meanwhile, at the showground the models were close to completion and set construction had begun at the studios in Queensland. Peter James had started doing camera tests.

Bruce's agent in LA told him that if the new controllers of DEG were trying to refinance the film, they should forget it. "Everyone in Hollywood is leery of it."

Terry Jackman warned DEG that the studio would never be used if *Total Recall* did not go into production there.

Fighting broke out between DEG and DEL, as DEG tried to get its hands on the funds which DEL had raised from the Australian public to make Australian films under 10BA.

"These guys will never do anything," Bruce said. "I'm so sick of them all."

On 26 November, a Thursday, I tried to ring Howard Koch. "Mr Koch is on the East Coast," his voicemail told me. "The office is closed for Thanksgiving and will reopen on Tuesday." Well, thanks for letting us know. Tuesday being Wednesday in Australia, this meant carrying on for a week without any news – or any money.

Terry Jackman called to ask me to fax a copy of the script immediately to a company called Carolco, in London. They wanted it that night. We got to page twelve and Carolco's fax ran out of paper.

Two weeks after the stock market crash, we sold 44 Liverpool Street. There was only one bidder. We were lucky to get out of it at all. We probably dropped 20 per cent by selling after the crash. It left a big hole to cover the cost of the new house. But Tom had *Stock Squad* coming up, and, just maybe, *Total Recall* would survive …

We flew to Queensland for the SPAA conference. The annual producers' conference was being held on the Gold Coast, with an advertised highlight of a tour for all the delegates of the new De

Laurentiis studios and the sets for *Total Recall*. On our way from the airport at Coolangatta to the hotel at Surfers Paradise, we stopped off at the studio office. There was a fax from the accountant at DEG telling us to reduce the weekly cash requirements or they would shut the picture down. This was like telling Qantas to keep flying but don't put any petrol in the planes.

The next morning I was stepping into the shower when the phone rang. "It's-a Dino here. Sue, you have to shut-a the picture down." Although he'd left DEG, he was still there. He said no one would ever raise the money for the film.

It was 5 December – eleven months to the day since Dino called my hotel room in Perth to start us on this diversion to nowhere. If we'd done *End of the Line* instead, it would have been ready for delivery just about now.

I called Terry. We agreed to sit on the news for a bit. Anything was preferable to telling 200 industry *schadenfreudeists* at the conference, here are the sets but the movie has just been cancelled.

We hosted brunch for the conference delegates at the studios. Tables were set up in the Last Chance saloon, with white tablecloths and flowers. A jazz band played on the saloon stage. The buffet of seafood and hot dishes was excellent. As I was helping myself to some food I did not want, Blake Murdoch, the deceptively amiable *Variety* correspondent, sidled up to me. "Money okay for *Total Recall?*" he asked.

"Sure," I replied. It was hard to make my lips move, but it says a lot that, in a business which leaks like the Titanic after it hit the iceberg, we had kept the problems so quiet that the news wasn't already page one in *Daily Variety*.

As we drove to the airport to fly back to Sydney, I was relieved to be able to stop smiling. My face hurt.

But it *still* wasn't over. On Monday I arranged a meeting of the staff to tell them the picture was finally, irrevocably, cancelled … but before we could meet, Terry called to say: could we put the shoot back four weeks. "Don't cancel, I'm trying to reach Stephen

Greenwald." Greenwald was the legal executive now running DEG.

"I have to. DEG have told me to shut down."

"Wait."

At five thirty he rang to say that he had found Stephen Greenwald, who had approved $150,000 to keep the doors open.

I walked over to the model shop, to tell them one more reprieve. The model makers were all drunk. They'd been drinking all afternoon, waiting for the axe to fall. They cheered.

The days drifted by. Terry Jackman came down with viral pneumonia.

Stephen Greenwald arrived from LA and we showed him the models – works of art, beautifully finished, ready for filming. We discussed the motion control rig, twenty-five metres long, which had been airfreighted from LA and was sitting in crates, $50,000 worth, ready to be assembled for filming the models.

At the end of the week we had a meeting with Stephen at the Regent Hotel. He told us it was finally over. DEG was still trying to find a partner for the film but they could not cashflow it any longer.

And that was how it ended, not with a bang but a whimper.

Farewell the models.

On Monday morning the packers arrived at Liverpool Street to move us to Bondi. At ten o'clock I called everyone together in the model shop and dropped the guillotine. *Total Recall* was over.

That afternoon Tom called from Independent Productions. *Stock Squad* had just been cancelled. Gene Scott's empire had collapsed like a pricked balloon in the wake of the stock market crash. Like us, he'd been floating on air for some time.

From two big budget productions which would have set us up for another year, we were unemployed, with a very large mortgage.

That night, the first in our new home, we walked down the back steps to the garden with a bottle of wine and sat by the little fishpond in the kind summer dark. We contemplated this huge old wreck of a house which had cost us more money than we had. What have we done, we wondered.

The next day, I was invited to attend a Board meeting of DEL at Terry Jackman's mansion overlooking the harbour at Clifton Gardens. While I waited to be called in to the meeting, Ngaire, Terry's wife, took the time to tell me what she thought of Dino.

Bruce came out of the meeting. He was dressed in black from top to toe. He escorted me into the room where the Board was seated, along with the DEG executive, Stephen Greenwald. Stephen's face was the colour of an overripe tomato. A pale New Yorker, he had spent too long by the hotel pool in the Sydney sun on Sunday.

The Board assured me that all bills would be paid, that everyone on the crew would be paid out their due and that I would get the appropriate part of my fee. I was grateful. So many movies collapse leaving everyone out of pocket, while the perpetrators just move on without a conscience. The Board of DEL did their best and they ensured that everyone was treated fairly.

We tried to sell the motion control rig but could not find a buyer. We moved it up to the studios in Queensland in the hope that someone might find a use for it. The last time I saw it, this beautifully made precision instrument was lying in the grass in a

corner of the back lot, rusting in the rain. The models were disman-
tled, packed into containers and stored on the outskirts of Sydney.
When Carolco took the project over we transferred ownership to
them and, for all I know, they are still there.

Village Roadshow bought DEL and took over the studio.
They formed a partnership with Warner Brothers and turned the
studio into a successful filmmaking centre, creating an industry in
Queensland.

Terry Jackman got to convert his shares in DEL to Village
Roadshow shares; he left the company a lot richer than he joined
it. He sold his house in Clifton Gardens and moved back to his
home state of Queensland where he became, among other things,
a very successful cinema exhibitor. No one could begrudge Terry
his success. He put his heart into Australian films and the disasters
which followed him were not of his making.

Carolco bought *Total Recall*, hired Paul Verhoeven to direct,
and Arnold Schwarzenegger to star. The script underwent a lot
of changes, but some traces of Bruce's dialogue remained. From
an elegant, spoofy Bruce Beresford film it became a violent action
adventure. It was a big success and made a lot of money. Who
knows if our version would have done as well?

In 2012 another version of the film was released, starring Colin
Farrell and Kate Beckinsale. This time the visual effects were out of
this world, but the story was more or less irrelevant.

In 2010, at the age of ninety-one, Dino de Laurentiis died in
his sleep. He resurrected his career after the collapse of DEG and
went on to produce several money-making films, including the
Hannibal spin-offs. He was still taking meetings up until a couple
of days before he died.

So far, Robert Hughes' book *The Fatal Shore*, probably the biggest rights purchase of any Australian work, has not been made
into a film.

SEVEN

Censorship Blues

Now Tom and I were the owners of three flats in Bondi. Flat three, we belatedly discovered, came with a tenant. George was an old-age pensioner whose tenancy was rent controlled, that is, pegged at World War II levels with tiny increments. We had him for life, as by law we could not evict him if he paid his rent, which he did meticulously, and we could not put the rent up until he left. His flat was built around the piles which supported the house below the street. It was dark, damp and the decor was vintage post-war. He had been there since 1948. He was a very nice old man who kept to himself and we became fond of him. He loved Rita, who used to pop round to say hello to him and probably share his breakfast.

Rita and I took to walking around the cliffs between Bondi and Tamarama in the mornings. We usually had the path to ourselves. I loved the expansive view of the sea in all its moods and the Aboriginal rock carving beside the path as you swung down to the Tamarama side where Rita swam in the rock pools of Mackenzie's Bay.

On winter Sundays she would come into the Icebergs pool with me and sit with my towel while I did my laps. The man who put out the lane ropes for the club races brought his little dog, who trotted up and down the side of the pool with him. I became part of a coterie of winter swimmers who met in the pool, knew each other's names and exchanged a few words and a joke or two as they shared the icy water. In the winter entry to the pool was free. When the temperature got down to 14 or 15 degrees, only the hardiest swimmers continued to brave the cold, adding a cap to their bathers. Some mornings I broke the meniscus and shared the pool with just a couple of seagulls.

We began the renovation to restore flats one and two back to the original Federation house, which took most of the year. I came to understand why wealthy women are always renovating. From the time you get up there are people around, needing decisions, wanting your opinion, deferring to you, making you feel important. You never have time to be bored.

We closed down the *Total Recall* office at the showground. I was lucky – I still had Film Finances, which kept our permanent office in Pyrmont open and covered Chris Gordon's salary. I was back to being a completion guarantor full time.

Production was down in 1988. Following the stock market crash and the tightening of the 10BA tax incentives, it was hard to raise money for films.

In March I was asked by the South Australian Department for the Arts if I would review the South Australian Film Corporation. SAFC had thrived in the 1970s with an astonishing number of successes, most notably *Storm Boy*, *Sunday Too Far Away* and *Breaker Morant*. It had been prolific in the 1980s at the height of 10BA, producing movies and mini-series, including *Robbery Under Arms*. However, the early successes had not been repeated and the organisation had become increasingly alienated from local filmmakers who, given it was run with SA taxpayer funds, not unreasonably wanted a seat at the table. The government decided it was time to take a look at its operation.

SAFC, founded by Don Dunstan in 1974 and set up by former ABC producer Gil Brealey, had been run by John Morris for the previous ten years. A former documentary producer at Film Australia with the height and build of a guardsman, John was a controversial figure. He could be charming, funny, charismatic and spectacularly rude. He had managed to put the local filmmakers right offside and there was a war going on between them and SAFC.

John was running SAFC as a studio, focused on bringing in talent from outside the state. To placate the locals, he had persuaded the government to set up an independent fund to assist their projects. It was plainly nuts to be subsidising two separate film industries in the one small state – something had to be done.

I did as I always do when charged with managing a situation with a lot of people involved. I talked to everyone with a vested interest, inside and outside the SAFC, and did a lot of listening. SAFC had offices and facilities which could be made available at a modest rent to the local producers, but they were barred from working there. It was also apparent that the ability of SAFC to create successful productions had run its course; it was time for a new arrangement. It wasn't rocket science to see that a collaborative relationship would allow the best of both worlds.

I said all this in my report which, while I was careful to give due credit to John and his staff, recommended that SAFC be opened up to new and varied creative inputs. I don't know what John was expecting me to say, but he was clearly shocked when I visited him after he had read the report, and before long he had resigned. He would never have agreed with me that I did him a favour, even unwittingly, because before long he became chief executive of the NSW Film Corporation, and following that he went to the top film bureaucrat job in Australia, CEO of the Federal Film Finance Corporation.

The government did not implement all my recommendations; the Corporation went through a few rocky years following John's departure. With the arrival of the convivial former head of the NZFC, Judith McCann, things started to come together again and SAFC has survived, evolved and prospered. The local filmmakers now work uncontentiously alongside those from outside the state who come to South Australia for finance, facilities and locations.

In October 1985 four Palestinians hijacked the Italian tour liner *Achille Lauro* in the Mediterranean off the Egyptian coast. They held the 380 passengers and crew to ransom, demanding the liberation of fifty Palestinian prisoners from Israel. When their demands were not met, they shot and killed an elderly American Jewish paraplegic, Leon Klinghoffer, and threw his body and his wheelchair overboard. The story horrified the world.

In 1988 American producer Tamara Asseyev secured the rights to the story from the Klinghoffer family and teamed up with an American production company, run by Michael Jaffe, to make a Movie of the Week about the event for NBC. They planned to make the film in Italy, but fear of reprisals from the Palestinians caused them to look for somewhere safer. And where else, but the bottom of the world?

Michael Jaffe asked me if I would put the picture together for Tamara. The fact that I was working full-time for Film Finances didn't stop me. I thought I was superwoman.

Tamara was a successful US producer. She had produced the groundbreaking Academy Award-winning movie *Norma Rae*, and a well received mini-series about the Kenyan adventurer, Beryl Markham, amongst many others. She was a short woman, small-framed and handsome with a lot of long black hair, a dry wit and a volatile temper. She always wore black: "I travel so much, with black it's just easier." I liked and respected her, but you had to watch it with her. One morning during pre-production I had to fly to Queensland for some Film Finances business. When I left home everything was under control. By the time I had checked in with Qantas at Sydney airport for the nine a.m. flight, Tamara had reduced the entire office to tears. Fortunately she spent a lot of the production time in Los Angeles, and we communicated amicably by fax.

The director was an amiable but quietly determined American, Robert Collins, who had also written the script. The cast was made up of fading American movie stars – Karl Malden, Vera Miles, E. G. Marshall and a star of Broadway, Lee Grant. The supporting cast, as usual, was Australian. The Americans were nice old pros, with the exception of Lee Grant. Although a name virtually unknown outside the US, Lee Grant had quite a track record. She had two Academy Awards, one for Best Supporting Actress in *Shampoo* and one for directing the documentary *Down and Out in America* for HBO. She had an Emmy for *Peyton Place* and several nominations for Academy Awards and Emmys. A feminist who fought hard for opportunities for women directors, she had been blacklisted in the McCarthy witch hunts for refusing to testify against her writer husband, and was prevented from working in film and television for ten years. It was this hiatus which presumably prevented her from becoming famous. Someone, you would think, with whom it would be a privilege to work. Not so.

Lee complained about everything and to our surprise we found her demanding, difficult and ungracious. Australian film crews are generally cheerful and kind, and they would do anything for the actors, but no one could relax around her. She drove Bob to distraction. She was, at the time, sixty years old, although she looked much younger. There are no secrets in the makeup van and her youthful appearance would have been remarkable without some cosmetic assistance. She wanted to dress and act like a thirty-year-old while playing a fifty-year-old, the wife of Leon Klinghoffer. Eventually Tamara told her that she looked too young and too beautiful for the role, whereupon she very professionally agreed to a little ageing.

The next problem was finding a ship on which to film. The story took place almost entirely on board the *Achille Lauro*, at sea. Therefore, while interiors could be built in a studio, some scenes, at least, needed to establish that this was, in fact, a *ship* on which the events were happening.

This was only three years after the real events; Palestinian terrorists had the world well and truly spooked. We decided that innocence was the best approach. When the office looked up tour ship schedules on the east coast of Australia, we found that the *Fairstar* was travelling at exactly the right time in our filming schedule. I rang them up. Would they be able to accommodate fifty people to do some filming on the Sydney to Brisbane leg?

Would they what ... they were *thrilled* with the idea. A film crew! No problem at all.

I put down the phone and looked at Adrienne Read, the production manager. "Do you think we should tell them what the film's about?"

We both knew the answer.

I rang the shipping company back. I could hear the atmosphere freeze over. Suddenly I was as popular as a maggot at a barbecue.

There wasn't a ship afloat that would let us film on it. We couldn't even get permission to use stock footage of a cruise ship. As soon as they knew what it would be used for, panic set in. No company wanted their ship used as the *Achille Lauro*. Not even the *Achille Lauro*.

In the end, Michael Jaffe's office dug up some stock footage of a liner for a few wide shots, and the *Achille Lauro* of our story was comprised of studio sets, a horizon swimming pool at Coogee, and a stinking old tramp steamer which we hired for a couple of days. This ship, which plied its trade between Sydney and Wollongong, was about to be decommissioned. The art department constructed some liner railings and a few other bits and pieces. We walked the actors up and down and filmed them with the wind in their hair and an ocean background. There were no facilities on this old wreck so they all had a terrible time. Lee cut her leg on a ship's ladder and then let it get infected by not following the unit nurse's instructions, but the footage sold the "at sea" situation.

In the end, the film was quite convincing for television, although we would never have got away with it in the cinema. It was nominated for three Emmys. Lee refused to pay the personal section of her hotel bill when she left Sydney, she lost her luggage on her flight to LA, and that was the last we heard of her.

Intense lobbying had been taking place with the Hawke Government to provide an alternative to 10BA. The incentive had been cut back so far that investors were no longer interested and another hiatus in production had developed. The outcome was the establishment of the Film Finance Corporation, on a plan devised by the head of the Australian Film Commission, Kim Williams. The system was a return to direct funding.

The FFC was established at the end of 1988 and was up and running by the start of 1989. It was well funded, and the industry quickly adapted to the new system. The staff of the new organisation were mostly from outside the industry, which caused plenty of teething problems. But at least the rules were clear. In order to access FFC funds, you went first to the commercial marketplace – distributors, sales agents, TV networks – and secured advances to the value of up to half the cost of the production, and then you went to the FFC and it kicked in the other half. The reasoning was that if the commercial marketplace made the decision about which films should get made, it removed the creative decision-making from the government bureaucrats, and from the "lawyers, accountants and their well-heeled clients", in Paul Keating's words, of the tax-based 10BA system.

One of the early films financed with FFC funds was interesting for the debut of a megastar. *The Crossing*, a story about two young men in a country town, was intended to feature a handsome young actor called Robert Mammone in the lead role. But from the moment the second lead walked into frame, there was only one person to watch. His name was Russell Crowe.

I was still on the SPAA council and working full time for Film Finances. Tom had taken a full time job as head of training at the Australian Film, Television and Radio School. The school had

had a troubled history, but for a while it looked as if the regime under the newly appointed head John O'Hara, with Tom as head of training and production accountant Penny Carl in charge of business affairs, could really change the culture of the school and do some great things. Tom threw himself into the task and worked mostly six days a week.

In May I was appointed by the Federal Government to the Film Censorship Board of Review which heard appeals from distributors when they didn't agree with the censorship rating applied to their films by the full-time Film Censorship Board. We were a part-time panel, convened when appeals were to be heard.

Appeals did not always come from mainstream distributors. A group thought they could see a way through the censorship laws legally to screen hardcore pornographic films to the public. They rented a small cinema in Melbourne and ran some videos. They were immediately raided by the police and closed down. They appealed. My first task with the Board of Review was to view ten half-hour hardcore pornographic videos – with elevating titles such as *Naughty Girls* and *A Star is Porn* – in the company of four men and one woman, only one of whom I'd ever met before the screening. That one was Evan Williams, journalist, film critic and Chair of the Board, whom I'd met a few times. In spite of the awkwardness of watching this material in mixed company, it wasn't long before boredom set in and the most interesting thing about it became the resourceful places the "filmmakers" managed to position a camera.

We had to view a certain amount of exploitation material for which decisions were mostly a formality. But many of the decisions we had to make were quite difficult because, while we were required to interpret guidelines, the only way to reach a conclusion was to be subjective about the content and its context. Over the five years I was on the Board, we dealt with a number of causes célèbres. Peter Greenaway's film *The Cook, the Thief, His Wife & Her Lover* wanted an M rating; the Board upheld the R due to its violence. *Henry, Portrait of a Serial Killer*, a powerfully made but disturbingly violent film, stayed banned.

We were able to play good guys for some quality filmmakers, reducing the rating on *Greencard* from M to PG (contained two uses of the world "fuck"), and also for *An Angel at My Table* from M to PG. We agreed that the rating for *The Silence of the Lambs* should be M rather than R. A few people didn't like that one. The Censorship Board gave Jane Campion's *The Piano* the first of the new MA ratings; this seemed ridiculous and the Board of Review overturned it, reducing it to an M.

In 1990 the Board was expanded to become the Film & Literature Board of Review, and in 1992 we had to consider a publication titled *Final Exit*, offering advice on various forms of suicide, imported by the Euthanasia Society. The Censorship Board had refused classification; the Board of Review granted it a Restricted category, available for sale to people over the age of eighteen. I was happy to support this decision as I believe that the right of a *compos mentis* person to take their own life, if the quality of that life has ended, should be one of the freedoms available to all.

The film which brought us undone was *Salo*.

Pier Pasolini's film, based on the Marquis de Sade's *120 Days of Sodom*, was a metaphor for the violence and depravity of the fascist regime in Italy. It had been banned in Australia since 1976, although available in the US, Britain, France, even Italy and a number of other countries. In 1992 it was re-submitted to the Censorship Board and, in a split decision, the Board refused it classification. A minority of the Board felt strongly enough to append a statement to the decision which said: "Whilst certainly challenging from a classification standpoint, (the film) could nonetheless be accommodated in the Restricted category, defined as this is to encompass material considered possibly offensive to some sections of the adult community. The minority argued that although the film deals with indecent and obscene phenomena, it does so in a manner which is neither indecent nor obscene in itself when viewed in the context of a film of merit where even the most problematic of elements clearly serve the director's metaphorical purpose. For the minority the film is neither exploitative nor voyeuristic, but a powerfully realised political statement on the violation of innocence and freedom."

The distributor, presumably encouraged by the minority view, appealed the decision; in January 1993 it came before the Board of Review seeking a restricted classification.

All the members of the Board of Review viewed the film – Evan Williams; Keith Connolly, film critic and journalist; Jan Williams, executive director of the Marriage Guidance Council; Father Michael Eligate, a Roman Catholic priest and chaplain to Melbourne University; Professor Brent Waters, director of psychiatric services at St Vincents Hospital in Sydney; and me. The Board's secretary, Joel Greenberg, also viewed the film. Joel's sober and detached interpretation of the censorship guidelines was always extremely useful when the Board found itself on the horns of a dilemma.

Having viewed the film, none of us wanted to see it again. But it was undeniably a powerful, intelligent and well-made film which did not set out to exploit its subject. We agreed with the minority opinion from the Film Censorship Board of Review (now known as the Classification Review Board), believing the decision to be at the heart of the matter of censorship in a free society – that is, the right of an adult to choose to see what they wish. There is a line between exploitative material and works of quality which push the boundaries but contain valid statements about the human condition. This, and the protection of children, is why censorship cannot be dispensed with altogether, and why arbiters are required to decide, however imperfectly, where that line falls.

After much consideration and soul searching, the Board of Review unanimously decided to give the film an R classification, with unprecedented further restrictions – that it be screened in one cinema only in each city, and that it never be disseminated electronically, either on video or broadcast television. In our view, *Salo* was on the side of the line which entitled adults to be able to view it if they wished. The R classification and consumer advice would enable the public to make an informed decision as to whether they wished to see the film or not. The additional restrictions would prevent inadvertent viewing by the young or those who would choose not to see it.

The decision provided an opportunity for a riot of political bandwaggoning. There was much beating of chests and outrage expressed in the popular press. National Party Senator, Julian McGauran, saw a chance to get his name in the papers by calling for Evan's sacking because (ignoring the rest of us) Evan had allowed "the artistic value of the movie and the freedom of expression of the director to override community standards." McGauran had not seen the film.

The matter was taken up by a group known as the Parliamentary Standing Committee on Community Standards. Their brief was television, not cinema. *Salo* was specifically banned from television. That didn't stop them. The attack was led by Liberal Senator John Herron and the Savanarola of Tasmania, Senator Brian Harradine, neither of whom had seen the film. They had a merry old time. Evan was hauled before the Committee and cross-examined theatrically by Harradine in a performance which would have made the Spanish Inquisitors look like the supporting cast from *Home and Away*. (The comedian Stan Freburg would have arrested Harradine on a four-twelve. What's a four-twelve? Overacting.) The experience was very unpleasant for Evan.

A newspaper report later claimed that when Harradine eventually saw the film, he commented that "it was not as bad as he expected".

Western Australia and South Australia invoked their territorial laws to prevent the film screening in their cinemas. Denver

Beanland, the Queensland Attorney General, who also had not seen the film, beat the drum to a noisy extent and exhorted the Premier, Wayne Goss, to intervene with his Federal colleagues to ensure such a thing did not happen again.

Because of all this attention, a film of unattractive subject matter but artistic merit which would otherwise have attracted only film buffs and a few curious members of the general public, did extended business and ran for much longer than anyone expected.

The upshot of all the hoo-ha was that when Evan's term as Chair was up, he was not reappointed; he was replaced by Barbara Biggins, a conservative campaigner for children's programs on television.

We were all in the *merde*; one by one my colleagues dropped off the Board or were not reappointed. For me, the final irony occurred early in 1994 when my film *Sirens* received an MA from the Censorship Board and the distributor, Village Roadshow, appealed. With my conflict of interest I could not be present at the appeal. The new conservative Review Board not only upheld the rating, they increased it! *Sirens*, which should have been rated M on the basis of its restrained, gentle and harmless eroticism, ended up with an MA 15+. Films of sadistic violence regularly get an M from the main Censorship Board, while we at the Board of Review had always taken the view that violence was of more concern than sex in context. My second term was almost up and there was no chance of me being reappointed. In April 1994 I resigned from the Board of Review, the last of my colleagues to depart. Eighteen months later John Howard was elected, and the forces of conservatism were rampant.

Curiously, I never heard of increased crime, violence in the streets or widespread depravity as a result of our liberal view of the censorship ratings of quality films, or from the access by persons over the age of eighteen to *Salo*. This has not, however, stopped many of the same forces of darkness from squealing to the press whenever they get an excuse to get their names in front of the public in relation to distribution of the film. The only thing it seems which will stop them, as it did with Senator Harradine, is death.

---◦◦◦---

Don Chaffey, the irascible director of *Ride a Wild Pony* and *Harness Fever*, reappeared briefly in our lives, having survived a helicopter crash in New Zealand at the age of seventy while directing a film, and bringing with him a new and beautiful young wife, following the death of his marvellous Edna. He was back to visit John Meillon, who had been diagnosed with a terminal illness. John's death did not come as a great surprise, his alcoholism pre-ordained it. Sometimes his inimitable voiceover for the VB commercial is still played; whenever I hear it I have the mixed feelings of admiration for that great voice and talent, and sadness for his self-destruction.

I attended a SPAA lunch at the Intercontinental Hotel for Senator Chris Puplick, the Coalition Shadow Minister for the Arts. He was very full of himself and very confident that the Coalition would win the next election. "Ask me for what you want now," he announced. "Once we're elected I'll be doing it my way and I won't be taking advice from anyone." Politicians' blind belief in their own omniscience never ceases to amaze me. Satisfyingly, Labor won the next election and Chris left politics, so we never found out what his expertise was in running a film industry.

At the same time, Peter Collins was Arts Minister in the Greiner Liberal Government in NSW. In a classic case of it's not the party who's in power but the people running it who matter, Peter was an excellent Arts Minister – accessible, informed and enthusiastic. And bad luck this time, Greiner was forced out and Labor won the next election. Bob Carr, in whom we had faith as a well-rounded individual who appreciated and would support all facets of the arts, could have been a boilermaker who failed the Intermediate exam for all the interest he showed in the area. Film in NSW has struggled ever since to compete with the more entre-preneurial governments of Queensland and Victoria – and indeed, South Australia and Western Australia, all of whom understand that if you want productions to come, you have to do something to attract them.

The 1989 pilots' strike made travel around Australia reminis-cent of Europe in wartime. When you left home you never knew when or if you would reach your destination, and if you did, when you would get back. Film Finances had productions in all main-land states through this period, which made for an adventure I could have done without. The airline would take your booking for a scheduled flight, but they would not tell you until you got to the airport that they had no pilots. I travelled from Melbourne to Perth in an RAAF Hercules, only slightly more comfortable than the one I had shared with Dennis the marauding camera-man on our visit to Lake Eyre. After a flight had been delayed in Perth for twenty-two hours, I flew to Adelaide via Melbourne and considered myself lucky.

The pilots' strike had a major impact on Australian tourism, es-pecially in the remote areas which are such a jewel in the Australian tourist landscape. It began the shakeout of the domestic airlines which leaves us with a very different infrastructure.

In November Tom and I unpacked our boxes of books which had been in storage for a year. The renovations at 26 Imperial Avenue were finished.

Tom put his back out at The Mountain on New Year's Eve; by 7.30 he was in bed with a Panadol and a hot water bottle. He showed no interest in celebrating. I saw the New Year in with Rita, sitting by the open fire at the back of the house, the lights of Forster far in the distance. I demolished our bottle of Bollinger, bought to share, and smoked a packet of cigarettes. I woke up on New Year's day feeling so ill that I have never had another cigarette. Mission accomplished, after a decade of trying.

I didn't give up Bollinger, though.

———— ✿ ————

My production manager from the Dino disasters, Helen Watts, started to work for Film Finances in January, and my life suddenly got a whole lot easier. Helen was one of the early group of film production managers who could have run Australia. Smart with money, they also understood the creative imperative which underpins filmmaking. They were brilliant organisers who could persuade virtually anyone to do anything, especially if a timely injection of cash went along with the persuasion. They were tough deal makers but good managers of people, and while organising the micro detail, they never lost sight of the big picture. I doubt we'll see their like again. Mostly women, they were of the last generation of bright girls who did secretarial courses instead of university. So without qualifications to become merchant bankers, lawyers or professors, they drifted into the film industry where they found a niche which not only allowed their talents full reign, but where they earned, for a few years, more money than they could have made in the professions.

Irony of ironies, the distributors of the film *Total Recall* were unhappy with the film's censorship rating and decided to appeal. So I found myself in the Censorship Board's screening room, viewing a print of a film which I had almost made, but hadn't quite … someone else had. It was a weird experience. Some scenes were as we had imagined them, but most were unrecognisable. And Schwarzenegger was great, but subtle he was not. I admired the film which was more about action and bad guys than a journey through the mind. I suppose I had a conflict of interest, viewing the film for the Board of Review, but no one seemed to care. We upheld the appeal so the distributors would have been happy.

EIGHT

Freezing Rain in Tadoussac

EARLY IN 1990 A CANADIAN producer called Robert Lantos contacted me. He had acquired the film rights to a novel by the Irish-Canadian novelist Brian Moore, *Black Robe*. He had offered it to Bruce Beresford to direct, but he was having trouble raising the money. Then he hit on the idea of making it under the Canada/Australia co-production treaty. This would enable the film to seek Australian government funds. Lantos had an Australian director and a Canadian writer, which was the start of the legal basis for a co-production. When he talked to Bruce about it, Bruce suggested me as the Australian co-producer.

Black Robe is set in the 17th century in northern Quebec, at the time a province of France. The Jesuits in Montreal send a priest out to a mission in the far north, as nothing has been heard from it for several months and, with the Indians having little time for these uninvited do-gooders, the Jesuits are worried that harm has come to the missionaries and their outpost. So Father La Forgue sets off up the St Lawrence river, too late in the season, with a young French boy and a small group of cooperative Indians as companions and guides. The film follows his journey and his crisis of faith in the unforgiving bitterness of the Quebec winter.

Not much Australian about this. But Australia had been using the co-production treaty with Canada very successfully to make and finance Australian films, and the philosophy of such treaties is to assist countries which cannot compete commercially with

Hollywood to team up to make films in the national interest. "On balance" the stories have to come from both countries in the partnership. It was arguably time for Australia to contribute to a Canadian story.

The rules and regulations for co-productions are quite strict. In the case of *Black Robe*, it was to be a 70 per cent Canadian, 30 per cent Australian co-production. Which meant that Canada had to come up with 70 per cent of the money and the creative talent, with Australia supplying 30 per cent. We had to spend this 30 per cent on Australians or Australian elements. This meant that I had to extract $3 million from the Film Finance Corporation and prove that it could be spent as the rules required.

As it happened, Peter Weir had just made the film *Greencard* as a co-production with France, using FFC funds, and some in the industry had criticised the FFC for "investing in a French film". (*Greencard* went on to become one of the FFC's eleven moneymakers.)

Bureaucrats always fear for their jobs first and foremost, and public criticism instantly reminds them that they are transient beings. The FFC never came out and said: we're scared that the industry will make a fuss if we give you money for *Black Robe*. The Board just decided to make it difficult for us in the hope, I suppose, that we would go away. However we had all our ducks in a row: official co-production status, finance and expenditure at the correct levels, and creative talent in line with the regulations. Why would we go away? At the first Board meeting which considered the film, a decision was deferred. At the second, investment was approved subject to a whole lot of absurd conditions, many of which we could not fulfil. There may have been a touch of payback from John Morris, now the CEO of the FFC, for my review of the SAFC, where he had also had a run-in or two with Bruce as well. "Bruce doesn't live here," John said to me at one of the many meetings I had with them to try to break the impasse. "He's not really Australian." Even for John, this was an outrageous statement.

Bruce was born in Toongabbie and had directed ten Australian feature films before he went to the US to make *Tender Mercies*. He had returned to make *The Fringe Dwellers*, and his children were at boarding school in Sydney. The fact that he had principally been living in the US, where he had been working for the past seven years, was irrelevant. Imagine saying, Nicole Kidman is not Australian, she lives in Tennessee.

Eventually I made an appointment to see the Chair of the Board of the FFC, Kim Williams, in his office at his day job, Southern Star Entertainment. When I arrived it was clear that Kim had no idea why I was paying him a visit, so I caught him by surprise. I put the case for investment in *Black Robe*. It may have been coincidental, but it went through the Board at the next meeting.

In order to make up the 30 per cent Australian spend, we took ten Australian film crew to Canada, including the director of photography, Peter James, and his team, and we did all the post-production in Sydney. We also cast in Australia the young Frenchman who accompanies Father La Forgue. Bruce was already in Canada preparing the film when casting director Alison Barrett and I screen tested two young actors for the role. We sent the tapes to Bruce in Montreal, and he chose Aden Young over the actor who had just surprised in *The Crossing*: Russell Crowe. Russell's test was every bit as good as Aden's; as is the fate of actors, Bruce chose Aden because he had a more European look than Russell's strong Aussie face and, at twenty, Russell was a little old for the part. Aden, as it happened, was half-American/half-Australian and had lived in Canada until he was fourteen. Now sixteen, he was delighted to be going back there for his first professional job.

I made several trips to Canada during the contracting process in order to speed up the finalisation of the agreements. The lawyers as always had a great time: a budget of $10 million, five contracting parties, two countries (three if you considered how Quebec sees itself in relation to Canada and four if you included one of the financiers, Englishman Jake Eberts). As usual, there were times when we thought it would never get done. Eventually a five-country teleconference which went for most of the day ironed out the final irrelevant points and the contracts were ready for signature.

The role of Father La Forgue proved surprisingly difficult to cast. The perfect actor for the role was Daniel Day-Lewis, but he passed. Eventually an intense young French Canadian actor, Lothaire Bluteau, who had just made an impact in *Jesus of Montreal*, was cast in the role. The remainder of the cast was made up of Canadian actors, with the exception of Aden and the

Aden Young in furs.

priest in the mission at the end of the film. For this role we cast the Australian actor Frank Wilson, whom Bruce had used in his early films, most notably in *The Club*. Frank gave a touching and sensitive performance as the dying priest.

The production crew was made up of Anglo-Canadians from Toronto and French-Canadians from Montreal. They were not particularly disposed to like each other, and when the Australians with their overtly happy-go-lucky attitude but disciplined professionalism were added to the mix, it was a bit like two kinds of oil and water.

I flew over for the last week of pre-production in Montreal at the end of October. There wasn't much for me to do apart from check the costs, take people to dinner and generally observe – a change from running the show. On the Saturday before shooting started, the unit moved to the location, an hour's flight north of Montreal. A mini-bus picked me and other out-of-towners up at our hotels, then drove to the rented house where the Beresfords were living. There was a certain amount of chaos as Bruce, Virginia, their five-year-old daughter Trilby and the nanny tried to cram two months' worth of acquired possessions into the van. Finally, in danger of us all missing the plane, they were ready.

"The agent said slam the front door and post the key back through the letterbox," Virginia said, doing as instructed. When we arrived at the airport, everyone heaved a sigh of relief that we'd made the check-in before the flight took off, but only with minutes to spare. Then, as the line of bags was shoved closer to the counter, Bruce suddenly looked around. "Where's my bag?"

A mixture of expressions crossed Virginia's face, in quick succession. "Still upstairs in the house," she said.

With the key safely posted inside the front door, there was no way of getting back into the house until Monday. So we took off for location with the director having only the clothes he was wearing. His bag eventually arrived four days later.

The unit was based in a village called La Baie, on the Saguenay

River, not far from the busy industrial centre of Chicoutimi. The Saguenay is very like the St Lawrence, on which the story is set. It is a broad, tidal estuarine river with a variety of landscapes along its banks, from high cliffs to dark, wooded islands. Its scale is dramatic.

Bruce, Virginia and Trilby moved into a rented house about twenty minutes' drive out of La Baie. Trilby, I noted with amusement, had rapidly acquired an authentic French-Canadian accent. A couple of years later when the family was living in Kensington in London, Trilby greeted me in the impeccable tones of middle-class England. When the family eventually settled back in Australia, so did Trilby's accent.

The first day of filming was exterior in the Quebec City set, built on a bay in the Saguenay River. Quebec City in 1670 was not much more than a few basic wooden buildings and a lot of mud, all faithfully realised by the Australian production designer, Herbert Pinter.

Worried about the budget, or just freezing? First day of filming on *Black Robe*.

Under grey skies, the weather was quite brisk and autumnal when I arrived on set. Then incredibly, at mid-morning, without warning the temperature dropped twenty degrees in about ten minutes. One minute I was comfortable in a sweater and a short coat, the next I was freezing to death. The Canadians were unperturbed but I noticed the Australians becoming quieter and quieter. I later learnt that the Canadians had offered to take them to the store on the weekend to buy winter gear. But the Australians had said, "No mate, we're used to all sorts of weather, we'll be fine." Now they were stuck on set, noses red and fingers blue, unable to go shopping till the end of the week. The Canadians were smiling to themselves. When I next saw my Aussies, they were kitted out fit for a year at the North Pole.

I flew back to Sydney, congratulating myself on a cushy job (how quickly one forgets the stressful financing fights) where all I had to do was telephone occasionally and keep an eye on the cost reports, then go back over at the end of the shoot to supervise the transfer back to Australia for post-production. I was driving contentedly north to The Mountain one Friday morning when my mobile phone rang. It was the *Black Robe* production manager, a quietly capable girl from Toronto, Susan Murdoch. This is odd, I thought. It must be very late at night over there.

"Hi, Sue," I said. "How are things?"

"Put it this way," she said, "If you could come back here earlier, I'd appreciate it."

"Like, how much sooner?" I asked.

"Well, straight away."

Robert Lantos, the Canadian producer, was a financier and deal maker, and the fine detail of keeping a film crew shooting was not his thing. He had promoted a production manager who worked on his TV series to the role of line producer, and things were not going well. I sorted out a few things in the office, packed my warmest ski clothes and flew back to Canada.

I found the usual problems when a big and complicated

production is in the charge of a weak producer. Not enough decisions, no anticipation, not a firm enough hand, not a lot of leadership, not enough information being communicated. There were some fine Canadians on the crew, but there were also quite a few from Robert Lantos' TV productions, and some of them were out of their depth. The Australians were the cream of the Australian industry, and by now they were sick of having to work with people less experienced than themselves who weren't particularly friendly. Susan Murdoch, being an Anglo, was often given a hard time by the Quebecois. Bruce was pleased to see me because the problems on set had been annoying him as well. Sue and I worked around the Canadian producer, who eventually was persuaded to put himself in charge of a long trip upriver with the second unit. This kept him out of the office, so Sue and I were able to settle down to keep the show on the rails.

An important element in the story of *Black Robe* is the transition from autumn to the depths of winter and, unusually for a movie, we were able to shoot in sequence. On this occasion the

No fake snow was used on *Black Robe*.

weather kept time with the shooting pretty much exactly. There were autumn colours all over the place when the filming started, and gradually it became grey and cold, and the leaves dropped from the trees.

On the morning we shot the scene where Father La Forgue is abandoned on an island in the river and left to die, under leaden skies it started to snow. From that day, about four weeks into the ten-week shoot, the sun never reappeared until the very last shot, and the temperature never rose above freezing. The last shot in the film is a crane shot, pulling up from the desolation of the abandoned mission and craning around to a cross, full frame. As the camera swung around the sun came out behind the cross, flaring into the lens. You could either put it down to God or Peter James' luck, but whatever, it was perfect.

The roads were icy driving out to location in the morning and it was normal for a car or two to slide off black ice into a ditch. Sue Murdoch and I walked 200 metres through knee-deep snow to check out a location; when we returned to film three weeks later our footprints were still frozen sharply into the snow. One morning towards the end, when we had moved to a bleak summer

resort near the mouth of the river called Taddoussac, I was sitting watching the filming when I became conscious of something sticky on my jacket. It was freezing rain, which arrives silently and coagulates into a thick layer of ice which sticks to everything. Bruce and the camera crew were in a rowboat on the river filming back towards the mission. They sat hunched over, freezing under a large black umbrella which was encrusted with ice, all around them snow, black water and grey wooden buildings under a slate grey sky. It looks sensational on film.

The Canadian wardrobe department was wonderful; their designs were dramatic and authentic, and they kept the actors warm throughout the coldest of days. They looked after Bruce, too. Two days running he walked out onto the ice on the edge of the river looking for a camera angle, only to go straight through. He had to be pulled out, dried off, warmed up and put back on the job.

Herbert's Canadian team of construction and props men also did a remarkable job, having to create everything, down to the tiniest of props, from scratch. The locations were a cinematographer's dream – Peter James won an AFI Award and a Canadian Genie

Award for his beautiful pictures, which he would be the first to tell you were enhanced by Australian Andre Fleuren's dazzling second unit shots of the canoes going up the river.

Brian Moore and his wife Jean came out for a few days to watch proceedings. He was a slight man with a soft Belfast accent, Jean a beautiful Canadian former actress. They shared a dry sense of humour and I became very fond of them both.

Susan Murdoch went on to become one of Canada's leading producers, and Robert Lantos to become a mogul. I have remained friends with Sue, and we meet occasionally if we are both in the same part of the world at the same time.

At the end of the shoot I flew to Banff with Bruce and Virginia for a few days' skiing before returning to Australia. It was early in the season, and bitterly cold. "This is the kind of holiday Father La Forgue would have enjoyed," Bruce said one freezing grey morning as we were hunched over, icing up on the chairlift.

In the late eighties I had taken up skiing after a gap of twenty years, but found to my chagrin that I had not returned to the easy skill of my youth. One week a year at Perisher wasn't getting me very far. This was partly due to a lack of natural ability, but because I loved the sport so much, I wanted to do better. I love the natural world that skiing takes you into, the silence, the intense concentration required, the pitting yourself against yourself, the thrill of speed combined with a little bit of danger, and the camaraderie of sharing something completely different to making films. I also loved that there were no phones or faxes on the mountain. Not then.

I heard about a group which ran tours to the USA, with the rather grand name of Steins World Ski Tours. A specialist company which arranged for up to 200 Australians at a time to ski on the best mountains in the world, the company survived on return business and many of the clients had been with them regularly for more than twenty years. The leader of the tour was a small, dynamic Austrian-Australian, Franz Pichler. Franz had run the ski school in Perisher; he'd been a racer and he was a brilliant teacher, with a uniquely graceful style on the mountain which he patiently transferred to his less talented customers. Each year Franz brought along with him instructor pals from Perisher and Thredbo. The boys also acted as guides, in theory knowing the best runs on the best snow, but quite often the customers, who had often skied the mountain for more years than the instructor, had to show them the best way down.

The Steins arrangement was convenient as I could, right up till the last minute, cherrypick the weeks that suited me, pay the money and show up. Everything else was taken care of. It also meant that if I didn't know anyone else who wanted to ski at the same time, I was assured of convivial companionship, as skiing is not a pastime to undertake alone. Tom had never skied and showed no interest in taking it up in middle age. I took the opportunity to learn to ski at the high level which Steins offered and became a regular – although, like a new arrival in a country town, it was about ten years before I was treated as one of the old hands.

In the northern winter of 1991 I booked a two-week ski holiday in Aspen and Vail, nicely timed to fit in with *Black Robe* post-sync sessions with the Canadian actors in Toronto, and the filming of the flashback scenes in Rouen, France. It had been agreed to edit the film first, and then decide whether to go to the expense of travelling to France for more filming. The scenes proved necessary and by now the Canadians had given up any pretence at producing, so I was the producer to oversee the French shoot. Rouen had been chosen because it had a magnificent unused cathedral in good condition, perfect for our purposes. There are not many of these lying around.

The cathedral had been unused, it seemed, for centuries. There were no pews and there was no heating. The old stone was impregnated with damp. It was so cold that the chill rose through the ancient flagstones and entered your bones, causing actual pain.

The hour or so I spent on set watching the filming is the coldest I have ever been. Ski lifts in a blizzard, the freezing rain in Tadoussac, swimming in snow melt in Interlaken – nothing ever felt like those medieval stones in Rouen. Somehow the crew and Lothaire made it through the day, but in any other industry they'd have called it off until the building was heated and floor dried out.

The second location was more amenable. It was a simple two-storey country house with a small drawing room where Bruce's elder daughter, Cordelia, played the recorder while Lothaire, dressed in ruffles as a young chaplain, listened attentively with the lady of the house.

Cordelia Beresford, an accomplished flautist, directed by her father.

According to the co-production regulations, the composer for the film should have been a Canadian, but Bruce wanted to use Georges Delerue, the legendary French composer with whom he had worked on *Crimes of the Heart* and *Her Alibi*. So we approached the co-production regulators and, as our points were in good shape, they agreed. The decision was helped by Georges' distinguished career – an Oscar and four nominations, and scores from *Hiroshima Mon Amour* and *Jules et Jim* to *The Pumpkin Eater*, *Women in Love*, *The Day of the Jackal* and *Silkwood*. Georges was tiny and round, almost hunchbacked, and a dynamo. He was totally organised and lovely to work with. We recorded the score in the main studio at the old Film School at Ryde, because there was then no recording studio in Sydney big enough to hold the full orchestra and choir of a hundred voices for the Requiem at the end of the film.

With Georges Delerue, in the recording studio at AFTRS.

Black Robe was nominated for ten AFI awards and won nine of its ten nominations at the Canadian Genie Awards, including best film, best director and best screenplay. The film is a masterpiece and considered by Bruce to be his best. "I don't think I can direct any better than that," he said recently.

NINE

Fantasy in the Blue Mountains

DURING THE SEVENTIES, talent agent Faith Martin represented most of the best actors in the business. Time and again, when I looked at the cast list of one of our productions, Martin Artists was the most represented agency. Faith had an unerring eye and she picked them young, straight out of NIDA. She eventually sold the business to Bill Shanahan, who developed the agency into the eighties and beyond. Bill, as Faith had before him, devoted himself to getting a fair price for his clients while making sure the deal got done with the producer. As the business became more sophisticated, with some of his actors working more in the US than Australia, Bill worked a supportive balancing act to give Australian producers a chance to compete. He became, like Bill Gooley, one of the integral cogs in the workings of the industry. But shortly after *Black Robe* was finished, he died, too young and greatly mourned. He bequeathed the agency, now called Shanahans, to his friend and colleague, Ann Churchill Brown. Ann had learnt the trade from Gloria Peyten at International Casting Service. She is a lot tougher to deal with but has maintained the quality of its actors and the agency's dominance in the business.

My friend June Cann, wife of Alex with whom I spent my first day ever beside a camera, eventually retired and passed her successful agency, June Cann Management, to her son John. Their clients included Jack Thompson, Bryan Brown, Rachel Ward, Naomi Watts and the brilliant Indigenous artist, David Gulpilil.

John became David's friend, minder, mentor and financial manager. John's empathy with Indigenous actors, and his love, patience and emotional and financial support for a generation of these brilliant but often troubled artists, is a legacy which has made the industry a better place. John also died too young and left a gap in our hearts.

Acting is an odd profession. Actors live with rejection and – unless they reach the top – they cannot control their own destiny. Producers and directors live with rejection too, but their success does not depend on their sex or how they look. Actors are always subject to someone else's perception of the role. An actor can be very talented, but the producer or director – or someone at the network or the studio – will say, "Mmm, I had in mind someone taller ... shorter ... darker ... blonder ... better known ..." as the despairing casting director goes back to the list one more time. As we have seen from the nonsense which went on trying to cast *Total Recall*. An actor will ring their agent in tears: "WHY didn't you put me up for X role? You KNOW I'd be perfect for it!" when in fact the agent has done everything possible to promote the actor for the role, but the director is just not interested and the casting director has told the agent, in desperation, "Nothing I can do about it, it's hopeless." If the agent told the actor the truth, the actor would probably commit suicide.

Then there's the X factor. Many actors have great ability, some are also handsome or beautiful. But they lack that indefinable element which is simply expressed as "the camera likes him". Without this X factor, there will be no stardom. A lucky break has to be underpinned by all these factors, otherwise the fame will not last. There is no accounting for "screen presence". Actors either have it or they don't. Even if they have it, they don't always get the successful films which combine with this special gift to push them to the front of the pack. Russell Crowe has the X factor in spades, along with stratospherical talent. He worked hard for his success, but he was lucky that *Romper Stomper* came along to show what an amazing impact he could make on the screen. Or maybe it was his mesmerising performance which made *Romper Stomper* a standout film. These things are never straightforward.

Agents have a tough job. They have to get their actors working and then keep them there. They have to support them through their insecurities, carry them through long periods of unemployment and sometimes advance them money to live on. They have to work out what they are worth to a production and not price the actor out of a job. They have to channel the often colourfully expressed opinions of producers, directors and casting people into something that leaves the actor with their self-respect intact.

When Noel Coward sang, "Don't put your daughter on the stage, Mrs Worthington," he knew what he was talking about. But kids who want to become actors are driven. Nothing will put them off, not even the worst horror stories.

I love working with actors. They are generally warm, vulnerable and very likeable. I understand their vulnerability, and try always to provide them with an environment in which they can get onto that set and give it their best. Sometimes nothing you do pleases them, but that is very, very rare. Usually the better the actor is, the nicer they are to work with.

It is the same with directors. The old cliché, "I've always wanted to direct" is a cliché because it is true – many are called, and most have no idea how hard it is to be even good, let alone great. The best directors, I have found, are the ones who knew that was what they wanted to do from the outset, but who did not let themselves get side-tracked on the way. Good directors must have a great visual sense and be natural storytellers. They must be intellectually rigorous. They are charismatic and manipulative, because charm is an asset which they need to persuade people to do what they want – everyone from financiers and studios to producers to actors to crew. They need to have the kind of brain that can visualise the script, then hold it all in their head in order to be able to drop in to any part of the story, and film it out of sequence so that when it is assembled, it fits with the bits around it, into one cohesive whole.

They need to be able to think on their feet. They need to be able to keep their head when things outside their control such as bad weather and crew or actor delays are wrecking their plans and a hundred pairs of eyes are looking to them for the next move. They need to be artful and flexible so that when there is not enough money to do everything they want, they can revise their plans to make the resources available work for them. They need to be able to pick up a good suggestion when it is offered, and strong enough to reject pressure when they know it is not in the interest of the end result. They need to be distinctively individual and still be able to work as part of a team. And then they need to be resilient enough to pick themselves up after the critics have panned their work, and start all over again.

While producers must also have good storytelling and creative instincts, a good general knowledge and taste, they come to the business with a different set of skills to a director. They also have to know the filmmaking process intimately, but must have a business brain, a knowledge of budgets, be persuasive with investors and be able to provide stable leadership to the director, actors and crew throughout all the problems and pressures of filming. They must be tenacious through the ups and downs of development and financing. They need to have good people-management skills, and be at once tough and considerate. They need to be able to establish that they and the director share the same vision for the film. If not, trouble! They need a good bullshit detector, because there is a lot of bullshit in the film industry. The producer is first in, last out on a project. The idea – wherever it comes from – doesn't start its journey to the screen until it has a producer, and they can still be managing the film's commercial life thirty years later. As the chief executive of the American Film Institute said recently when asked what do producers do: "Whatever it takes."

Who can say what makes a good film? If it was easy to figure out, there would be a lot more. No one ever starts out to make a bad film. But ego, greed and errors of judgement all contribute to bad films. Sometimes, just the desperate need to earn a living drives films into production before they are ready. Even the best talents, the greatest rigour and the highest ideals do not always combine to make a great end result. I have always felt that it can only be explained by magic. There is magic in the air. If it gets into the film during production, the film will be good. If not, the best it will be is okay. Like life, you do your best, but it is a crapshoot.

When Tom's mother died, it was unexpected but not surprising as she had been ageing rapidly and had become very frail. The same week that Ma died, Rita the wonder dog had begun behaving strangely; one morning when we woke up her eyes were open but she could not move. The vet thought she had had a stroke. We decided to hold on for a little while to see if she would recover. However, on our way home from Ma's funeral when we stopped at the vet, little Rita was dead. She was thirteen, on the younger side of a full life for a cattle dog. The vet was puzzled but an autopsy revealed a brain tumour. We mourned Tom's mother, a gentle, patient woman, the daughter of a bishop, who had suffered a pompous and humourless husband for sixty years, and we mourned Rita as well. You get one dog like her in your life, if you're lucky, and we missed the click-clack of doggie toenails following us as we moved around the house and the morning walks around Bondi with this beautiful animal, her white tail up, looping the loop with happiness.

After a couple of months, I found the emptiness around the house too much and decided we had to get another dog. Tom was not keen. He had been raised without animals, and for him Rita was the dog of a lifetime. Which was unfortunate, because no dog could ever measure up.

I wanted another cattle dog but decided to go for a blue this time so that it would not have to be compared to Rita, at least in looks. I talked to Evanne who said she would like a blue pup as well. I started buying *The Land*, and when nothing suitable appeared, I placed an advertisement for two female blue cattle dogs. I got a call and drove out to Young, returning the next morning with two very annoyed puppies on newspaper in the back of the station wagon, protesting energetically from both ends. I called them Jessie and Joycie; a few days later I drove to Nowendoc to deliver Joycie to Evanne.

Jess was a very different dog to Rita. While having all the intelligence, charm, humour and manipulative characteristics of the breed, she was highly strung and often unpredictable. She had a battle in our house for not being perfect Rita, and I loved her the more for that. She also had as many lives as a cat, using up the first one by chewing through the electric radiator cord in the dining room on one of the rare times when I had switched it off at the mains rather than, as I usually did, at the radiator itself. Had I done that she would have fried.

Joycie shared her sister's hyperactive personality, leaping from the seat of a horse-drawn coach at full gallop during the filming of a scene on *The Man from Snowy River* TV series and surviving the flying horses' feet beneath. She lived a happy life among the horses and camels, but her demise was inevitable when she dived in for a nip of a horse's heels once too often.

Our lawyer, Dick Toltz, called me. "I don't know what to do about Stephen," he said. Stephen, his son, had finished university and didn't know what he wanted to do but thought he might want to work in the film industry. "I'm worried about him – is there any way you can find him a job on a film? Anything will do." Stephen came to see me and sat slumped in the chair opposite my desk.

"I'll see if I can find you something," I said. I persuaded the production manager on one of the films we were guaranteeing to take Stephen on in an assistant's job, to see if he had any potential.

"Don't do that to me again," she said when the job was over. "That guy is useless."

Stephen is now Steve Toltz, the best selling author of *A Fraction of the Whole* and a short-listed Booker Prize nominee. A case of right key, wrong door.

One day early in 1992 I was opening my mail in the office when out slid a script, accompanied by a note in handwriting which looked like an ant had accidentally stepped in ink on its way home from the pub. The note was from John Duigan, director of *The Year My Voice Broke* and *Winter of our Dreams*. By now I also knew him as Virginia Duigan's brother and Bruce Beresford's brother-in-law. The note said, "Sue, do you think we could do this?"

When I read it I thought, I do hope so. The script was called *Sirens*. It was a fantasy based on the world of the artist Norman Lindsay, a charming story about sex, religion and repression. Tom and I had tried to make a film from Lindsay's comic novel *Redheap*, without success, and I had researched the artist's life and work and admired his multi-talented genius across the fields of art, literature, sculpture and political cartooning. Although much of his painting borders on the kitsch, this is not true of everything he did. His novels are fun, *The Magic Pudding* is an iconic story for children, and his cartoons for *The Bulletin* were biting and satirical. Some of his etchings are masterpieces. He had an insouciant taste for life and a long time to practise it, living for almost ninety years.

John suggested we do the film as a co-production with the UK, as it would suit him to live in England while doing post-production; two of the lead roles were English and could be cast from there. This would make it a reverse co-production to *Black Robe*, making a nice symmetry for me, and it meant we could access UK government finance. It also meant we could get visas for the two English actors without being screwed around by the union. We would need an English co-producer. John's agent had suggested Sarah Radclyffe, a well-known producer who had recently parted company with Working Title, which she had founded with Tim Bevan. Sarah and I had a talk on the phone, liked each other and agreed to go to work to get the film financed. Thus began a year of nightly phone calls about how to raise the money – usually just as our dinner was on the table, which annoyed Tom – and a friendship which endures.

Sarah put together the UK finance; in December the FFC approved the final tranche of investment and, with some constructive help from Greg Smith at the NSW FTO, we were on our way.

Casting for *Sirens* was handled by Liz Mullinar, whose job it was to find the three models who had to be stunningly beautiful, able to act and willing to take their clothes off. Liz pulled off a coup by getting Elle Macpherson to play one of the roles. Elle was already a superstar, but she wanted to try movies. Kate Fischer was a top international model, and Portia de Rossi was a rising actor and model. Portia went on to fame and fortune in the US in *Ally McBeal* and in the arms of Ellen de Generes. Elle went on to become an even bigger superstar, and Katie has made a career for herself as a TV personality and the former fiancée of James Packer. They were great girls and a lot of fun to have on the film.

John had identified a young actor who had done only one film of interest up to that time, called Hugh Grant, to play the parson. Not only was Hugh perfect for the role, but he was a nobody so we could get him and afford him. Tara Fitzgerald was chosen to play Estella, the parson's wife. She had been in a charming small English film called *Hear My Song*, and was considered on the brink of stardom. She was a very serious girl and she had a great voice with mellifluous timbre and perfect diction.

Sam Neill and Pamela Rabe played Lindsay and Rose. Pam got her clothes off with the other girls without inhibition when required, and with a body like hers, who wouldn't? Sam decided to play Lindsay with some kind of strange accent which he claimed was the way Lindsay actually sounded in old recordings. I couldn't see it myself, but John was happy with it.

Most of the film was set in and around Norman Lindsay's house at Springwood, which was now a museum, open to the public. So we set out to find a country house of the period with an appropriate

The adorable Hugh

garden, somewhere within reach of a town with accommodation for the crew. Shouldn't be too difficult, we thought. However, the search went on for weeks and, frustratingly, the location people could come up with nothing that worked. They would be on the road for days on end and return with bags full of photographs, but none of them seemed to be right. As time marched on, I started to worry that we might have a crew and a cast and money, but nowhere to film.

One afternoon when the art director was visiting the Norman Lindsay gallery to pick up some reference material, he got chatting to the caretakers. He happened to mention that we were having trouble finding a location which measured up to the real thing. "Why don't you film it here?" Mrs Caretaker said.

There it was, under our noses, all the time … what we didn't

Sam Neill not looking much like Norman Lindsay, with Portia, Elle and Kate.

know was that the gallery was not doing particularly well and the Board was interested in the fees we could pay. The Lindsay family was not thrilled at the idea, I suppose because they did not like the liberties which John had taken with the story, but we were able to negotiate the closure of the gallery to the public for the five weeks we needed, in return for our substantial location fee.

Sirens took as its starting point a true controversy over Lindsay's pen drawing, "The Crucified Venus". In the film a young English parson, en route to a new parish with his new wife, is asked by the "Bishop of Sydney" to stop over at Springwood and try to persuade Lindsay to remove the offending drawing from an exhibition at the Art Gallery of NSW. There is a train strike and the parson and his wife are stuck at the house for a few days, during which they both, in their own ways, discover things about themselves which will change their lives.

Filming at the house was a charmed time. The weather was warm, early autumn with a touch of crispness, and steady blue skies. For once we weren't rainmakers. John was an enjoyable director to

John Duigan directs Elle in the Lindsay garden.

work with – he knew exactly what he wanted, communicated well and everyone liked him.

For the fee we could pay him, Sam Neill, through his agent, Ann Churchill Brown, would only agree to work for two weeks out of the seven-week schedule. Which meant that we had to squeeze all of the scenes that Lindsay appeared in into that time. This was a nuisance, but the alternative was to pay Sam a lot more money than we could afford to have him for longer. Once he had finished all his scenes, he used to turn up on set to visit his wife, Noriko, who was the film's makeup artiste. He would complain about having nothing to do and being bored. We ground our teeth …

When Hugh Grant arrived in Sydney from London, we booked him into a first-class hotel in the city for rehearsals and wardrobe, and the filming at the art gallery. He never complained to the office about his room, but he must have made a nuisance of himself to the management because when he left the manager said, "We like Hugh, but if he ever comes back to Sydney, please don't book him into our hotel." He was no trouble at the Fairmont, where we stayed in the mountains. When the crew came in from work he always bought me a cocktail in the bar, something he had invented called "Milliken's Madness", accompanied by a couple of adorable kisses, which I used to line up for. When his girlfriend Elizabeth Hurley came out to visit, Hugh was very happy to see her. Elizabeth was easygoing, friendly and funny.

Elle's problem at the Fairmont was teenage boys. They used to go completely gaga when they knew she was there. I heard a mother say to one, "Go on, go up and say hello!" as he hung back, mouth agape, while Elle swept past. When they did pluck up the courage, she was completely charming to them, leaving them with a moment, I imagine, which would remain with them into very old age.

The production executive from our German investors paid us a visit. He arrived with the news that they had sold the film to Harvey Weinstein at Miramax for the USA. It meant that we were already part of the way to recoupment, and Harvey's legendary

Sam and John

promotional ability would be good for the film.

On the day he left, the executive told the office staff to arrange gifts from himself, in the way of Hollywood executives – a bottle of champagne each for John, Sam and Hugh, and flowers for the production manager, me and the actresses. He charged the gifts to the production. What was even more annoying was that all the girls would have preferred the French champagne.

The last few days of shooting were at Sofala, out of Bathurst, in the street so loved by Russell Drysdale. Then we packed up all the film and shipped it to London for editing.

————

On my way back from Colorado before starting *Sirens* I had stopped over in Los Angeles for my regular meeting at Film Finances' head office, and on this occasion I had dinner with a woman called Ellen Freyer. Dr Patricia Edgar from the Australian Children's Television Foundation had put Ellen in touch with me. Ellen was a television producer who had done mostly children's programs. She had optioned the acclaimed memoir by the dynamic Australian/American academic and businesswoman, Jill Ker Conway, *The Road from Coorain*, which she wanted to make into a film. I loved the book; I found it almost overwhelming in its depiction of the tragedies of a farming family in the years of the Depression and the war. The death of Jill's father, worn out by the problems of an immeasurable drought, and the uncomfortable portrait of her complex mother, made it an extraordinary piece of writing. I had considered trying to option the film rights to the book myself but I had held back, because there were structural problems with the story which I could not figure out how to overcome in translating it to film. Ellen thought she could. If that was the case, I was happy to be involved and see what we could do together.

I suggested a writer who was very experienced and, being of an age with Jill, I thought she might bring an insight into the times in which the events took place. I explained to the writer that Ellen had a very strong view of how to structure the adaptation, and that she would be required to write to this brief. Jill was coming out to Australia at the end of February so we arranged a visit to Coorain. We would all see the real place where the events took place, and where very little had changed in the ensuing forty years; we could also spend time with Jill, which was a good way to start the process.

We flew to Griffith with Barry, Jill's brother, then rented two cars to drive the couple of hours to the property. About halfway out, I got the feeling that Jill wanted to drive, so I offered her the wheel. As she took off down the narrow bulldust road at high speed, I tightened my grip on the door. Before long she misjudged the road and the car went into a furious spin, lurching from side to side as red dust flew around us. Oh shit, I thought, imagining us cartwheeling across the landscape. But with the will that got her to the top of American academia, Jill wrestled the vehicle back on to the road and drove a little more sedately after that.

We stayed as guests on the next-door property where Jill and I shared a room with double bunks. We drove over Coorain, its bare paddocks and half-empty dams bringing the past to life. The homestead, empty now, was still very much as the Kers had left it, but with almost nothing left of her mother's beloved garden. Jill and Barry were easy to get along with and open about the past. It was a good start and everyone left feeling positive.

Ellen had talked at length to the writer about the shape of the adaptation, but for some inexplicable reason the writer went off on a tangent of her own, and when I read the first draft I thought, this isn't what we were after. Nevertheless I sent it to Ellen without comment. It is impossible to predict reactions to scripts, so I waited to hear what she thought.

Disaster. Ellen hated it. Without talking to me, she sent it straight to Jill. More appropriately, Ellen should have discussed it with me and we should have gone to another writer before showing anything to Jill. Portraying someone's life is always tricky and has to be handled with great care. In this case, we were dealing with a dynamic, brilliant, ego-driven woman who understandably had a very strong view of her own image.

No surprises – Jill hated the script too. Ellen and I parted company, Ellen taking the project with her. Before long Jill and Ellen fell out and the option lapsed. Notwithstanding this rocky episode, Jill remained keen to have the film made, but the moment had passed. And I was right, there was a problem with the material which could not be overcome. Some years later the book was made into a rather disappointing telemovie. I was sorry. Jill is an extraordinary Australian and she had a great story, but not everything translates well into film.

Around this time I was asked by the Arts Department of the Western Australian Government to chair a review of government support for film in Western Australia. The WA Film Office was a basket case. It had a tiny budget which permitted it to do nothing but develop scripts to first draft, upon which they were generally deposited somewhere and forgotten. I had a conversation with a WA writer which went like this:

"What do you do?"

"I'm a scriptwriter."

"What films have you written?"

"Oh, I haven't written any *films*. I get one grant a year from the WA Film Office and I live on that."

After much lobbying by the small but vociferous WA film community, the government had decided it was time to do something. It was agreed that the best way to proceed was to form a committee of representatives of the vested interests and have it formulate some ideas for a new approach. But as most of the Western Australian groups were barely speaking to each other, it was thought a good idea to bring someone in from outside to run the committee. I was invited.

I was greatly helped by Chris Keely, the astute young adviser to the Arts Minister, Kay Hallahan. It also helped that I knew most of the Western Australians through my work as their completion guarantor and, irrespective of their feelings about each other, I liked them a lot.

In so many ways Western Australia has been shaped by its isolation; the film industry there was no exception. Perth is one of the loveliest cities on earth, and the most isolated. Western Australia is a natural environment of endless surprises, from the Kimberley to Esperance and Eucla. It is a filmmaker's paradise.

The review took me back to Perth several times for meetings in which everyone had a say and contributed ideas. It was a positive experience with a satisfying outcome. The recommendations of the review (known to posterity as The Milliken Report) which included a new, revitalised film support organisation and an incentive-based employment scheme funded through Lotteries WA, were implemented by the incoming Liberal Government in 2003, following the loss of the state election by the Labor Party. Such bipartisan support was both rare and exemplary, and because of it, as well as consistently appropriate funding over the ensuing years, Western Australia now has a small but solidly productive film industry with some of Australia's best documentary filmmakers, and some successful drama producers, including Sue Taylor and the unsinkable Paul Barron. I have felt close to the WA filmmakers ever since.

Early in 1993 I was appointed to the Australian Film Commission as a part-time commissioner. The AFC had been the main deliverer of Federal subsidy to the industry until the creation of the Film Finance Corporation, which took over the role as the industry bank. The AFC had then reinvented itself as the development agency, responsible for scripts, young filmmakers, film culture and co-productions.

It didn't take me long to realise that the organisation I had just joined was in trouble. There seemed to be a lot of unhappiness and quite a bit of infighting among the staff. Commission meetings were interminable and boring. For a while I considered bailing out. Then, when the Chair, Chris Noonan, announced that he was resigning to direct *Babe*, I put my hand up to take his place. I had the support of the Chief Executive, Cathy Robinson, and a benign Labor Government endorsed the appointment.

One of the first things we did was to move the organisation out of its old premises in West Street, North Sydney. Spread over three floors, there was an ageing, negative culture embedded in the furniture. A few key staff changes made a major difference, and by the time the AFC was settled in William Street, Woolloomooloo, in premises which were conducive to communication and interaction, there was a more energetic, collaborative atmosphere. I had a great Commission who, given the opportunity, contributed ideas and took the tough decisions when required. Cathy developed into a clever, collaborative CEO who admired filmmakers without wanting to be one, or resenting them – rare in a bureaucrat. When a vacancy arose I managed to get the first Indigenous Commissioner, the writer/director/actor Bob Maza, appointed. This gave weight to the newly formed Indigenous Branch, which was the beginning of opportunities for Indigenous filmmakers to tell their own stories.

The system of subsidy for the Australian film industry at that time was widely recognised as the best in the world. Both the FFC and the AFC were adequately funded and they worked in reasonable cooperation to give filmmakers the best opportunities. The word I used most at Commission meetings was "flexible". Talent and ideas do not always fit the neat boxes so loved by bureaucrats, but mediocrity will quickly work out how to operate the system. It is necessary to have guidelines, policy and a framework to operate in, but rules are made to be broken, or at least bent, in the interest of assisting success.

Cathy and I were helped in our endeavours by the fact that Chris Keely, the arts advisor from WA, was now working for the

Federal Arts Minister, Michael Lee, and both Chris and Michael were supportive of the film industry. When Paul Keating decided to placate the television networks which were demanding a reduction in licence fees by creating a new fund for the production of television drama, logic dictated that it should be administered by the FFC. However, Cathy and I put our hands up for it and the government put the AFC in charge of the Commercial Television Production Fund with its own budget of $20 million a year. This was an opportunity to run a fund the way I thought it should be run, with minimal administration and maximum flexibility and support for the program makers.

The CTPF was very popular, and it worked. This was partly because it was designed to make it easy for the networks to get their hands on the money, but also because they had to access the fund through independent producers, and we at the AFC set it up to work for them. It was administered by one senior project officer and an assistant, with accounting and legal backup from AFC staff. It had its own Board of experienced television people, and it ran like a well-oiled clock.

Another popular initiative Cathy and I introduced and our Board supported, which also crossed the demarcation between AFC and FFC, was pre-production cashflow. The FFC was prohibited, or so it claimed, from advancing any funds to a production until every last contract was fully executed. Sometimes creative requirements – a key person's availability, a particular season, the date of some external activity featured in the film – meant that the pressure between starting pre-production and getting those signatures was immense. AFC therefore made funds of up to $100,000 available to a production where it was obvious even to blind Freddy that the contracts were going to close, so that they could get started. The AFC lawyers took a responsible but pragmatic approach to checking out the contractual situation, Cathy and her staff made a quick decision and the money flowed to the production, enabling them to get going. We figured that we would only get caught once, and it was worth the calculated risk of $100,000 to assist good films to be made. We never had a problem getting the money returned when the first drawdown was received.

In March 1996 the Labor Government, the arts' friend, was voted out and the Liberals voted in. It took us a while to realise just what a disaster this was as our new Minister, Richard Alston, seemed friendly and on side. John Howard wasted no time getting rid of the CTPF. David Gonski was put in charge of an industry review. In spite of being invited, he never bothered to visit the AFC. Cathy and I were granted an audience at his office where we sat like primary school students in front of the headmaster's desk. The outcome of the review was less money for the AFC and the introduction of the FLICS – the Film Licensed Investment Scheme. The FLICS was a time-wasting, money-wasting *flop*. It began to dawn on us that the industry was in trouble.

As *Sirens* was being edited in London, I flew over to view the cut and to be present at the music recording and sound mix. That summer in London was breathlessly hot, and the English do not know how to do hot weather. The streets and the tube, and Sarah's office up five flights of narrow stairs in Soho, were hotter than Sydney in February. Luckily for me, my room at Browns Hotel had an ancient air conditioner which made a noise like a steam roller and blew coolish air to relieve the stickiness.

Harvey Weinstein was now on board, by virtue of paying for the US rights to the film, and he approached the post-production of the film with the enthusiasm he brought to everything. He assigned a young executive, Trea Hoving, to be present, representing Miramax. Trea was the unassuming daughter of Thomas Hoving, the innovative former director of the Metropolitan Museum in New York, and granddaughter of the head of Tiffany & Co. She knew everyone and told stories of her father travelling to Moscow with Jackie Kennedy. She also had a nice sense of humour and she fitted in happily with John, Sarah and me.

The film came up well and at the various screenings of the cut everyone laughed in all the right places. But later, when we screened it with the full soundtrack to Harvey and a small audience, no one laughed. The film wasn't funny any more. We all emerged from the screening room feeling glum. What had gone wrong? "I think it's the music," I said. The score by the British composer Geoffrey Burgon was very grand, a kind of imperial empire sound with lots of brass, which worked against the subversive, rather silly goings-on at the artist's house in the Australian bush. After some discussion, Harvey agreed to pay for a new score, and Rachel Portman's lighter treatment better suited the mood. It lifted the film and set it back on the rails.

Harvey had a lovely time arranging for Herb Ritts to do a photo shoot with the girls for *Vanity Fair*, and the film got a great launch in the US. It performed very well at the box office, becoming one of the FFC's profit makers.

The summer of 1994 brought the worst bushfires Sydney had experienced. The Film Australia studios at Lindfield nearly burned down in a fire which cut through Lane Cove National Park, taking several houses with it, and many houses were lost in the southern suburbs and the Blue Mountains. A fire came up to the garden of Norman Lindsay's house at Springwood, which was only saved by the volunteer firefighters. The smell of smoke drifted right through our house at Bondi and I kept finding fire-blackened gum leaves in Jess' water bowl on the back verandah. Chris Gordon was evacuated twice from her house in Como, after saying that there was no possible chance the fires could reach them. My brother drove past families in Mowbray Road, Chatswood, packing their cars for evacuation. He said they had a look of disbelief on their faces. Adrienne Read was producing a film called *Country Life*, being shot in the Hunter Valley over December/January. When the crew tried to return to location after Christmas, they could not get back for three days. All the roads out of Sydney to the north and west were cut by fires.

At the end of January, Harvey was screening *Sirens* at the Sundance Film Festival in Utah. Film Finances had rented a house for its staff so I moved in with them, my skis and boots in my luggage. John Duigan, Hugh Grant and Elle Macpherson were also there for the screenings and publicity. We dined each night at Harvey's table in the hottest restaurant in town, and I usually found myself sitting next to Tim Jeffries, Elle's boyfriend of the time. The handsome heir to the British Green Stamps fortune was friendly and self-effacing, used to Elle being the main attraction. He and I compared notes about being the one they never wanted to interview.

Park City was bursting with festival attendees. Traffic was at a standstill. You could not get a table at a restaurant unless, like me, you were with Harvey or someone almost as important (there wasn't anyone more important), and even making a mobile phone call was a challenge because the network was jammed and continuously collapsing. One night I went to a party hosted by Film Finances in one of the town's ski lodges. I got there late, after dinner, and was told by the doorman that I couldn't go in. About a dozen other people were milling about outside the front door in the sub-zero night. I protested that I was one of the hosts of the party.

"No one goes in till someone comes out," the doorman said. "The floor's about to collapse as it is."

When I did get in the stairs were jammed with people, not moving, stuck halfway up or halfway down. Above the roar of the party, conversation was impossible. I never found anyone I knew, so I left as soon as I could work my way back out again.

On another night on a wider set of stairs, at a much grander party, I passed Elizabeth Hurley, inching her way up as I abseiled down. "Have you seen Hugh?" she mouthed at me.

"Yes. He's up there somewhere." We were carried past each other.

In May *Sirens* screened in the marketplace at the Cannes Film Festival which I attended as the Chair of the AFC. Being there as the Chair was the next best thing to having a film in competition, as there was always something to do. When Phillip Adams was Chair and Kim Williams was Chief Executive, they used to attend Cannes together dressed all in black with matching white panama hats, and they would parade up and down the Boulevard de la Croisette looking pleased with themselves. Cathy and I did not try to emulate them. The year 1994 was good for Australian films, with *The Adventures of Priscilla, Queen of the Desert, Muriel's Wedding* and *The Sum of Us*. These successes, made possible by Keating's financial support for the industry and a constructive bureaucracy, in turn encouraged the commercial marketplace to have faith in the potential of Australian films and to continue to invest in them.

I hosted the AFC party, a tradition at Cannes, to facilitate Australian filmmakers' meetings with buyers. This year the party was held in the ballroom at the Majestic Hotel in the presence of the Australian ambassador to Paris. We had tea with the director of the festival, Gilles Jacob, whose continued support for the Australian presence paid off in opportunities for Australian films and filmmakers. With the help of marketing manager Sue Murray and her wealth of knowledge about buyers, markets and the people who mattered, we made sure that the AFC office was a resource which benefited all the Australians selling their films at Cannes.

Back in Sydney, I decided it was time for the AFC to do something about the AFI – the Australian Film Institute. The AFC was responsible for administering the budget of the AFI, whose brief was film culture, a creaky old film library and the annual film awards. The AFI was badly run and always in financial trouble.

I was told when I joined the Commission that Phillip Adams, when he was Chair, used to fling himself on the sofa at the end of the boardroom whenever the agenda reached the item AFI, groaning, "OHHH, THE AFI!!" When I became Chair, I quickly understood why.

The organisation should have been put down, its library transferred to Film Australia and the awards run by the AFC. But I felt that it had rattled along for thirty-five years, and you destroy something with caution as, once gone, you never get it back. I was reluctant to take the tough, smart decision, so we decided to try and fix it. Well, repair it. We instituted a review run by a professional accountant, together with an experienced film producer, Margot MacDonald.

Their report made a number of recommendations. The first one was, abolish the AFI. The second one was, if you don't do that, get a new director. This should have been relatively straightforward as the report confirmed that there was no contract with the incumbent.

We sent the report to the Board of the AFI. By the time Cathy, my Deputy Chair Christopher Stewart and I arrived at the AFI's offices to meet with the Board, they had put the director on a two-year contract. Checkmate.

Eventually, we instituted reforms which made the organisation more efficient, but not much more effective. And so it continues to lurch along. It is a dinosaur left over from the sixties and seventies, and should have been dealt with in the major shakeup of Federal funding agencies in 2008. It has recently sought to reinvent itself with the establishment of the AACTAs – a new and silly name for the AFI Awards, but I don't see a lot to justify its continuing existence.

In spite of my leading the charge against the AFI, at the end of 1993 I was presented with the Raymond Longford Award at the annual Australian Film Awards, run by the AFI. The award is named after the eponymous pioneering Australian filmmaker of the silent era, and is awarded to someone from the industry who has made a contribution. It is a huge honour, and it was an unexpected one. Unexpected, because it would never have occurred to me that I had done anything to deserve it, and because Tom knew but kept it such a secret that I had not an inkling. I was furious with him because it meant I had to get up in front of the industry and make a thankyou speech which I had had no time to prepare. There were many gracious, articulate and grateful things I would love to have said, most of which were lost in the shock of the moment. By a nice coincidence, on the same night, Evanne received the Byron Kennedy Award, given for inventiveness and innovation, the only animal trainer ever to be so recognised.

TEN

It's a Film About a Choir

SOME TIME IN 1994 I was in Brisbane taking part in a seminar at the Queensland Film Office. "There's a couple of guys want to see you before you leave," the receptionist said. When the session was over, I looked around and found two men lurking by the door, waiting for me. I said hello, and they said, mysteriously, "Come with us", and led me outside into a quiet corner of the office corridor. So what's all this about, I was thinking, when one of them produced a Walkman and handed me the earphones.

What I heard was a woman's voice, saying, "Imagine that you are in a prisoner of war camp, a prisoner of the Japanese. You have been there for two years. You are living in filth, among rats and bedbugs. You are starving. You are wondering, will the war ever end? Then one night, you assemble in the parade ground, and this is what you hear ..." The tape then played women's voices singing, without words, the Largo from the "New World Symphony". The words of the song written to Dvořák's music came to mind – "Going home, going home, I'm just going home ..." Shivers went up my spine.

Finally, my two new acquaintances explained themselves. Martin Meader and David Giles had written a script about a vocal orchestra created in the women's prison camps in Sumatra, during World War II. The voice introducing the music on the tape was that of Sister Vivian Bullwinkel, the Australian army nurse who had survived the massacre of nurses by the Japanese on Banka

217

Island a few days after the fall of Singapore. The recording was made at a re-creation of the vocal orchestra in Perth. I knew the story of the murdered nurses. What I didn't know was that two English women, Margaret Dryburgh, a missionary with perfect pitch, and Norah Chambers, a classically trained violinist, had devised a way to create music without instruments in a world where their captors were doing their best to starve everyone to death. I immediately saw that here was a way to tell the story of the Australian nurses and their fellow captives. My next thought was that the subject might interest Bruce to direct, given his love of music and his interest in films about women. I was given a copy of the script and I said I would give it to Bruce.

Happily, he liked the idea. However, he wanted to write a new version of the script. In the Meader and Giles script, the story focused very much on the two English women. Our interest was to feature the heroism of the Australian nurses whose strength and spirit helped everyone to keep going. The writers understand- ably wanted their script made into a film, and for about a year the project disappeared from my life. But then it resurfaced. Meader and Giles had taken it to Village Roadshow, who passed it to Greg Coote, then CEO at Village Roadshow Pictures, Village's production arm in Los Angeles. Greg liked the idea and bought the rights. He then asked Bruce if he'd like to direct. Bruce told Greg he wanted to write the script and he wanted me to produce. Greg asked me if I would co-produce with him; I readily agreed.

So we started from scratch and began a period of research, during which we met with women who had been in the camps, including Betty Jeffrey, who had published her prison diary as *White Coolies*, a classic never out of print, and Vivian Bullwinkel. I read *While History Passed*, an account of the experience by another of the nurses, Elizabeth Simons. While in Perth to meet Vivian, we met Edie Leembruggen, a retired headmistress who had been a girl in the camp. Edie was thirteen when captured, and nearly seventeen when rescued. She told us of walking down the stairs at Raffles Hotel after her release and not recognising her own reflection in the mirror. She had not seen herself for three and a half years, during which time she had changed from a girl into a woman. Sitting over morning tea on a sunny morning in Vivian Bullwinkel's comfortable house in Peppermint Grove, we listened as she recounted in detail the events of that terrible day when she had regained consciousness in the sea, wounded and the only survivor from nineteen young Australian women whose only purpose in war was to save lives.

We spent a day in Melbourne at the Nurses' Centre in St Kilda Road with the indomitable Betty Jeffrey. Betty told us stories about life in the camps, and did not mince words about the less than heroic behaviour of some of the women captives. From her, we first heard about the German doctor and her controversial approach to survival. After the war, Betty and Viv spent a year travelling around Victoria, raising money for the Nurses Centre as a memorial to their lost colleagues.

"I always ring Viv on the sixteenth of February," Betty Jeffrey told me, a look of grim memory on her face. "Still swimming?"

"Still swimming," Viv would reply. This was the date on which the *Vyner Brooke* was torpedoed and sunk by the Japanese, pitching 350 women and children into the sea.

While in London after Cannes, I met with television producer Lavinia Warner, who had written a book called *Women Beyond the Wire* on which the successful British drama series *Tenko* was based. *Tenko* was evolved from the same set of circumstances as the story we were about to tell, although it focused entirely on the British women in the camp. Lavinia had researched in detail the story from the English side when many more of the camp inmates were still alive, and her book was an invaluable resource. I took a train to Walmer in Kent to meet the gentle widow of a parson, Sheila Lea. The characters of Celia and Mrs Roberts, played by Tessa Humphries and Elizabeth Spriggs in the film, were based on Sheila and her mother, who was a classic colonial matriarch.

I took this photo at an Anzac Day march in the nineties. I don't know who these women are, but they bring a lump to my throat, as they exactly convey the spirit of the nurses of Paradise Road.

We visited the Australian War Memorial, where Vivian's nurse's uniform, with bullet hole, is reverently preserved.

The women we met who had survived humiliation, starvation and torture, were exceptional human beings. Now elderly, nothing had diminished their spirit and their emotional strength. The surviving nurses. although scattered around Australia, all stayed constantly in touch, a close bond that could never be broken, for the remainder of their lives.

When we had the basis of the research together, Bruce went off to write the script. This did not happen quickly though, as he was directing a movie called *Silent Fall*. A year passed.

Meanwhile, it had been known for some time that the Royal Agricultural Society was keen to move its activities, including the Annual Show, from its historic location in Moore Park in Sydney. There was talk that the State Government would sell off the site to help pay for the 2000 Olympics. There was a real concern that it would end up as high-density housing. I had talked to Wendy Machin, a Wingham girl and a minister in the State Government, about preserving the horse pavilions and precinct. Wendy was a rider of considerable talent and she readily took the cause on board. For once we got lucky, because when the Showground changed hands, the horse precinct was excised and preserved.

Because of my familiarity with the site through keeping horses at the stables and through the productions I had based there (not forgetting the depressing months of *Total Recall*), as well as the productions I had visited for Film Finances, it was a short leap to realising that it would make a great film studio, which would also save it from the property developers. I took the idea to Greg Smith at the NSW Film and Television Office and he asked me to write a report which he could take to government. This I duly did, and an industry movement began to save the Showground for the film industry. We conceived a naïve and optimistically simple operation to be administered by the NSWFTO which kept things pretty much as they were and gradually converted the existing buildings to studios and offices. A special word has to be said for Greg Smith, who ran the NSW Film & Television Office in the tradition of the old NSW Film Corporation, the way all government agencies should be run: simply, openly and helpfully.

Cathy Robinson and I went to Canberra to attend a major cultural policy statement by Paul Keating at the National Gallery. It was here he announced the "Keatings" – his controversial musical scholarships, and gobsmacked the film industry by announcing the transfer of the Sydney Showground to Rupert Murdoch for the purpose of establishing Fox Studios in Sydney. Imagine our surprise! Very different from the outcome we had planned but, we had to admit, a lot better result than blocks of town houses marching up and down the show ring.

The decision nevertheless was controversial, as many in the industry feared the "Americanisation" which Fox would bring with its money and its clout. The neighbours in Moore Park feared noise and industrial intrusion on their suburb. Bitter disagreements followed the announcement. While the transformation of the site is hardly a thing of beauty, in a pragmatic world it was the best outcome both to prevent over-development and to provide a facility for the film industry. The various facilities at Fox Studios are now used by all and sundry, and crews are grateful for the work in the big budget offshore productions which use the studios.

—⁂—

In the course of my Film Finances work, I had read a script I really liked by young writer director Megan Simpson, called *Dating the Enemy*. It was to be produced by Phillip Gerlach. The film was almost financed but the money fell through and the project lapsed. At the time, I remarked to Phil how much I enjoyed the script and that I wished I was making it. This happened only very rarely, as taste is a peculiar thing and a story about which one person is passionate can just as easily leave someone else cold. Sometimes it's a bit like seeing a painting in an art gallery. I really *want* that. But you can't have it, so you have to move on.

Now Phil called me. "Were you serious about wanting to produce *Dating the Enemy*? Would you like to do it with me?" I said yes and yes.

Phil and I had had our differences, and we disagreed a lot when we were both on the SPAA council. I had worked happily as vice-president to Ross Dimsey who had been president for a year, and when Ross said he was going to stand again, I agreed to stand as his vice-president. What neither of us foresaw was that Phil, then managing director of the production and distribution company, Beyond, was also planning to stand for president. Phil was elected. At the time I thought that he was a bombastic loudmouth and the last thing I wanted was to spend a year yoked to him on council. However, I could either resign in a fit of pique, which would look childish, or stick it out. I decided to stick it out. When I got to know him a bit better I found that there was a nice and very decent man underneath the kamikaze front, and eventually we became good friends. But when it became known that I was co-producing *Dating the Enemy* with him, there was considerable amusement from the people who had witnessed our adversarial relationship. It was said that the film was aptly named and applied to both of us. But we worked well together. Phil looked after the finance and I made the film. Perfect teamwork from my point of view.

Bruce sent me an email from London to say that he had just read a novel by an old university friend, Madeleine St John, and he thought it would make a wonderful film. Would I read it? It was called *The Women in Black*. Set in a Sydney department store in the 1950s, it was a fairytale about the clash of post-war migrants and the old Australia. I thought it would make a charming film. We set about acquiring the rights.

———

Meanwhile Greg Coote continued to work on the financing of the women's prison camp project. In June he called me to say that Tom Rothman at Fox Searchlight had agreed to finance the film, subject to casting, and he wanted more work on the script. Fox Searchlight would pay for another draft if we got another writer to work with Bruce, who brought in Alfred Uhry, the Academy Award-winning writer of *Driving Miss Daisy*. Alfred Uhry flew to Sydney and they worked at Bruce's house in Balmain. We thought carefully about including the massacre of the nineteen nurses on the beach at Banka Island, but because the story was about the prison camp and how the choir helped the women to survive, we could not give such a terrible event the emphasis it deserved. Rather than do it injustice, we left it out. We felt that you couldn't just mention it in passing without trivialising it. It was a difficult decision.

Phil brought the French distributor, Ernst Goldschmit of Pandora Film, into *Dating the Enemy*, which closed the finance. After the usual contracting hiatus we started pre-production. *Dating the Enemy* is a romantic comedy about the war between the sexes. We were extremely lucky to get the two best actors possible for the film. Claudia Karvan, as beautiful on the inside as she is on the outside, played Tash, and Guy Pearce, prominent from his role in *Priscilla, Queen of the Desert* but not yet internationally famous for *L.A. Confidential*, played Brett. They both were wonderful at playing each other, and the special effects company, Animal Logic, did a fine job of making them magically switch bodies – easy-peasy now, but tricky and expensive in 1995.

I had hired production manager Anne Bruning for *Dating the Enemy* and we were having a lot of fun working together. So now I asked her if she would come onto the women's prison camp film, now titled *Paradise Road*, with me as line producer. We spent weeks working on the budget and having it reduced by Fox, until we reached some sort of compromise where we thought we could probably make the film for $25 million, and Fox agreed. It was only made possible, though, by the contribution of $6 million from a Singaporean businessman, Andrew Yap. So in effect, Fox got the movie for $19 million.

Eventually, Greg Coote called from LA to say that we had been given the green light by Fox. We took off immediately for a location survey to Queensland.

Location surveys are the best time in the filmmaking process. They come in the euphoric period after the money has been raised and before weather, greed, egos and inhuman working hours wear you down. All your illusions intact, you have your team around you and you all revel in the prospect of realising a dream after months, or more often years of struggle, setbacks and disappointments. On this occasion, there was a holiday atmosphere as we set out in a rented mini-bus driven by location manager Phillip Roope from Cairns to the Daintree, checking out locations.

In Cairns, we found the wharves for the scene of the departure of the ship from Singapore without difficulty. Trouble arose, though, when Bruce and cinematographer Peter James fell in love with a location for the prison camp which Anne and I knew was logistically unworkable. On the side of a hill outside Cairns, it had a spectacular view across a wide green valley to violet mountains which, on the day we were there, were wrapped in cloud and mist, looking layered and tantalisingly Sumatran. It also had a public road around three sides on which noisy traffic whizzed by, and the soil was a soft loam which, after a shower of rain, would bog everything in sight. Anne and I argued against it, Peter pushed for it. Production designer Herbert Pinter sat on the fence. Herbert would have to deal with both the look of the sets and the logistics of making it work. The arguments for and against went back and forth. You never like to say no to a great idea, but someone has to be practical when everyone is getting carried away. That is Anne's job, and the producer sometimes has to play Solomon. Finally, Herbert pointed out that the view was so beautiful it would look as if the prisoners had strayed into *The Sound of Music*. We settled on a less scenic but more appropriate valley outside Port Douglas, which worked much better on every level.

A couple of weeks later we flew to Singapore. A condition of Andrew Yap's contribution to the budget was that we film some sequences in Singapore which, after all, was where the real story began. Bruce had set the beginning of the story in the Raffles Hotel, and he had bookended the script with a modern scene in the streets of Singapore. We also wanted to film the girls staggering through some rice paddies, to add authenticity.

I had not been to Singapore since the 1970s. It had transmogrified from a charming colonial city to a place of glass towers and designer shops, indistinguishable from any other modern metropolis. There were few relics of the past left, but Raffles was still there. We quickly settled on the exterior of Raffles, but soon established that filming the big opening dance scene set in the Raffles ballroom was impossible in the real hotel because there was no such room. That would have to be found elsewhere.

We flew to Penang where, in addition to the rice paddies, we were to look at a square in which the women are rounded up before being herded off to prison, and to try to find an exterior for the Japanese brothel scene.

Modernisation was overtaking Penang as well, with a CBD of glass towers, but from our rooms at the new Hyatt we could look down on to the terracotta roofs of the old city. We drove past an area in the nearby suburbs where there were streets of enormous Victorian houses, mansions which would dwarf anything in Toorak. Each was set in about five acres of grounds and they were all empty and slowly decomposing in the tropical damp. A relic of the British Raj, they would soon disappear forever. Bruce chose one of these houses to use as the exterior of the brothel. As we walked around the deserted garden, I looked through the windows. I could see a great central reception area or ballroom, with a ceiling two storeys high. There were hundreds, possibly thousands, of bats flashing through the gloom, lit by rays of the sun where blinds and curtains had rotted away. The floor was covered, wall to wall, in bat poo a metre deep. That's a lot of work by bats. No one had inhabited this house for a very long time.

We crossed over the causeway from the city and spent a day on the mainland, driving around the countryside looking for rice

Batpoo House, as it appears in the film.

paddies. Here was old Asia with kampongs, narrow roads, paddy fields, chickens and motor scooters. Every time we had to turn around, the van reversed to within millimetres of the deep monsoon drains before lurching forward to safety. When we stopped by the roadside for an ice cream, a young couple riding a motor scooter puttered past. They both had helmets on, hers screwed down firmly over her veil, but their tiny child, riding perched between the handlebars in front of her father, wore just a T-shirt and little trousers, and was not even strapped on.

As the survey proceeded it began to dawn on me that this picture was bigger than us. The logistics of the film meant that we would spend 30 per cent of the schedule filming 10 per cent of the story, leaving seven weeks to film 90 per cent of the script when we got to Port Douglas and the camp. The numbers were ominous.

About this time the Australian dollar began to rise, leaving me with a half-million-dollar currency loss. Fox refused to cover it. I knew I couldn't do the picture without it. Most directors would throw a tantrum when faced with these problems and say, you fix it. Bruce, one in a million, never uttered a cross word. We were in it together, and he would do his best to manage with whatever we came up with.

While all this was going on, there was the casting. Again. Along with the Australian nurses, the characters in the film included English, Dutch, Chinese and Japanese. The union, true to form, determined to make the process of importing actors as difficult as possible. Fox was determined to get as many Americans into the cast as possible. We just wanted to cast the best actors for the role, with the emphasis on Australians wherever we could.

The first problem came with the casting of Susan Macarthy, the Australian nurse who was one of three central characters in the film, and who was inspired by those heroes, Betty Jeffrey and Vivian Bullwinkel. Bruce wanted Cate Blanchett for the role. Cate had done only theatre and Australian television to that time. But Bruce and casting director Alison Barrett knew she was a major talent in the making. The executives at Fox, never having heard of her, were not interested. (*Plus ça change …*) Arguments raged backwards and forwards across the Pacific. "What about Minnie Driver?" Joe, the Fox production executive, asked. No. "Well, what about Kate Winslet? She's a New Zealander" (i.e. that should shut you up). No, Kate Winslet is English. She was in a New Zealand film, *Heavenly Creatures*. Bruce dug his toes in. It was Cate or nothing. Joe was angry. Bruce wasn't budging.

Meanwhile, a similar argument went on about the role of Adrienne Pargiter, the violinist based on Norah Chambers who was, in real life, English. Bruce wanted to cast an English actor, but no one that the casting agents in three countries could come up with would satisfy Fox. Eventually, the studio sent the script to Glenn Close who agreed to do it. We were realistic about the fact that unless Fox was happy with this role, the picture would not go ahead. Glenn was a fine actor and, with the right accent, right for the role. She was nothing like the real Norah Chambers, but at this point we just counted our blessings that someone talented who could play the part satisfied the studio.

We offered the role of the German doctor, Dr Verstak, to Anjelica Huston. She showed interest, but when she wanted more

With Glenn Close on set.

profit share than we had left to give, she dropped out. Frances McDormand, who had just won an Academy Award for *Fargo*, happily accepted the deal and was cast.

The ageing star Jean Simmonds was cast as Margaret Drummond, based on the middle-aged missionary, Margaret Dryburgh. Jean Simmons was really a little too old, but the studio was happy and so was Bruce. That is, until a week before she was to catch the plane, when her agent rang to say she had to withdraw due to illness. There was a scramble to recast. The studio wanted Joan Plowright.

"Too old," we said.

"But Jean Simmons was old," they said.

"Jean Simmons was sixty-seven. Joan Plowright is *seventy-four!* Margaret Dryburgh was fifty when she was imprisoned. Seventy-four for this role is ridiculous."

The studio wanted Joan Plowright because the head of Fox Searchlight, Lindsay Law, was away and Joe had flicked the decision to the head of the whole studio, Peter Chernin, for approval. Of the names on the casting agent's list, the only one Peter Chernin had heard of was Joan Plowright.

Fortunately, in the nick of time Miss Plowright was made another offer which she preferred, thus avoiding the embarrassment of trying not to cast her. Pauline Collins, star of the hit film *Shirley Valentine*, agreed to do the role and Fox concurred.

As soon as we got the okay, I rang Pauline in London to say hello and welcome her to the film. She was not at home. By the time we tracked her down, she was at the hairdresser. Oh no ...

"Pauline, I hope you're not doing anything to your hair. Our hair people want to style it for the film when you get here."

"Oh heavens no, darling. Just getting the roots done."

Oh yes ... what she was doing was having her hair coloured a vibrant reddish brown. Her role was a middle-aged Anglican missionary who had been in the Far East for most of her life, and who was to be shipwrecked, imprisoned and starved to death, out of sequence. Our hair department had to spend seven hours stripping out the colour and putting in grey, hair by hair. Actors! You love them, and Pauline Collins is one of the nicest, but sometimes ...

Eventually the studio gave in on Cate, and they were not interested in the smaller roles, leaving Bruce to cast the best actors. In the end we imported seven of the nineteen female roles, plus the four Japanese-speaking parts, as their performances were critical and we could find no appropriate Japanese actors in Australia.

Suzie Porter, Cate Blanchett and Lisa Hensley

Paradise Road was totally financed without government subsidy, bringing $25 million of foreign currency into Australia. It was a coup to get an American studio to fully finance an Australian film at this budget level; until that time it was the most expensive Australian film ever made. None of this mattered to the actors' union, the MEAA, which gave us no quarter. Our friends in the Federal Labor Government were no help; they would never intervene with the union. I've no idea what the MEAA hoped to achieve. A high school student could figure out that the film would not be made without significant imported cast – all of whom, with the exception of the two biggest stars, were playing ethnically correct roles. But I seriously believe that if the MEAA could have sunk the production altogether, they would have felt they'd had a victory. Their staff were rude and obstructive, and they kept us waiting to approve the foreign actors' visas until three days before they were due to catch a plane. Then I got a call from the union official which went like this:

Me: "Hello, Rachel."

Rachel: "That's fine."

What's fine? That you've kept us waiting three months for approval to import some actors, that you've made us run casting sessions all over Australia to humiliate Australian actors who we are never going to cast, that you've held up visas so that actors from another country are stressed and angry? That you've never said so much as sorry for the inconvenience?

"If you have a lot of power, you should exercise it gracefully," I said.

We got the artists into the country, but the union didn't give up. It advised the local agents not to sign contracts with us (they sensibly ignored it), and during the filming in Sydney two of their officials arrived, unannounced and uninvited, on the set and started handing out flyers about what a bad production we were. Asked to leave, they handed a bunch of the flyers to one of the actors and told her to hand them out to the cast and crew. The actor, bless her forever, gave them to one of the production staff who brought them into the office, where we threw them in the bin. The day we were moving the unit from Sydney to Cairns – a hundred people, tons of equipment, a massive job for a production office which was, like all production offices, understaffed – a letter was delivered by courier from the head of the union stating that we were in breach of various clauses of the feature film agreement. Perfectly timed to be as disruptive as possible. We were not in breach of anything, as they well knew. Once we were in far north Queensland it was harder for them to harass us, particularly as their members were well paid, well fed, and well accommodated in one of the most beautiful places on earth. But they still sent a local organiser out from Cairns to waste our time.

We had nineteen female actors for the entire Australian shoot, and I'm sure that if the film had not been about saintly self-sacrifice and heroism, we'd have had at least some movie star behaviour from the girls, human nature being what it is. But whenever trouble threatened, they remembered that no matter what their problem was, it was piffling compared to what the real people they were playing went through, and rarely did the office have to intervene.

Which is not to say that all was sweetness and light at all times. One of the wardrobe girls heard the following exchange between Jennifer Ehle, star of *Pride and Prejudice*, and Julianna Margulies, star of *E.R.*:

Jennifer: "How long does it take you to shoot an episode of *E.R.*?"

Julianna: "Eight days."

Jennifer: "Eight days for *that* stuff?"

One of the actors who was required to appear in the shower scene waited until she was cast and contracted before telling Bruce that on no account would she take her clothes off. Another one in a supporting role dug her toes in and insisted on single card billing. Negotiating the billing for all the cast was like solving a Chinese puzzle. Everyone wanted to be above everyone else.

Glenn Close was one of the biggest stars in the world and great to work with; she set the tone for everyone else. Her accent was perfect and she dedicated herself to the demands of the role, working tirelessly. We got off to a rocky start, all the same. Glenn started work in Penang. We had a read-through of the script with the cast and Bruce the afternoon before filming began, and as it went on, Glenn became less and less animated. Late that evening she rang me, in a state. Although she was playing the main character in the film, it was an ensemble piece and she had just realised that her role was smaller than she had thought. She said

232

The crew sets up a tracking shot of the women being marched to captivity.

that when she first read the script at home in New York she was so moved by the story that she didn't stop to think just how little of it she was involved in. She didn't think she could do the film, and she wanted to go home.

This was a seriously terrifying moment. I had already spent several million dollars on preparation and contracted commitments for the film, I had a full crew and a large number of cast in a foreign country ready to shoot the next day. If Glenn left, the picture would collapse. We could never recast in time to save it. I didn't tell her this, though. Trying to disguise the panicked thumping of my heart, I asked her not to do anything until I talked to Bruce.

I called Bruce and together we discussed some new scenes which would build her role – and in truth, she was right, her character needed more to do. Bruce got to work; late in the evening we took the new scenes to Glenn and asked her to think about the situation. The next morning I went up to her room in trepidation, not knowing whether my producing career would fly off from a runway in Penang with our star, or we could get on with the day.

Glenn said of course she realised she could not leave, and the show lurched on.

Our budget problems were solved, temporarily, by Bruce contributing part of his fee. (All he said was, "It's amazing we got it up at all." What a guy! No other director in the world would do this.) Andrew and Fox eventually kicked in some more as well. But the roller-coaster did not end. The ten-week schedule should have been fifteen, so the pressure stayed on until the very last day.

The management of Raffles Hotel refused us permission to film when they found out what the story was about. They didn't want to offend the Japanese ... Andrew Yap worked some miracle there. A long search for the interior of the ballroom which matched the exterior of Raffles ended at the Marrickville Town Hall, which looked as if it had been built at the same time and by the same architect as Raffles (which it probably had), so it was a perfect match. We filmed the splendid opening sequence there. Julie Anthony sang "Mad About the Boy", and when offered a car to drive her from her trailer to the set, Glenn said, "Oh, I'm happy to walk." So Marrickville was treated to the sight of a Hollywood star, in full period ball gown and makeup, strolling up Marrickville Road.

I was planning to tell this little anecdote to Alan Jones when he interviewed me on the radio about the film but every time I started to say something he talked right over me, so I assumed he was more interested in what he had to say than listening to me and I gave up.

In one of the research photographs, Bruce had noticed a colonial wife holding a small dog. He latched on to this and wrote in a dog for Mrs Roberts, played by the Shakespearean titan, Elizabeth Spriggs. The logistics and expense of hiring a dog outweighed its value to the film, so, ever-optimistic, I figured I would be able to persuade Bruce to write the dog out again. In general, directors can be led, but they can never be pushed. My approach when there is a conflict between the budget and the vision, and persuasion fails, is to say yes, and mean no. This usually works, as time often results in the director losing interest in the thing they were so passionate about and so they think that giving it up is their idea. Object achieved without the unpleasantness of confrontation. So I took the cost of the dog out of the budget and put the money somewhere it was needed more, thinking I would win in the end. However, on this occasion my strategy did not work. Bruce was determined that the dog stay. You can't win them all.

Evanne provided us with Creature, an extremely sharp and well-trained small brown poodle and two stand-ins, Kerry-Anne and Darren. Creature, Kerry-Anne and Darren had to have their own wrangler, their own house in Port Douglas and a car for the wrangler to drive them around.

We could not take our poodles to Penang, where the dog was needed for continuity, because of Australia's quarantine regulations. So the art department was charged with finding a poodle locally which could double for Creature. It turned out that poodles were not the dog *du jour* in Malaysia. After weeks of searching, they turned up one miniature poodle called Russell, owned by a doting Chinese couple. Unfortunately Russell was the wrong colour, so he had to be dyed to match Creature. There was immense difficulty about getting Russell dyed; it's not something you do every day. Eventually his owners took him to their own hair salon, who turned him out a tasteful chocolate brown.

"Russell's getting his own campervan," Terry Ryan, the costume designer said.

It turned out that Russell had never in his small life been out of the air conditioning, and after one day of being clutched to Elizabeth's expansive bosom in the heat and humidity of the paddy fields as the women were marched to captivity, he had a heat attack and had to be laid off. Elizabeth had to soldier on carrying a pyjama bag, which left me wondering why she hadn't been given that from the beginning, which would have saved us quite a bit of time and money.

We were asked by Andrew Yap if, on their way back to Sydney from Penang, the stars could attend a dinner in Singapore specially arranged for forty of his friends and business associates to showcase his involvement in this film. This was terribly important to him, and for $6 million I'd have given him anything – within reason. I talked to the girls – Glenn, Cate, Elizabeth Spriggs, Julianna Margulies, Jennifer Ehle, Wendy Hughes and Pauline Chan, and, good sports, they all agreed to be in it, where they could just as easily have said no way, it's not in our contract.

Because they were all required every day of filming, we could not spare time out to accommodate this event, so the dinner was planned to follow the end of work in Penang. When the day's shooting was completed we would fly to Singapore, do the dinner, stay the night, then go on Sydney the next day. The dinner started at eight. If we left Penang at six, we would land at seven and be at the restaurant comfortably by eight o'clock. Even if the flight was a little late taking off, we would arrive by eight thirty and make an entrance.

After wrap we all changed into our dinner finery, the makeup girls put the actors' faces on and we raced to the airport, only to be told when we got there that the flight had been delayed by three hours. It was now due to land at ten, which would put us in the restaurant around eleven p.m. Frantic calls were made to Andrew Yap, desperate attempts were made to change airlines. Somewhere in the middle of all this, Jennifer Ehle realised that her suitcase had been left behind at the hotel. Stressed, jet-lagged, exhausted, she turned scarlet and rushed for the toilet where she threw up. On a moving footway as we raced between airlines trying to find another flight, Elizabeth Spriggs, 115 kilos, resplendent in a full-length dinner dress, tripped over like a rubber toy and travelled several metres on her back, legs and arms waving, until she was rescued by her much smaller travelling companion, Murray, and bravely pressed on.

All to no avail. There were no earlier flights out of Penang. I rang Andrew one last time to tell him it was hopeless. I felt dreadful for him. He had spent weeks arranging this event and there was a lot of face involved. He was gracious and philosophical on the phone, but I could imagine his embarrassment when he had to tell his guests what had happened. Once we realised there was nothing more we could do, we settled back in the airport lounge with a drink and everyone cheered up at the thought of not having to attend the dinner. Elizabeth, unfazed by her stunt on the moving footway, regaled us with stories of touring the world with the Royal Shakespeare Company in the 1960s.

The next day, before we left Singapore for Sydney, the actresses attended a press conference arranged by Andrew. It was a small compensation for the evening's disaster and they all, bless them, gave it the full treatment. With the help of our makeup, hair and wardrobe staff, they arrived at the press room at Raffles Hotel looking achingly beautiful and they were patient with the local press. Glenn, whose makeup accentuated her blonde beauty, glowed. "I

Cate and Bruce demonstrate their extraordinary concentration.

Bruce behind the camera, with operator Brad Shields.

just feel you've got to give them a movie star," she said, "rather than a bag lady, which is how I usually am."

Because of the Marrickville location for the ballroom scene, we had to take the travelling circus to Sydney for three days before moving on to Cairns and the wharf where the women board the *Vyner Brooke* to escape Singapore. While we were travelling to Sydney, the freight company helpfully sent the camera equipment – a container load of it – to Cairns. Another sleepless night for Anne.

While in Sydney, I attended an Australian Film Commission meeting. Pauline Chan, who played Wing in the film, was a member of the Commission. It was funny to see her, immaculate and chic, attending to her Board papers when a few days before she had been dragging a suitcase through the heat of Penang in a coolie hat.

On the flight to Cairns, Glenn was invited into the cockpit for the landing by the flight staff. The plane came down with a thump. "Maybe the pilots were getting Glenn's autograph," Anne said.

It was raining in Cairns. Drizzle, enough to be annoying. But we had no time to wait and filmed on, in the rain. "One hair will go frizzy, one will go straight," the hairdresser said. "All I can do is lurk over them with the tongs."

While we were in Cairns, crammed into an overcrowded temporary production office at a hotel, a new drama erupted when Cate Blanchett's agent had an assistant phone to say that Cate had been booked out on another film the day after her contract with us ended. This meant that if we didn't finish with Cate on exactly the contract date, we could not complete her role in the film, which might mean the film made no sense and could not be released. Films go over schedule all the time; I had slipped up by not putting a "days over schedule" clause in Cate's contract, something I always did, but in the chaos of setting up the picture it had somehow been overlooked. However none of the agents I had ever worked with would knowingly book an actor out the day after the contract ended without discussing it first and giving you a chance to rectify it – at a cost, usually, but you expected that. Bond companies, for obvious reasons, will never agree to it.

"Don't worry about it too much," Richard Soames said when I informed the guarantor. "Possession is what counts, and you have to keep her until her role is completed."

It put us under a lot of pressure, though, towards the end of the film when it became obvious we would need Cate for a few days beyond her contract. And I worried all right – I lay awake at night, my stomach in a knot, wondering how I would explain to Fox, Village Roadshow and Bruce that we couldn't finish the picture because this actress, whom we had fought so hard to have and to whom we had given her first break in a big movie, left before her role was completed.

The problem finally solved itself because the only way to clear her on time was to cut one of her biggest scenes, where she is stood in the sun by the Japanese and tortured. When I told Cate this is what we had to do, she cried and said she would stay. I didn't blame her; it was the agent's job to manage the situation.

Eventually we made the final move to Port Douglas where

everyone was able to settle in to permanent accommodation, all of which was A-class, because in Port Douglas there isn't anything else. The weeks on the road had been hard on everyone. "It will be better when we get to the camp," the actors would say. Meaning, when they could settle in to the long schedule in the prison camp and sleep in one place. Julianna Margulies arranged for Nike, with whom she had some kind of commercial arrangement, to produce T-shirts for the cast and crew which said "Paradise Road" and Nike on the front, and "It will be better when we get to the camp" on the back.

There was no let-up for the production office, though. Once we started filming the prison camp sequences, there were 200 extras every day, as well as a cast of thirty, all in period wardrobe with period hairstyles and starving makeup. Catering for 300 cast and crew every day was handled without fuss by the brilliant Kerry Fetzer, although even that was not without its tension. The actors were all on strict diets to get their weight to approximate that of starving prisoners of war. They would come to lunch and look at the actors' table, with its raw carrots and lettuce leaves, and across at the table where the crew were loading their plates with delicious pasta and pies and meat and sauces and roast potatoes ... we quickly learnt not to speak to the actors while they ate their lunch. The dietician, visiting to check on the actors, paid a visit to Elizabeth Spriggs' trailer at lunchtime just in time to see an empty dinner plate being passed out to an assistant who passed in a new full one from the crew table, then the door slammed shut. The dietician knew when she was beaten. Everyone else, though, took their dieting seriously, and Glenn was particularly dedicated.

For once in my career I had a house which befitted the status of producer – a large, comfortable bungalow a few metres from the main beach, with a green slate floor and French windows, surrounded by cool green palms. Glenn had the best house we could find, with a spectacular view and a pool. Her agent, Fred Spektor, came to visit; unfortunately it was on the only two days of the

No computer effects here, or stuntmen. The girls all did their own jumps into the sea.

shoot I had to leave the set for an AFC meeting in Sydney. Fred Spektor is one of the legendary heavies of Hollywood. When I returned to Port Douglas I got a phone call from him. He was now back in Los Angeles. "Glenn hates that house," he said. "Move her to the Mirage." I opened my mouth to protest and then thought better of it. Don't take him on, I said to myself. You will lose. So I said okay.

"Glenn wants to move to the Mirage," I told the production office. "Get her a suite, and tell the runners they can move out of their motel and into Glenn's house until we can get out of the lease. Let me know when you've done that and I'll tell Glenn when she can move." Pained faces stared rebelliously at me, then collectively sighed and got on with it. The runners – the bottom of the pecking order on any film – were ecstatic at the prospect of moving to nob hill. I drove out to the set to see Glenn. "We've made all the arrangements," I said. "Paul will be round tonight to move you and Annie to the Mirage." Annie was her small daughter, who was visiting.

There was a pregnant silence while Glenn stared at me. Then, "Did Fred tell you to do this?" I nodded. Yup. "Bloody Fred," she said. "The house is fine. I might have complained a bit about it while he was here (actorspeak for had a huge whinge) but I don't want to move. And Annie loves the cat. She'll be devastated if she has to leave it. Can we stay?"

Back to the office. "Cancel all that." More sighs. But my

With my co-producer, Greg Coote and Bruce on set.

amateur psychology told me that if I'd gone to Glenn and said we don't want to move you, if she'd been having a bad day she might have said, "But I insist."

One of the biggest moments in the film was the night when the choir, which had been rehearsing secretly so as not to attract the antagonism of the Japanese, performed for the camp. The first piece they were to sing was the fabled "Largo" from the *New World Symphony*, and everyone was looking forward to the scene being shot. It is the emotional highlight of the film. So when I arrived on set to find that the sound recordist had not brought the correct equipment, I could be heard all the way to Cairns.

"It's a film about a choir!"

Because I was now settled in Port Douglas and Tom was doing a lot of travelling, he decided I should have our dog Jess, so he put her on a plane and I drove into Cairns to pick her up. She had

Sue with Cate Blanchett, Julianna Margulies, Lisa Hensley, the mighty Elizabeth Spriggs and Creature the dog.

never flown before but the flight didn't faze her. She leaped out of the Pet Pak, wagged her tail and took off at a gallop to do a circuit of the freight shed. My heart was in my mouth as she headed for the door onto the runway, but she heard me yelling at her, wheeled round and came bounding back. "If the dog had gone on the runway we would have shot it," the freight handler said.

She liked my house and we both enjoyed our early morning walks along the beach, sometimes accompanied by Creature, Kerry-Anne and Darren with their wrangler, Glennys, and Glennys' brown kelpie, Meg.

About halfway through the Port Douglas shoot we got a call from the Roadshow office. One of the top executives was coming to town and would like to take "the girls" to dinner. He meant Glenn, Frances, Julianna, Jennifer and probably, as an afterthought, Cate. But as all the cast were in this together, I wasn't prepared to leave anyone out. Many telephone calls and faxes followed, as it was pointed out that there were nineteen actresses, and several of them had partners staying with them. Eventually we booked

Producer and assistant, after a hard day in Paradise.

Nautilus, the legendary open-air restaurant in Port Douglas, for a party of thirty. An extremely pleasant evening was had under the palm trees and the stars, on a perfect tropical night. The executive paid the bill with a flourish.

A few weeks later the production accountant handed Anne an invoice. "What do you want me to do with *this*?" he asked.

Anne was in my office in a microsecond. "We've been charged for the dinner at Nautilus," she said. Nothing unusual in that. They all do it.

"Yes, but this invoice is for $10,000."

Thirty people at Nautilus was never going to be cheap, but $10,000 did seem excessive. When phone calls were made, it was established that the bill was actually for the executive's party on a charter boat to the reef earlier on the day of the dinner. Oops ... although of course it might really have been an accident ...

Whenever the irreconcilable twin problems of not enough money and not enough time threatened to overwhelm us, Anne Bruning and I would sneak out of the production office in Macrossan Street to a café across the road where no one could overhear our worries, and calm ourselves in the time-honoured way, with fat food. I was particularly fond of a *specialité de la maison* of creamed sweet corn covered with melted cheese over bacon on toast, about a million calories, which always cheered me up.

If you have to be working at high levels of stress, there are worse places in the world than Port Douglas to be doing it. The climate, the views, the beaches, the Sunday markets, the cafés and restaurants – although the pressure never let up until the last shot was in the can, we all remember the time in Port Douglas with affection, and I'm sure we'd have had a lot more problems with everyone involved if they hadn't been in such a beautiful place.

Bruce did a brave job of coping on set with the pressure of the schedule, and after finishing shooting we returned to Sydney to begin the editing. The film was completed in early 1997. Fox was so pleased with it that they decided to open it in the US rather

My friend from Wingham, Lesley Roxon, visited while we were filming. These shots were taken fifty years apart.

than, as caution would have dictated, opening it first in Australia where it would have a sympathetic audience and awareness from the in-shoot publicity.

We were all, therefore, shocked at the reviews in the US press. For some bizarre reason the Americans decided that we had made the story up, that such things never happened, and they professed outrage at such duplicity. Controversy raged for a brief period while Fox tried to counter the criticism – the fact being, of course, that no film could ever reproduce the horror and cruelty of the real events. Even the bad publicity didn't help. The film did poor business in the US and from then on, its commercial life was doomed, as critics elsewhere followed the US lead.

Critics or no critics, it is the film I am most proud of, and I am proud that we were able to create a lasting memorial to the courage of the women who endured their captivity with such fortitude and heroism.

The arrival of the new Liberal Government brought the end of my time as Chair of the AFC. I was extended for a while, then told I would not be reappointed. The new Chair quickly got rid of the CEO, Cathy Robinson, as well. The long slow slide into mediocrity, which marked the Howard years in the film industry, had begun.

In May, before I left for location, Tom and I had had a civilised dinner at the Imperial Peking and decided, mutually, to end the marriage. It had not been working for a while and, as there were no children, there was no reason to continue. We agreed that we would split up when I returned from filming.

In amongst the very busy post-production for *Paradise Road*, I had to find a new house. When I found an Edwardian cottage near Queens Park, I remembered how Tom had bid for Imperial Avenue; I just kept bidding until I got it. Jessie the dog and I moved in December to start our new life together.

ELEVEN

Bumps in the Road

ONE OF MY WORST YEARS was 1997. Post-production on *Paradise Road* was as busy, in its own way, as the filming. There were lots of arguments with Fox about the final cut. Throughout the whole process, Greg Coote and Village Roadshow Pictures backed Bruce and me, and it would have been a lot more miserable without them.

I had, over the years, employed top production managers to look after the day-to-day supervision of Film Finance projects while I was off producing. Now the latest incumbent, Adrienne Read, was ready to move on. I could find no one suitable who was available and willing to take over. Helen Watts kindly came in to help out when Adrienne left, but she could not stay. I was panicky about whether I could hold the business – and my life – together.

Then I thought about Anni Browning, who had worked in the art department on big pictures like *Mad Max II*, and who had produced some small films as well as having worked for some government agencies. When I talked to her she was enthusiastic. Finally I had found someone who was not wanting to go back into production and who was happy to become a full-time completion guarantor.

Some time later, Chris Gordon decided to retire and while I could not imagine the business with her, I understood that there is only so long you can be the lightning rod for an operation like mine. Incredibly, we found "another Chris" – the wonderful

Roberta McNamara, to take over as office manager. Roberta has made the job her own and we have all come to rely on her. The Chris story had a sad end, when she died of cancer just a few years into her new life.

In 2009, Richard Soames retired as CEO of Film Finances in a management buyout by his two senior employees, Steve Ransohoff and Kurt Woolner. The UK manager Graham Easton had become a consultant. I decided that when I turned seventy it would be an appropriate time for me to step back as well. With Richard's departure, I was the longest-serving member of the international Film Finances family. Steve and Kurt very generously agreed to my becoming a consultant, and in 2010 Anni Browning took over the management of Film Finances Australasia.

Film Finances is such a wonderful company, in my heart I will never leave. Nor could I ever forget the great years I had working with Richard, Steve and Kurt, Graham Easton, David Korda and James Shirras and all the other international staff. Lloyd Hart, Film Finances' indefatigable Australian lawyer, was always there for support in the many tricky contractual situations that are an inevitable part of the bond business.

Australian independent producers need more than one string to their bow to keep afloat between times of film income. My balancing act between producing and bonding kept me on my toes, but my early lessons in employing the best people and then backing them, got me through many a tight corner. And some of my best memories of the business are of flying around Australia with Richard, visiting film sets and our clients, and finding the funny side in even the darkest disasters.

In 1997 I made my last trip to Cannes for the AFC. John Morris departed the FFC. As CEO he had run the organisation competently, but it is a job that can never please everyone. John was no exception, and his occasionally intemperate way of calling a spade a shovel did not endear him to the majority of filmmakers. In any event, he had been in the job for seven years and it was time for a fresh approach.

A fresh approach proved hard to come by. After a couple of false starts the Board appointed Catriona Hughes, the Senior Investment Manager, to the job. Catriona had been with the organisation since its inception, and she knew the deal side of the business backwards. She was brilliant at her job and of immense value to the industry. I admired her intellect and her quick wit.

Slowly, I began to get my life back under control. Scary as it first appeared, being on my own was not so bad. With the help of Chris at the office, the support of my brother, some good friends and the ever-loving Jessie, I began to build a new and manage-able – and ultimately happy – life.

— ⁂ —

Financing for the film I now most wanted to do, *The Women in Black*, remained elusive. Through Richard Soames I met a New York lawyer called Janet Jacobson who worked for Hallmark Entertainment, one of the biggest producers of television drama in the world, and the company behind *The Hands of Cormac Joyce*, back in the seventies. Janet travelled the world looking for tax deals or currency rates which would assist the financing of Hallmark's production slate.

Through Janet I became involved with a science fiction tel-evision series which was made in Australia by the Jim Henson Company for the Sci Fi network in the US, and deficit-financed by Hallmark. *Farscape* was an amazing opportunity for Australians to spend big dollars to try out things that could never be afforded on local productions. The budget was an astounding $2 million per episode, and eighty-eight episodes were made before the Sci Fi channel pulled the plug.

The story was about an American astronaut who had acciden-tally, while fooling around in his space ship, got shot through a wormhole into a parallel universe. The series was about his adventures in space and trying to get back to earth. It was a clever premise as the time setting was the present, rather than away in the future like most science fiction, which meant a lot of contemporary references could be woven into the scripts. As the astronaut was the only human in the show, the Americans were happy for all the aliens to be played by Australians, which they did with their customary talent, good humour and aplomb. When we asked Claudia Karvan to do an episode, she grinned and said, "I want to play a monster," so the visual effects department tricked her up in an outfit which took her an hour to get into and even longer to get out of, but she made a happy baddie. Justine Saunders likewise was happy to play an alien, as a change from only being cast in Aboriginal roles. The star of *Farscape*, an American actor called Ben Browder, was handsome, wonderfully well trained and incredibly hard working, and the crew were dedicated and achieved fantastic things.

It could have been a great experience, but *Farscape* was a runaway roller coaster which constantly threatened to cartwheel off its tracks into the vortex. The script department – the heart of any television series – was a crisis-driven horror movie, which made management a nightmare and ensured that no one could ever relax. The Sci Fi network chose not to take up its option on a fifth series in 2003, and when the Australian dollar rose against the USD, Hallmark and the Jim Henson Company departed our shores for more financially fertile territory.

At the end of 1999 I was appointed to the Board of Screen West, the organisation which had resulted from the review I had chaired in 1992. With Perth being so far from anywhere, the Board decided to have one appointee from the east to help keep them in touch. I was delighted to be asked as, one way and another over the years, Perth had become a home away from home. I spent five happy years commuting once a month for Board meetings and during this time, with the support of CEO Tania Chambers, Screen West instituted a program of short dramas written and directed by Indigenous filmmakers, which continues.

In 2000 the wonderful Bob Maza, writer, actor, activist, star of *The Fringe Dwellers* and first Indigenous Board member at the Australian Film Commission, died of kidney disease, aged sixty. His funeral filled St Mary's Cathedral and lifted the rafters. A highlight was a ceremony by dancers from Mer, Bob's homeland, and while it may not have been the first, it was a welcome sign of the future when the tribal and religious could share an important moment together to honour someone who lived both cultures.

Blackfellas do not make old bones. In 2007, Justine Saunders OAM (she returned her Order of Australia in protest at comments made by the Howard Government), died, aged fifty-three. She had been a pioneer for Indigenous artists, and she fought to ensure worthwhile roles for black actors. One of the stolen generation, she carried a lot of pain which she hid behind a generous, fun-loving persona. She called me Warranoo, sister girl. I loved her and I miss her.

With my brother Robert and Virginia Duigan (Bruce was, as so often, in some other country) I joined the quarter of a million Australians who marched for reconciliation across the Harbour Bridge in 2000. The march was an incredible experience, an important moment in public support for a better future for Aboriginal Australians.

Early in the new millennium, a conversation with someone from the Melbourne company Artist Services led to me producing a remake of *My Brother Jack*. For complicated financing reasons, Artist Services needed an independent company to be the production vehicle, so it was agreed that I would make it through Samson Productions.

My Brother Jack was directed by Ken Cameron. It starred Matt Day as David, with Claudia Karvan, the only actress in the country beautiful enough to play the incomparable Charmian Clift, making an appearance as Cressida.

There have been few remakes in the Australian film and television industry. It was a curious experience. I looked at Storry Walton's version, made for the ABC more than thirty years before. Some of it was inevitably dated but some scenes were as fresh as tomorrow, and could not be improved upon. I did my best to measure up both to the earlier version and to the memory of George Johnston and Charmian.

The show won Best Mini-series at the Australian Film Awards and won its ratings when screened on Channel Ten.

In 2007 the Rudd Labor Government was elected. Over the previous couple of years the Coalition had been planning a major change to the way film subsidy was delivered, and the change was in the pipeline by the time of the election.

Most agreed that it was time for a change. It was hoped that the amalgamation of the operations of the Film Finance Corporation and the Australian Film Commission, along with the introduction of the new tax offset to replace what was left of the old 10BA structure, would result in a new dynamic for film assistance.

Unfortunately, the transition fell between the outgoing and incoming governments, and the new organisation, Screen Australia, retains many of the problems of the old organisations. It was a disappointing waste of a rare opportunity to revitalise subsidy to the film industry. The tax offset has many benefits, but it is cumbersome and complicated, and I can't help wondering if direct subsidy, and simplified administration, might not give as good or better a result while directing more of the taxpayer funds where they should go – onto the screen.

The current breathtaking technical changes in filmmaking are revolutionising the industry for the first time since the introduction of sound. Between 1929 and the early 2000s, the mechanics of filmmaking barely changed at all. Black and white changed to colour, film stocks became more flexible, digital sound made for better soundtracks. But that was about all. Cameras still had to be big enough to accommodate bulky magazines of 35mm film, rushes were sent to the lab and processed overnight, a Bill Gooley phoned a report on the negative to the production office the next morning, the crew together viewed the raw footage at the end of each day. Visual effects were done in cumbersome and expensive laboratory processes, film to film.

When digitisation of motion picture was introduced, it was the beginning of the end of a hundred years of common activity. Now cameras are lighter, digital recording is cheaper, you view the results either simultaneously or on instant replay. The director reviews the day's footage at home on a DVD. The old camaraderie of rushes screenings has gone. Digital effects have allowed images to change faster than Ben Browder flying down that wormhole.

As the avant-garde artist Ken Jacobs said, cinema doesn't have to be film; it has to be magic.

It is a natural thing for each generation to look back with rose-coloured glasses and forward with lemon-tinted ones. I read a quote from Joy Cavill, talking in the 1970s about how much more fun it was making films in the fifties. To me, the seventies was a golden age. That was when Australian film was recovering from a generation of neglect. While we were discovering the wonder of making movies, the world was discovering Australian talent.

Now, any kid with a mobile phone and a computer can film a story, edit it, add visual effects and screen it on the internet. The future is infinite. Filmmakers who are growing up in today's visual revolution may one day say, as we did, that this was a golden age.

It is beginning to look like a golden age in television drama, too. The standard of TV drama in recent years has increased exponentially, and Australian television audiences once again have really excellent Australian drama which reflects themselves, past and present, good and bad, to delight in.

No matter what the technology, to be a great and enduring filmmaker you have to have something to say. The new generation of Indigenous filmmakers does, in spades. And they are finding an audience. Watch their future. I am, through rose-coloured glasses.

I have just received a call that a project has been cancelled, after months of work. I am standing in a horse-yard, holding a poodle in a blanket and a mobile phone. It says everything about producing.

INDEX

C